Lo, I Tell You a Mystery

Princeton Theological Monograph Series

K. C. Hanson, General Editor

Related titles in the series

Richard Valantasis
The Subjective Eye: Essays in Honor of Margaret R. Miles

Stephen Finlan and Vladimir Kharlamov
Theōsis

Sam Hamstra Jr.
The Reformed Pastor: Lectures on Pastoral Theology by John Williamson Nevin

Paul O. Ingram
Constructing a Relational Cosmology

Caryn Riswold
Coram Deo

Byron C. Bangert
Consenting to God and Nature

Michael G. Cartwright
Practices, Politics, and Performance

Philip Harrold
A Place Somewhat Apart: The Private Worlds of a Late Nineteenth Century University

Mark A. Ellis
The Arminian Confession of 1621

John A. Vissers
The Neo-Orthodox Theology of W. W. Bryden

Lo, I Tell You a Mystery

Cross, Resurrection, and Paraenesis in the Rhetoric of 1 Corinthians

David A. Ackerman

PICKWICK PUBLICATIONS
An imprint of *Wipf and Stock Publishers*
199 West 8th Avenue • Eugene OR 97401

LO, I TELL YOU A MYSTERY
Cross, Resurrection, and Paraenesis in the Rhetoric of 1 Corinthians

Princeton Theological Monograph Series 54

Copyright © 2006 David A. Ackerman. All rights reserved. Except for brief quotations in critical publications or reviews, no part of this book may be reproduced in any manner without prior written permission from the publisher. Write: Permissions, Wipf & Stock Publishers, 199 W. 8th Ave., Suite 3, Eugene, OR 97401.

Pickwick Publications
A Division of Wipf & Stock Publishers
199 W. 8th Ave., Suite 3
Eugene, OR 97401

ISBN: 1-59752-435-2

Cataloging-in-Publication Data

Ackerman, David A.
    Lo, I tell you a mystery : cross, resurrection, and paraenesis in the rhetoric of 1 Corinthians / by David A. Ackerman.

    Eugene, Ore.: Pickwick Publications, 2006
    x + 171 p. 23 cm.
    Princeton Theological Monograph Series ; 54
    ISBN 1-59752-435-2
1. Bible—N.T.—Corinthians, 1st—Criticism, interpretation, etc. 2. Paul, the Apostle, Saint—Theology. 3. Rhetoric in the Bible. I. Title. II. Series.

BS2675.3 A24 2006

Manufactured in the U.S.A.

For my beloved Rhonda, Shan, and Joel, for their love and encouragement

Contents

Abbreviations / viii

1 A Conflict of Ideologies / 1

2 Concern for Conflict Resolution / 14

3 Revealing the Mystery in the Paradox of the Cross (1 Corinthians 1–4) / 38

4 Completing the Mystery with the Resurrection of Believers (1 Corinthians 15) / 76

5 The Paraenesis of the Mystery for the Community (1 Corinthians 5–14) / 108

6 Paul's Boundaries of Holiness and Love / 136

7 The Essential Paradigm Shift / 146

8 Conclusion / 158

Bibliography / 162

Abbreviations

ABQ	*American Baptist Quarterly*
AGJU	Arbeiten zur Geschichte des antiken Judentums und des Urchristentums
AJA	*American Journal of Archeology*
BAGD	Walter Bauer, William F. Arndt, F. Wilbur Gingrich, and Frederick W. Danker, *Greek-English Lexicon of the New Testament and Other Early Christian Literature,* 2d ed. (Chicago: University of Chicago Press, 1979)
BETL	Bibliotheca ephemeridum theologicarum lovaniensium
BHT	Beiträge zur historischen Theologie
Bib	*Biblica*
BSac	*Bibliotheca sacra*
BTB	*Biblical Theology Bulletin*
CRINT	Compendia rerum Iudaicarum ad Novum Testamentum
CTJ	*Calvin Theological Journal*
CBQ	*Catholic Biblical Quarterly*
EHPR	Études d'histoire et de philosophie religieuses
EvQ	*Evangelical Quarterly*
FRLANT	Forschungen zur Religion und Literatur des Alten und Neuen Testaments
GBS	Guides to Biblical Scholarship
GNS	Good News Studies
HTR	*Harvard Theological Review*
Hesperia	*Hesperia: Journal of the American School of Classical Studies at Athens*
IBC	Interpretation: A Bible Commentary for Preaching and Teaching
ICC	International Critical Commentary
Int	*Interpretation*
JAAR	*Journal of the American Academy of Religion*
JBL	*Journal of Biblical Literature*
JSNT	*Journal for the Study of the New Testament*

JSNTSup	Journal for the Study of the New Testament: Supplement Series
JSOT	*Journal for the Study of the Old Testament*
LEC	Library of Early Christianity
LCL	Loeb Classical Library
Neot	*Neotestamentica*
NICNT	New International Commentary on the New Testament
NIGNC	New International Greek Testament Commentary
NovT	*Novum Testamentum*
NTM	New Testament Message
NTS	*New Testament Studies*
PittsTMS	Pittsburgh Theological Monograph Series
PTMS	Princeton Theological Monograph Series
SBLDS	Society of Biblical Literature Dissertation Series
SEÅ	*Svensk exegetisk årsbok*
SNTSMS	Society for New Testament Studies Monograph Series
ST	*Studia theologica*
TDNT	*Theological Dictionary of the New Testament*, edited by Gerhard Kittel and Gerhard Friedrich, translated by Geoffrey W. Bromiley, 10 vols. (Grand Rapids: Eerdmans, 1964–76)
ThTo	*Theology Today*
TJ	*Trinity Journal*
TZ	*Theologische Zeitschrift*
TynBul	*Tyndale Bulletin*
WTJ	*Westminster Theological Journal*
WUNT	Wissenschaftliche Untersuchungen zum Neuen Testament
ZNW	*Zeitschrift für die neutestamentliche Wissenschaft und die Kunde der älteren Kirche*

All biblical translations are the author's own. The sources for all other translations can be found in the bibliography.

New Testament translations are based on the fourth edition of *The Greek New Testament* published by the United Bible Society, 1998.

Old Testament translations are based on the *Biblia Hebraica Stuttgartensia* published by the Deutsche Bibelgesellschaft, 1983.

1

A Conflict of Ideologies

Paul's first canonical letter to the Corinthians is about *conflict* and *conformity*. His goal is for them to have "the mind of Christ" (1 Cor 2:16) by growing from their immature state as spiritual infants into spiritual adulthood. Their immaturity was apparent in their quarreling (chs. 3–4), acceptance of immorality (chs. 5–7), selfishness (chs. 8–10), disorderly enthusiasm in worship (chs. 11–14), and incorrect understanding of resurrection (ch. 15). Growth into spiritual maturity (3:1-3; cf. 2:6) should have been evident in their communion with and devotion to Christ and in their fellowship with one another through love, unity, holy living, and concern for others.

Paul received bad news of problems in the church and determined the basic cause to be a lack of spiritual maturity. These believers had not allowed the Holy Spirit to grow them into Christ-likeness but were living too much like the world around them. Paul cautions against this and calls them to follow his standard of holiness and love. This standard did not originate with him but with Christ himself, embodied in the message of Christ's death and resurrection. This standard and the behavior of the Corinthians clashed, resulting in a conflict of ideology. Paul attempts to resolve this conflict by urging them to accept his interpretation of the gospel.

The Need for Change

Paul's pattern for spiritual maturity is contained in the *kerygma* of divine wisdom revealed with the death and resurrection of Jesus Christ. Paul writes in 2:7, "But we speak of the wisdom of God *in mystery* which has been hidden, which God has destined before the ages for our glory." Paul consistently applies the example of the "divine mystery" revealed in Jesus Christ as the goal for the spiritual development of the Corinthian community. The Corinthians failed to appropriate this message in their lives and church, and as a result, were experiencing problems within their community.

Paul's basic message is that the divine plan was *revealed* in the past with the death and resurrection of Christ and will be *fulfilled* in the future with Christ's return. In the *meantime*, believers must live in a way consistent with this revelation and grow into spiritual maturity in imitation of Christ. Paul uses this scheme of time as his basic approach to the problems in Corinth. Spiritual maturity for him is summed up in his concept of "fellowship with Christ." When a person is in fellowship with or "in" Christ (1:9), he or she is in the *sphere* of the lordship of Christ (12:3) and possesses the mind of Christ through the Holy Spirit (2:16). The divine mystery for Paul is the possibility of fellowship with God through the mediation of Christ (8:6) for those who put their faith in Christ and identify with him in his death and resurrection (Gal 2:20; Col 1:27). Paul bases his definition of spiritual maturity on his interpretation of the revelation and meaning of Christ's death and resurrection. He applies this definition to the situation at Corinth with the goal that the church there would grow into a unified community in fellowship with Christ (1 Cor 1:9-10).

What prompted Paul to write this letter was information he had received by way of a letter brought by Stephanas, Fortunatus, and Achaicus (7:1; 16:17) and from verbal reports from Chloe's people (1:11). When he received this news, he knew things were not going as he had hoped. To borrow from his metaphor in 3:6, the seeds of faith which he had planted among the Corinthians had either not yet taken root or had sprouted and were growing wildly. Their faith in Christ had not reached the level of maturity for which he had hoped. Therefore, he had to *remind* them from where they had come and to where they were going by exhorting them to live according to the gospel in the present time. His primary means for accomplishing this goal is to remind them of their past, present, and future.

The underlying issue faced by this church was spiritual immaturity, which created tension between the present status of the Corinthians and Paul's expectations for them. The majority of interpreters of 1 Corinthians have emphasized the conflict within the church itself, a position supported by strong internal evidence. For example, in the opening section of the letter in 1:10-17, Paul sets out the issues to be addressed in the letter by beginning with an appeal to unity in response to news that there were quarrels and divisions in the church (1:10-11) with people claiming either Paul, Apollos, Cephas, and Christ as their leader (1:12). Paul deals with this divisiveness specifically in chapters 1–4, and indirectly throughout the rest of the letter.

Since the early nineteenth century, interpreters have suggested many theories about the causes and people behind the divisions in the Corinthian church. These investigations have been helpful for interpretation but are only tentative theories. Inadequate information concerning the precise situation that lies behind 1 Corinthians warns against giving any definitive answers to the problems of divisions or parties in the church. It is more methodologically sound to examine the problems mentioned or implied in the text itself between Paul and the Corinthians rather than the problems in the community seen vaguely through Paul's reactions in the letter. By investigating the first, considerable insight and a more balanced method can be achieved for understanding the second.

The awareness of the complexity and uncertainty surrounding the theories on parties and divisions has led some interpreters to argue that the difficulty for Paul was not the leaders of the parties or the various groups in the church, but the problem of *division* itself in that the Corinthians were acting according to the flesh (*sarx*) and not according to the Spirit (3:3-4).[1] By examining Paul's reactions and counsel through his letter, it becomes apparent that his relationship with this church was strained at points. His ideal of life in Christ was different than the behavior of some of the Corinthians. His language is quite combative and sarcastic at points because the situation was very critical to him. The Corinthians were not living up to his expectations, and his preaching and example had not produced the changes in their lives that he had anticipated. They continued to be adversely influenced by their pagan environment with its lifestyles which were contrary to Paul's ideal of holy living. Their relationships, behavior, and worship had not been adequately transformed to the holy lifestyle resulting from communion with the risen Jesus Christ (15:17, 34). At the deepest level, this situation was caused by not being in close fellowship with and in Christ.

Paul's Understanding of Time and the Resolution of Conflict

Throughout the letter, Paul focuses upon the *present* behaviors and beliefs of the Corinthians. He refers to the *past* specifically in chapters 1–4 and the *future* in chapter 15 in order to influence the *present* situation in Corinth. The divine plan was *revealed* in the past (*apekalypsen*, 2:10) with Christ's death and resurrection and will be *completed* in the future (*telos*, 15:24) with Christ's coming again and the resurrection of those "in Christ." Paul's expressed purpose for the Corinthians, then, is for them to live as believers in communion with Christ in the *interim* time between these two points in history.

Paul's concept of *time* revolves around these two major moments in the one grand story of God's revelation of the divine plan or "mystery" through Christ. The first moment of the death and resurrection of Jesus Christ serves

---

[1] John C. Hurd, *The Origin of I Corinthians* (New York: Seabury, 1965) 114; Gordon D. Fee, *The First Epistle to the Corinthians*, NICNT (Grand Rapids: Eerdmans, 1987) 5–15.

as the basis for the many verbs in the indicative mood in his letters and refers to the status or state of those who put their faith in Christ.[2] The significance of this first moment in time for Paul can be seen in his statement that the one who exists "in Christ" is a new creation, meaning that the old way of living in sin and condemnation has passed away and a new life of forgiveness and freedom has begun (2 Cor 5:17; cf. Rom 6:4-5). The second major moment has yet to take place and will happen with Christ's *parousia*. At this point, those "in Christ" will experience the resurrected state with Christ, and the divine plan revealed on the cross will be completed (1 Cor 15:20-28). Paul's future hope is to participate in this resurrected state (Phil 3:10). His concern for his churches is what takes place in the interim. It is here that he especially uses imperative verbs of command and a paraenetic style of writing.[3] Based upon the past event of Christ's saving activity and the future hope of resurrection with Christ, those "in Christ" should live in the present by a certain paradigm which Paul attempts to articulate throughout the letter.

Paul tries to convince the Corinthians of his ideology by several means.[4] One tool is simply his *letter* and the ability of his words to persuade since he could not immediately come to Corinth in person (16:5-9) nor send an apostolic emissary (4:17; 16:10-11). A second way is by appealing to his *authority* as apostle and founder of the church in Corinth. He appeals to his authority in many places in the letter, often with irony and sarcasm. His authority comes mainly by his association and fellowship with Christ. A third means of persuasion is by using his *example* which is worthy of imitation. Since he follows the example of Christ, the Corinthians should then follow him (11:1). He also uses methods of persuasion in his letter common in rhetoric during

---

[2] The indicative mood in Greek is generally used to indicate a statement of fact, and the imperative mood is used for a command or exhortation. The term "ethic" refers to a pattern or norm for life. "Ethics" are more the conclusions or systematic account of right or wrong conduct. Victor Paul Furnish states that Paul's "ethic" is never formulated by Paul himself, but "it is still present in the dynamic of the indicative and imperative which lies at the center of his thought" (*Theology and Ethics in Paul* [Nashville: Abingdon, 1968] 211; see also 224–27; cf. William D. Dennison, "Indicative and Imperative. The Basic Structure of Pauline Ethics," *CTJ* 14 [1979] 55–78).

[3] Paraenesis is exhortation or instruction used by a speaker or author to urge an audience to act in an acceptable manner often with examples given of proper behavior. See Abraham J. Malherbe, *Moral Exhortation, A Greco-Roman Sourcebook*, LEC 4 (Philadelphia: Westminster, 1986) 124–25; Stanley K. Stowers, *Letter Writing in Greco-Roman Antiquity*, LEC 5 (Philadelphia: Westminster, 1986) 91–152; and David E. Aune, *The New Testament in Its Literary Environment*, LEC 8 (Philadelphia: Westminster, 1987) 191.

[4] Ideology refers to a belief system, presuppositions, or set of values by which a person or group orders their universe. It is influenced by one's theology but not exclusive of this theology since it involves matters of human relationships and choices. Cf. John H. Elliott, *What is Social-Scientific Criticism?* GBS (Minneapolis: Fortress, 1993) 130; Vernon K. Robbins, *Exploring the Texture of Texts: A Guide to Socio-Rhetorical Criticism* (Valley Forge, Pa.: Trinity, 1996) 95–96.

his time. These methods were pioneered by Aristotle, who lived in the fourth century BCE, and built upon by others, including Cicero and Quintillian, who were roughly contemporary with Paul.

If Paul's words were effective, they would result in an intentional conflict between himself and the Corinthians. Paul uses at least two ancient models of relationships in his attempt to create conflict with the Corinthians with the purpose of urging them to change and conform. One is the honor/shame model. Paul seeks to shame the Corinthians by assessing them as living in a different paradigm than his own and, hence, of Christ. His is the position of honor and theirs is the position of shame. They could be in a position of honor before Paul—and ultimately before Christ and God—by living according to Paul's paradigm.

A second ancient model by which Paul tries to create conflict is the relationship between a patron and client. This relationship was governed by the dependence of a client upon the patron for some necessary thing. Paul essentially calls himself the patron and interpreter of the gospel for the Corinthians (4:1). His interpretation, and not the Corinthians', is the correct one. He, as patron, attempts to shame them into accepting his position and thereby resolving his conflict with them.

Finding Paul's Solution

It becomes evident in reading this letter that Paul expects certain changes in the way the Corinthians were living. His expectations can be determined by asking four questions. First, what is his *ideology* as he expresses it in this letter? Second, what are the *problems* with the Corinthians based on his assessment of them? Third, what are the differences between him and the Corinthians, and how do these lead to a *conflict* of ideologies? Finally, what is his *solution* for resolving these differences? It becomes apparent in answering this final question that Paul's solution is based upon the revelation of God in the death and resurrection of Jesus Christ.

Two approaches to the letter help answer these questions. One is to consider how Paul constructs his letter, and the other is to evaluate the social relationships and changes presumed in the letter. Determining how Paul constructs his letter is important because what can be known about his relationship with the Corinthians comes through his written correspondence with them; all other data is secondary and only supports or clarifies the written text. Without a positive change in the relationships involved, Paul's words lose their power to transform. Two methods of interpretation address these two perspectives: rhetorical criticism and social-scientific criticism.

Rhetorical Criticism

Rhetorical criticism is the field of study that can reveal the effect of a speaker's or author's words. This approach is quite diverse and involves many aspects of interpretation. In the classical terms of Aristotle, rhetoric is *the art or means of persuasion*.[5] Rhetoric describes the way a speaker or author attempts to convince an audience to agree with her or him about a topic or action. According to Aristotle, rhetoric consists of five major parts.[6] The first is called *invention*. Invention determines the best way to communicate a subject by determining how arguments are developed and what issues are to be argued in a discourse based on internal or external proofs. External proofs come from outside the author (e.g., quotations). Aristotle gives three modes of internal or artistic proof: *ethos*, *pathos*, and *logos*, roughly corresponding to speaker, audience, and discourse. *Ethos* is the moral character or credibility of the author, the trust in the author which the audience has or develops. *Pathos* is the emotional response of the audience. *Logos* is the logical argument found in the discourse. Logos is divided into two forms: inductive, a series of examples which point to a general conclusion, and deductive, a conclusion drawn from premises most likely acceptable to the audience. Deductive proof, called an *enthymeme*, comes in the form of a statement and a supporting reason, otherwise called a syllogism. The speaker uses what Aristotle called "topics" (*topoi* or *loci*) or headings in constructing inductive and deductive arguments.

Several elements of Aristotle's insights into invention are significant for interpreting 1 Corinthians. One is the concept of ethos. Paul devotes a significant amount of attention in the letter to establishing his character. His example, authority, and relationship with the Corinthians are significant forces for persuasion. Since Paul is the prime example to them of Christ, his words, message, and theology should be followed. If the Corinthians disagree with his interpretation, not only does conflict with him result, but more significantly, they will find themselves out of fellowship with Christ himself. The logic of Paul's argument is also significant. The basic enthymeme he uses begins with the common premise held between himself and the Corinthians: *faith in Christ is the way to be redeemed from the power of sin and experience salvation* (1:30; 15:11). The second part of this syllogism is that *Paul is the father, founder, and apostle of the Corinthian community, and the best example to the Corinthians of how a believer in Christ should live*. The third part of the syllogism is that *the behavior of the Corinthians shows that they were not living consistently with Paul's way of life*. The conclusion to the syllogism is that *the Corinthians are thus out of step with the ways of Christ*. This position

---

[5] Aristotle, *Rh.* 1.2.1255; cf. Quintillian, *Inst.* 2.15.38.
[6] Aristotle, *Rh.* 1.2; Quintillian, *Inst.* 3.3.1.

is unacceptable to Paul and also should be unacceptable to the Corinthians. Along the way in developing this enthymeme, Paul uses pathos to shame the Corinthians into seeing the faults of their ways.

Furthermore, under invention for Aristotle are found three species or genres of rhetoric applicable to all discourse. In *judicial* rhetoric the speaker seeks to accuse or defend and to persuade about events that happened in the *past*. This type of rhetoric involves the question of truth or justice and often occurs in the setting of a courtroom. *Deliberative* rhetoric seeks to persuade about *future* action and involves the question of self-interest and future benefits. No judgment is passed, but only an appeal is made to the audience to make the right decision. The setting for this type is the forum. Finally, *epideictic* rhetoric seeks to persuade or educate the audience to hold or reaffirm some point of view in the *present* and is characterized by praise or blame. It involves a change of attitude or the deepening of values. The setting is the marketplace or amphitheater.

Paul uses some of each of these types of rhetoric in his letter. His overall purpose is to persuade the Corinthians to accept his standard of behavior which then will alter the way they live now and in the future. Thus, the basic type of rhetoric in the letter is deliberative rhetoric.[7] Yet, Paul also uses the other two types throughout the larger deliberative argument. For example, at specific points in the discourse, he uses epideictic rhetoric intentionally to shame the Corinthians into seeing the faults of their ways (6:5; 15:34). At other times, he uses judicial rhetoric with the image of the courtroom (4:1-5) or with references to past behavior (6:9-11) in order to convince them of a better alternative for the future. His purpose in using all three types of rhetoric is to convince them of the fault of their ways. In the process, he moves toward the conclusion of the enthymeme in order to convince them that they were not living the way those in Christ should live. They needed to change their ways and live in community according to Paul's interpretation of the divine mystery of Christ.

The second major element of rhetoric is called *arrangement*, which involves putting the various parts of a speech into an orderly and effective structure. According to Aristotle, a speech needs four parts. Using the terminology of the ancient rhetoricians, the first is called the *proem* or *exordium*. This part of a discourse serves as the introduction and attempts to grab the attention of the audience, to establish goodwill or sympathy toward the speaker, and to provide the desired goal of the speech. The next is the *narratio* of facts, which provides the background information and includes the *propositio* (thesis state-

---

[7] Margaret M. Mitchell, *Rhetoric of Reconciliation: An Exegetical Investigation of the Language and Composition of 1 Corinthians* (Louisville: Westminster John Knox; Tübingen: Mohr/Siebeck, 1991) 20–64.

ment) that gives what the speaker wishes to prove, often with a *partitio* (division) of it into separate headings. Then, the main arguments are presented in the proof or *confirmatio*, which is followed by a *refutatio* (refutation) of opposing views. A speech may include analogies, examples, or citations to provide supporting data in the proof. Finally, the epilogue or *peroratio* summarizes the argument and seeks to arouse the emotions of the audience to motivate them into taking action or making a judgment.

The third element of rhetoric according to Aristotle is *style*. Style involves both choice of words and the arrangement of words into sentences, including the use of appropriate figures of speech. Style is concerned with correctness, clarity, ornamentation, and propriety. *Memory*, the fourth element, consists of the preparation for natural delivery through memorization. The last element is *delivery* which governs the rules for control of the voice and the use of gestures appropriate for the occasion. How the fourth and fifth elements of rhetoric affected Paul's churches is difficult to determine and not directly relevant for this study since all we possess are written documents and do not know how the letter was verbalized to the Corinthian church.

Using the concepts of Aristotle and those who followed him in interpreting Paul's letters has proven to be an effective approach in determining how Paul addressed the issues and problems of his churches.[8] He wrote during a period when rhetoric was one of the standard subjects of Greek education and provided the rules for public discourse. Not everyone was formally trained in the finer points of rhetorical theory, but most were exposed to rhetoric in the public arena in the Greco-Roman culture and had ears attuned to ways of communicating.[9] How much Paul and other New Testament authors understood and consciously used ancient rhetorical theory cannot be known with certainty, but they persuaded their audiences using shared cultural norms about appropriate discourse.[10]

Moreover, most of Paul's churches probably did not at first see or read the manuscripts of his letters but heard them read publicly.[11] His letters served as substitutes for conversation and built upon the foundation of his personal presence.[12] Ancient letters were often seen as written speeches and show many

---

[8] For example, see Hans Dieter Betz, *Galatians: A Commentary on Paul's Letters to the Churches in Galatia*, Hermeneia (Philadelphia: Fortress, 1979); see also his "The Problem of Rhetoric and Theology According to the Apostle Paul," in *L'Apôtre Paul: personalitié, style et conception du ministère*, ed. A. Vanhoye (Leuven: Leuven University Press, 1986) 16–48.

[9] Burton L. Mack, *Rhetoric and the New Testament*, GBS (Minneapolis: Fortress, 1990) 31.

[10] George A. Kennedy, *New Testament Interpretation through Rhetorical Criticism* (Chapel Hill: University of North Carolina Press, 1984) 9–11.

[11] Reading a letter was an oral event that involved verbal and physical gestures. See John L. White, "Saint Paul and the Apostolic Letter Tradition," *CBQ* 45 (1983) 437.

[12] Seneca, *Ep.* 1.263-64. Demetrius of Phaleron (b. 350 BCE) writes that "a letter ought to be

characteristics similar with oral communication.[13] This makes rhetorical criticism even more important for Paul's letters since he was, in essence, "orally" arguing his case with written words by trying to persuade others to accept his views.[14]

Social-scientific Criticism

Paul's letter could fulfill its purpose if the Corinthians would modify their behavior and live according to his paradigm of the divine mystery of Christ. The letter implies significant differences of perspective between Paul and the Corinthians. Social-scientific criticism can help find these differences and determine Paul's answer for this troubled church. Social-scientific criticism of the New Testament recognizes that to appreciate and understand what Paul meant in his letters, one must ascertain, to some degree, his and his readers' social setting. In other words, to understand Paul and his letters, one needs to learn as much as possible about the ways people related in the first-century Mediterranean world.

Social-scientific criticism is a cross-cultural discipline that attempts to determine the reasons and ways people interact with one another.[15] It tries to explain human behavior in terms of typicalities or models by exploring the world behind the text and the narrative world within the text.[16] This approach returns to the world of the first-century and allows Paul and his churches to be seen as real people dealing with real issues in a real world. Social-scientific models attempt to put complex social relationships into understandable terms by examining the similarities and differences between ways of living.[17] Models also help bridge the gap between one culture, time, or social situation and another. No matter how sophisticated models are, however, they can

---

written in the same manner as a dialogue, a letter being regarded . . . as one of the two sides of a dialogue. . . . The letter should be a little more studied than the dialogue, since the latter reproduces an extemporary utterance, while the former is committed to writing and is sent as gift" (Demetrius, *Elec*. 223, 224). Robert W. Funk argues that the primary way Paul showed his authority was through his presence, but letters and emissaries were also effective ("The Apostolic *Parousia*: Form and Significance," in *Christian History and Interpretation: Studies Presented to John Knox*, ed. William R. Farmer, Charles F. D. Moule, and Richard R. Niebuhr [Cambridge: Cambridge University Press, 1967] 249–68).

[13] Raymond F. Collins, "Reflections on 1 Corinthians as a Hellenistic Letter," in *The Corinthian Correspondence*, ed. Reimund Bieringer (Leuven: Leuven University Press, 1996) 57–58.

[14] James D. Hester comments, "If one accepts the notion that Paul's letters are rife with oral expression or style . . . one had better begin to take seriously the possibility that Paul saw his letters as speeches" ("The Use and Influence of Rhetoric in Galatians," *TZ* 42 [1986] 389).

[15] Bruce J. Malina, "Why Interpret the Bible with the Social Sciences," *ABQ* 2 (1983) 128.

[16] Malina, "The Social Sciences and Biblical Interpretation," *Int* 36 (1982) 232.

[17] John H. Elliott, "Social-Scientific Criticism of the New Testament: More on Methods and Models," *Semeia* 35 (1986) 3.

never completely unravel the complexities of any given social situation. What model to use depends upon what questions one wants answered or what social phenomena one wishes to explore. Three models are especially helpful in delineating the conflict between Paul and the Corinthians over issues of spirituality and community.

The first is the *conflict* model which maintains that social systems are in a continual state of transition, inevitably leading to conflict. The presupposition is that all units of social organization are continuously changing unless some force intervenes to stop the change. Constraints hold social systems together and eventually create conflict. Bruce J. Malina writes, "Conflict is everywhere because constraint is to be found wherever human beings set up social organizations."[18]

Sociologist Lewis Coser has advanced several propositions, based on the work of the German sociologist Georg Simmel, that are useful for interpreting 1 Corinthians.[19] According to Coser, conflict helps a group establish self-identity and also distinguishes the group from outsiders.[20] Coser, paraphrasing Simmel, writes, "Conflict with other groups contributes to the establishment and reaffirmation of the identity of the group and maintains its boundaries against the surrounding social world."[21] The fellowship of believers with Christ and in Christ is paramount in Paul's agenda in this letter. The Corinthians were in danger of living like people of the world or, in Paul's words, people of the "flesh" (*sarx*, 3:1), the opposite of being "in Christ" (cf. Rom 8:1-11). These two realms of existence are mutually exclusive for Paul. Existence in Christ creates a boundary around the believer that sets him or her off from the world around (1 Cor 5:9-11; cf. 2 Cor 5:14a; Gal 5:19-24).

In another proposition, Coser writes, "The more tightly structured and primary the relations in a system, the more likely coalitions [between individuals or parties] are to develop common norms and values and form a more permanent group."[22] Paul considers and hopes himself to be in close relationship to the Corinthian church. This closeness can be seen in his terms of fictive kinship ("father," "children," "brothers," etc.), his terms of authority ("father," "apostle"), and his relationship as founder and spiritual mentor. Since most of the Corinthians likely had different perspectives than Paul due to the fact of their different settings in life, conflict resulted. Paul also attempts to create social cohesion by creating group solidarity through his modeling of the ways of Christ. The Corinthians could resolve their differ-

---

[18] Elliott, "Social-Scientific Criticism," 235.
[19] Georg Simmel, *Conflict* (Glencoe, Ill.: Free Press, 1955).
[20] Lewis Coser, *The Functions of Social Conflict* (Glencoe, Ill.: Free Press, 1956) 34–35.
[21] Ibid., 38.
[22] Ibid., 176.

ences with one another by being like-minded (1:10) and by growing into the spiritual maturity Paul describes (cf. Phil 2:1-5).

One final, helpful proposition is that conflict reaches its greatest intensity when competing viewpoints confront each another over the issue of ideology.[23] Paul's spiritual ideology is one of *paradox*, modeled after the death and resurrection of Christ. This ideology is characterized by love and consideration of others. Some of the Corinthians appeared to have an ideology of individualism, without consideration of those "weaker" in their community (8:12). They boasted in their human achievements which kept them from experiencing the power of the Holy Spirit (4:8-13). Paul's ideology of love and interdependence conflicted with their ideology of human achievement and understanding (*gnōsis*, 13:2). This was a significant problem in Paul's view that needed to be resolved lest the community be dissolved in dissension.

A second social-scientific model that shows how Paul's attempts to resolve his conflict with the Corinthians over ideology is the model of honor and shame. Malina comments that various groups with some degree of power "use coercive tactics on each other to get their own goals realized. Each of the various groups includes disagreement, strain, conflict, and force—as well as consensus and cooperation."[24] Paul uses his position of honor to shame the Corinthians into seeing the immaturity and futility of their position. At times this shaming comes across in a positive way and other times in a sarcastic, ironic, or caustic way. Although he mentions in 4:14 that his purpose is not to shame them, that is the intended effect his letter appears to have. His position of honor is marked by his status as apostle, his fellowship with Christ, and his lifestyle of humility empowered by God's strength. He uses the so-called "game of commitment" to appeal to the Corinthians' sense of obligation and loyalty to him, Christ, and one another. This "game," as Jerome Neyrey writes, concerns "getting results in social interaction" by appealing

> to another's sense of obligation, duty or belonging, i.e., loyalty as a genuine member of clan and family or as member of a fictive kinship group. Loyalty is urged by means of internalized sanctions such as guilt feelings, feelings of shame and disloyalty, or fear of disapproval.[25]

The third model of the relationship between patron and client illustrates well the basis for Paul's appeal to honor and shame. John K. Chow provides seven general characteristics of a patron-client relationship. First, it is an ex-

---

[23] Ibid., 111.
[24] Bruce J. Malina, "'Religion' in the World of Paul," *BTB* 16 (1986) 98.
[25] Jerome H. Neyrey, "Social Science Modeling and the New Testament," *BTB* 16 (1986) 109.

change relationship in which each has something the other needs. Second, it is an asymmetrical relation in that the parties are not equal in terms of power. Inequality exists especially in access to scarce material or spiritual resources. The client depends on the patron for either the provisions of the resources or the mediation to receive the provisions. Third, it is a particularistic and informal relation by which resources are channeled to specific individuals or groups and not meant to be bestowed universally. Fourth, it is a supra-legal relation, that is, a subtle and not fully legal relationship based on understanding. Fifth, it is often a binding and long-range relation with a strong sense of interpersonal obligation. Sixth, it is a voluntary relation and can be abandoned at any time, although a client may have no choice but to ask the patron for help. Lastly, it is a vertical relation whereby a client is bound to one patron; horizontal group organization and solidarity of clients are discouraged.[26]

In his relationship with the Corinthians, Paul considers himself to be the patron of the divine mysteries of God's plan (4:1). He uses coercion through his strong rhetoric to encourage the Corinthians to experience this mystery of Christ as their own. He appeals to shame in order to force the Corinthians to change their theology. According to Malina, a change based only on an abstract theological truth is of little value unless it includes challenging a person's or group's honor, social standing, influence or reputation.[27] From Paul's perspective, the resolution of the conflict over spirituality must be one-sided. He has the correct and only answer for the Corinthians, and it can be found in the divine mystery of Christ.

The Approach of this Study

This study attempts to determine Paul's solution for the troubled church in Corinth by examining how Paul uses his scheme of time as his reference point for change. His message of the divine mystery *in Christ* was revealed in the past through Christ's death on the cross and resurrection from the dead. Christ's death and resurrection brought the possibility of new life for believers marked by fellowship with Christ through the Holy Spirit. Christ conquered the power of sin and death through his resurrection. Believers participate in this victory, *in part*, in this life. When Christ comes again, believers will be resurrected, death will be defeated, and victory will be complete. Meanwhile, believers should live as holy people between the time of Christ's death and resurrection and his coming again.

---

[26] John K. Chow, *Patronage and Power: A Study of Social Networks in Corinth,* JSNTSup 75 (Sheffield: JSOT Press, 1992) 31–32.
[27] Malina, "'Religion' in the World of Paul," 98.

It may not be arbitrary that Paul begins and ends the body of his letter with significant theological claims. The first moment in time for Paul is the Christ-event, described in chapters 1–4. The position of these chapters in the letter is important because they establish the basis for change urged throughout the letter. The paradigm of the divine mystery revealed upon the cross is of primary importance to Paul's message. The Corinthians evidently missed the implications of this message and failed to grow to spiritual maturity. Paul intentionally creates a conflict of ideology with the Corinthians because of his concern for them. He creates this conflict by shaming them because he has a better alternative in mind. He attempts to resolve this conflict by appealing to the revelation of the divine mystery of Jesus Christ and the opportunity for relationship with him through the Holy Spirit.

Paul ends the main body of the letter in chapter 15 looking forward to the resurrection of believers when Christ comes again and God's plan is completed. Paul sees two basic paradigms at war during the interim period: one represented by Adam and the other by Christ, the second Adam. If the Corinthians continued to live and believe as they were, they were in danger of living according to the paradigm of Adam and, thus, still under the power of sin. Looking ahead to the hope of resurrection and looking back to redemption on the cross should impact the present situation.

Paul looks to the past and future for a reason. His explicit concern is for the spiritual maturation of the Corinthians evidenced by holiness and love in the community during the interim period. He looks backward and forward for his ideology of spiritual maturity for the present. If the Corinthians would agree with his interpretation of the divine mystery and act accordingly, their problems could be solved.

This study follows Paul's scheme of time in order to determine the means and goal for transformation in Corinth. When Paul says 15:51, "Lo, I tell you a mystery: we will not all sleep, but we will all be transformed," he has in mind the source for this change: the power and wisdom of God at work in the death and resurrection of Jesus Christ. The Holy Spirit could make this power be at work in the growth of the community from immaturity to maturity, from being indistinguishable from the world to being a holy community of love. The divine revelation in Jesus Christ is Paul's answer for this process. The imperative was given; it was then up to the Corinthians to act upon it.

2

Concern for Conflict Resolution

Paul's effort at reconciling the differences between himself and the Corinthians comes from his concern that they mature spiritually and communally. They had failed to grow closer in fellowship with Jesus Christ and with one another, primarily because they were not conforming to Paul's "ways in Christ" (1 Cor 4:17). Along with this stinging evaluation, Paul also offers a better way of living. His pervading concern in the letter is for them to conform to his interpretation of God's revelation in Christ. He wants the Corinthians, as believers in Christ, to be holy and set apart morally from the world around them, to conform to a different standard, and to live within the boundary of being "in Christ." Since it would be impossible for them to leave their pagan environment, they could at least become a holy community, empowered by the Holy Spirit to live free from immoral contamination (5:9-11; 6:11, 19-20). What were the cultural and religious pressures upon the Corinthians and how did Paul view them? How did he intend to resolve the tension between his concept of a holy church and the Corinthians' failure to live up to this standard? Answering these questions reveals Paul's concern that the Corinthians conform to his interpretation of the divine mystery of Christ.

The reason why Paul wrote this letter can be seen most succinctly in the thanksgiving section in 1:4-9. In these verses, Paul gives thanks to God for his grace in Christ Jesus that enriches and empowers the Corinthians to live as holy people in fellowship with Christ until Christ returns. In this section, Paul appears optimistic in the power of grace to transform the community into imitating him as he imitates Christ (4:16; 11:1). Yet, his optimism turns to sarcasm as he is forced to censure the Corinthians for being immature because their behavior was contrary to the model of the cross.

Paul received reports by way of Chloe's people that some in the community were quarreling and the possibility of division existed (1:10-12). This and other problems addressed throughout the letter cause him to label the Corinthians as spiritually immature. He writes in 3:1-3,

> I was not able to call you spiritual people but as fleshly people, as infants in Christ; I fed you milk and not solid food, for you were not yet able [to eat it], and you are still not able, for you are still fleshly, for when there is jealousy and quarreling among you, are you not fleshly, merely living according to the ways of humanity?

The reports about the Corinthians' behavior suggest that they had failed to see the implications of Paul's preaching after he left Corinth (2:1-5). The situation had to be reversed so that the community might be united and holy, fit for fellowship with the Holy Spirit (1:2; 3:16; 6:19). Paul's apprehension about the church leads to a conflict of ideologies between himself and the Corinthians over what it means to be in fellowship with Christ as a "church" (*ekklēsia*), called out from its environments and old ways of living to a new existence "in Christ."

The underlying cause of this conflict, from Paul's perspective, was that the Corinthians failed to live out the gospel in obedience to the leadership of the Holy Spirit (cf. 2:1-16). Some of them remained adversely influenced by their culture. They were not living by a new paradigm in conformity to Paul's interpretation of the gospel. This is illustrated with problems over immorality (chs. 5–7). Others thought they were beyond the influence of their pagan environment when they ate food sacrificed to idols (chs. 8–10). This lack of growth after Paul's ministry among them was the basic cause of their spiritual immaturity, lack of holy living, and disregard for community and authority.

A more apparent reason for this conflict arose from the different perspectives and influences upon Paul and the Corinthians. This surface symptom contributed to the deeper illness of immaturity. On the one hand, Paul viewed life through the event of Christ's death and resurrection. He, like other first-century Jews, had apocalyptic hopes of God's restoration of Israel and final triumph over evil, but these hopes were significantly altered when Paul had a visionary experience of the risen Jesus (Gal 1:11-17; Acts 9:1-9). This vision convinced him that Jesus was the messiah and object of revelation in the divine plan for restoration. Paul then became one of the most influential interpreters in the early church of this fulfillment of apocalyptic hopes.[1]

The Corinthians, on the other hand, came from a syncretistic environment with a religious mix of Roman, Greek, Eastern, African, and even Jewish religious elements. In Paul's judgment, they were indistinguishable from their

---

[1] See J. Christiann Beker, *Paul the Apostle: The Triumph of God in Life and Thought* (Minneapolis: Fortress, 1980); idem, *Paul's Apocalyptic Gospel: The Coming Triumph of God* (Philadelphia: Fortress, 1982).

cultural environment and acted like the pagans around them because of their behavior contrary to the mystery of Christ. Even those who thought they were free from their world acted no differently from those of the world because of their lack of love for their brothers and sisters (8:9-12). Paul uses his authority as founder and apostle of the church to convince them to accept his interpretation of spirituality and assumes that the power of his rhetoric will be effective for change.

Paul's Christ-Ideology

The letter suggests that behind Paul's concern for the spiritual maturity of the Corinthians was his motivation for providing them a better paradigm by which to live, a paradigm based upon the revelation of the "mystery of God" through the death and resurrection of Jesus Christ (1 Cor 2:1). When Paul writes about the "wisdom of God in mystery" (2:7), he uses language common to religious movements of his time. The following section examines the background of this thought in order to distinguish how Paul may have contextualized it as the solution for the problems in Corinth.

The Background and Content of Paul's Ideology

One of the major debates during the twentieth century was over the background and influences upon Paul's thought. Was Paul's religious hermeneutic more influenced by Hellenism or by Judaism? Was Paul a Hellenistic Jew or a Jewish Hellenist? Or, should such a distinction even be made? Can the ideological background of Paul actually be determined? A second major area of debate, related to the first, has been over what constitutes the center or core of Paul's faith. Was christology, anthropology, eschatology, apocalyptic, or something else Paul's main concern and focus? Is there even an essential "core" or "center" to Paul's thought? These are important questions to consider because their answers provide insight into Paul's basic ideology which then must be examined in the context of 1 Corinthians.

At the end of the nineteenth and beginning of the twentieth centuries, scholars in the history-of-religions school (*Religionsgeschichtliche Schule*) contended that Paul's background could be traced to the Hellenistic religions of the period.[2] Other scholars argued that Paul's background was Jewish and

---

[2] Wilhelm Bousset, for example, concluded that Paul's religion was the cult of the Risen Christ patterned after the mysteries (*Kyrios Christos: A History of the Belief in Christ from the Beginnings of Christianity to Irenaeus*, trans. John E. Steely [Nashville: Abingdon, 1970] 153–69). The heritage of the history-of-religions school has continued even up until recent decades. For example, J. H. Randall maintains that Paul formulated "the whole Christian system of salvation from sin and the whole framework of the redemptive system" in parallel if not even borrowed from "the many mystery cults of the time with their widespread myth of the dying

that the only thing he had in common with the religions of his day was terminology. Richard Kabisch, for example, concluded that Paul's eschatology arose out of the Judaism of his day which looked forward to the revealing of the messiah. Paul also looked forward to the restoration of Israel but believed that Jesus was the messiah who had already come, setting the end of time in motion.[3] Kabisch argued that Paul's whole theology revolves around this eschatological expectation.[4]

Albert Schweitzer was the next to assert extensively Paul's Jewishness and argued that Paul's thought developed out of Jewish apocalyptic hopes, although expressed with Greek religious terminology.[5] For Schweitzer, the clue to understanding Paul comes from his context of Jewish and early Christian apocalypticism and not from the Hellenistic mystery religions.[6] Paul's apocalypticism was expressed in his "Christ-mysticism," the identification of the believer with Christ resulting in the assurance of resurrection and participation in the kingdom of God.[7] This fellowship or solidarity of the church with the messiah in this present, natural world guarantees fellowship with him in the future. After Christ's death and resurrection, there is a new mode of existence that makes it possible for those who are in Christ to enter this new existence and thereby live in the resurrected state even while still living in the present evil world. The Spirit is the manifestation of the power of the resurrection and the guarantee of the future eschatological glory.[8] According

---

and rising savior or Lord . . . Christianity at the hands of Paul became a mystical system of redemption, much like the cult of Isis, and the other sacramental or mystery religions of the day" (*Hellenistic Ways of Deliverance and the Making of the Christian Synthesis* [New York: Columbia University Press, 1970] 152, 153, 154).

[3] A key passage articulating Paul's concern and hopes for the restoration of Israel is Romans 9–11. That this was Paul's concern before his transformation (Gal 1:11-17) can be gathered from his life as a Pharisee concerned for the purification of Israel and persecution of the heretical Christian movement (Phil 3:3-6), and from his going first to Jews and then having to be called to the Gentiles (Rom 1:16; Acts 18:6).

[4] Richard Kabisch, *Die Eschatologie des Paulus in ihren Zusammenhängen mit dem Gesamtbegriff des Paulinismus* (Göttingen: Vandenhoeck & Ruprecht, 1893). William Wrede, *Paulus* (Tübingen: Mohr/Siebeck, 1904) also contributed to the early exploration of eschatology in Paul.

[5] Albert Schweitzer, *Paul and His Interpreters*, trans. William Montgomery (New York: Macmillan, 1912) x, 239.

[6] Schweitzer writes, "Paulinism and Greek thought have nothing, absolutely nothing, in common. Their relation is not even one of indifference, they stand opposed to one another" (*Paul and His Interpreters*, 99).

[7] Albert Schweitzer, *The Mysticism of Paul the Apostle*, trans. William Montgomery (New York: Holt, 1931) 3.

[8] Schweitzer says, "The Spirit of God is in men only since men have been 'in Christ Jesus,' and in union with His corporeity have also part in the Spirit of God by which this is animated. The Holy Spirit, therefore, comes to the believer from Christ and as the Spirit of Christ. It is through the being-in-Christ that they have part in it. Not as natural men, but as those who

to Schweitzer, Paul's mystical doctrine of redemption in Christ stands at the beginning and center of all of the other themes in his letters. For example, Schweitzer calls Paul's doctrine of justification by faith, "a subsidiary crater, which has formed within the rim of the main crater—the mystical doctrine of redemption through the being-in-Christ."[9] With this new existence in Christ, the dominion of law and sin are destroyed. Both baptism and the Lord's supper are means by which one can enter into union with Christ in the present. Believers in union with the resurrected Christ can experience in this life an eschatological ethic of liberation from sin and the flesh promised in the eschaton.

Unfortunately, Schweitzer's insights were to be neglected by many scholars over the following decades with the dominance of the gnostic approach of Richard Reitzenstein and the existentialist approach of Rudolf Bultmann.[10] However, interest in Paul's Jewish background was not entirely eclipsed, and explorations of the relationship of Paul's thought to Jewish apocalyptic again were still pursued. Significant ground was broken by Erwin Ramsdell Goodenough, who argued that the concept of the mysteries had taken hold within first-century Hellenistic Judaism, with Philo of Alexandria being the prime example. The desire for the Hellenistic person was to experience true reality, existence, or knowledge, often symbolized in the gods of the mysteries.[11] In more recent decades, William D. Davies has asserted that Paul's background came specifically from Pharisaism and that everything in Paul can be understood solely on Jewish grounds. This thesis suggested to Davies that Paul only used terms and concepts that existed in the milieu of his day.[12]

Another modern voice in support of Paul's Jewishness is Johan Christiann Beker, who argues extensively that the core of Paul's thought

---

are actually dying and rising again with Christ, are they vehicles of the Spirit" (*The Mysticism of Paul*, 165).

[9] *The Mysticism of Paul*, 225.

[10] Richard Reitzenstein, *Hellenistic Mystery-Religions: Their Basic Ideas and Significance*, trans. John E. Steely, PittsTMS (Pittsburgh: Pickwick, 1978) 84–89; and Rudolf Bultmann, *Primitive Christianity in Its Contemporary Setting*, trans. by Reginald H. Fuller (New York: Meridian, 1957) 170–77.

[11] Erwin Ramsdell Goodenough, *By Light, Light: The Mystic Gospel of Hellenistic Judaism* (New Haven: Yale University Press, 1935).

[12] Davies criticized those who view Paul as relying upon the mysteries because of (1) the late date and lack of information of the sources, (2) the silence of Christian writers about the mysteries until the end of the second century, (3) the lack of certain Pauline features in the mysteries, (4) the vast difference between the historical Christ and the mythical gods of the mysteries, (5) the lack of absorption into the divine through union with Christ, (6) the failure of outward sacraments to unite mystically believers and Christ, (7) no loss of personal identity in Paul as in the mysteries and no faith like that in Paul to be found in the mysteries, and (8) no clear link between Paul's vocabulary and the mysteries (William D. Davies, *Paul and Rabbinic Judaism: Some Rabbinic Elements in Pauline Theology* [London: SPCK, 1980] 89–98).

comes from his apocalyptic hopes in the coming kingdom of God. Beker has drawn attention to the neglected eschatological emphasis of Albert Schweitzer. According to Beker, the coherent center of the gospel revolves around the apocalyptic interpretation of the Christ-event with the imminent triumph of God. Beker argues that modern critics have taken apocalyptic out of the center of Paul's thought and have "collapsed apocalyptic eschatology into christology." The one feature Paul kept after conversion was his apocalyptic thought structure, which he modified based on the Christ-event and its profound influence upon human history. Christ initiated the eschatological shift from the "not yet" to the "already," but the "not yet" was not lost.[13]

A danger that arises when considering the apocalyptic structure of Paul's thought, as Beker does, is that it is easy to lose the content of that thought in the structure or replace the content with the structure. Not all of Paul's thought can be easily categorized as apocalyptic, a problem Beker recognizes.[14] Paul shares some similarities with the structure of apocalypticism by way of terminology and imagery, but he modifies some of the content of that structure to focus upon Christ. If there is such a thing as the "core" or "center" of Paul's thought, it is the Christ-event, the divine mystery of God revealed in the death and resurrection of Jesus Christ.[15] Consequently, as Leander Keck has recognized, the primary difference between Paul and Jewish apocalypticism is the death and resurrection of Christ. Keck writes that Paul "rethought everything in light of Christ's death and resurrection. In short, if we find apocalyptic theology in Paul, it will have been transformed."[16]

Alan F. Segal has also recently attempted to pinpoint Paul as an apocalypticist. Segal begins with the presupposition that Paul should be understood from the context of the Jewish apocalypticism which preceded him.[17] He writes, "There is no need to posit any particular relationship between Paul and any known or unknown mystery cult. The vocabulary was probably generally available throughout the Hellenistic world to express mystic empathy with the divine." Segal's point of departure is that "the language probably already existed in the Hellenistic church that Paul joined and that would have baptized him."[18] According to Segal, Paul was a Jewish apocalyptic mystic who had visions of the *merkabah* or throne chariot of God mentioned in Ezekiel 1, Daniel 7, and Exodus 24, and the later object of visionary desire

---

[13] Beker, *Paul the Apostle*, 18, 139, 145.
[14] Ibid., 58.
[15] See Dean Flemming, "Essence and Adaptation: Contextualization and the Heart of Paul's Gospel" (Ph.D. diss., University of Aberdeen, 1987).
[16] Leander E. Keck, "Paul and Apocalyptic Theology," *Int* 38 (1984) 231.
[17] Alan F. Segal, *Paul the Convert: The Apostolate and Apostasy of Saul the Pharisee* (New Haven: Yale University Press, 1990) 34.
[18] Segal, *Paul the Convert*, 136.

in Jewish mysticism.[19] One of the most significant problems with this is that Paul makes no explicit reference to ever seeing in a vision Jesus sitting upon the throne chariot of God. Although Paul did have visions, he is frustratingly silent about them.[20] The link can be made between Paul and apocalyptic thought, but the link between Paul and the later Jewish mystics is strained. Paul's ideology lies somewhere in between the apocalypticism out of which such texts as *1 Enoch, 2 Enoch, 2 Baruch,* 4 Ezra, and other apocalyptic texts emerged, and the more developed Merkabah mysticism of the centuries after him.[21]

Contextualizing Paul

Paul should not be isolated from his environment and could have been influenced from any number of directions. However, his ideology is expressed through the filter of his concern for his churches. His ideology is always given from his own perspective. The "Paul" seen in the New Testament is a selective "Paul," the image of himself he intends to be seen. Beker has emphasized the contingent nature of Paul's letters, that Paul wrote to specific situations with specific purposes in mind.[22] For example, some of the imagery and terms Paul uses in Romans are not found in 1 Corinthians. Even the two epistles,

---

[19] Ibid., 40–52.

[20] C. K. Barrett writes, "To Paul, the spiritual world was unmistakably real, and from time to time he experienced it in an ecstatic way; but so far from cultivating this kind of experience he rather disparaged it, and laid no weight on it in his exposition and defense of the gospel" (*The Second Epistle to the Corinthians* [London: Adam and Charles Black, 1973] 34). For similar views, see Davies, *Paul and Rabbinic Judaism,* 87, 196–97, who argues that Paul's visions do not form the basis of any of his teaching; James D. G. Dunn, *Jesus and the Spirit* (Philadelphia: Westminster, 1975) 213–16, 339; Russell Spittler, "The Limits of Ecstasy: An Exegesis of 2 Corinthians 12:1-10," in *Current Issues in Biblical and Patristic Interpretation,* ed. Gerald F. Hawthorne (Grand Rapids: Eerdmans, 1975) 259–66; Andrew T. Lincoln, *Paradise Now and Not Yet: Studies in the Role of the Heavenly Dimension in Paul's Thought with Special Reference to His Eschatology,* SNTSMS 43 (Cambridge: Cambridge University Press, 1981) 71–86.

[21] Another notorious problem which plagues discussion on whether or not to call Paul an apocalypticist without any qualification is the enigmatic nature of "apocalyptic." Recently, scholars have come to somewhat of a consensus concerning the definition of "apocalyptic" and have distinguished between apocalyptic literature as a literary genre and apocalypticism as a mindset or ideology that lies behind the literature. Paul shares more with apocalypticism than with apocalyptic literature. See further John J. Collins, ed., *Apocalypse: The Morphology of a Genre, Semeia* 14 (Missoula, Mont.: Scholars, 1979); John M. Court, "Paul and the Apocalyptic Pattern," in *Paul and Paulinism: Essays in Honour of C. K. Barrett,* ed. M. D. Hooker and S. G. Wilson, 57–66 (London: SPCK, 1982); Richard E. Sturm, "Defining the Word 'Apocalyptic': A Problem in Biblical Criticism," in *Apocalyptic and the New Testament, Essays in Honor of J. L. Martyn,* ed. by Joel Marcus and Marion Soards, 17–48 (Sheffield: JSOT Press, 1989).

[22] Beker, *Paul the Apostle,* 11. See also William G. Doty, *Letters in Primitive Christianity,* GBS (Philadelphia: Fortress, 1977) 37–38.

which seem to be similar in theology, Romans and Galatians, use different terms and imagery. This contextualization by Paul is a significant matter in reference to his paradigm for the Corinthian church.

Dean Flemming has argued that at the "core" or "center" of Paul's contextualization is the Christ-event, the death and resurrection of Jesus Christ. While Paul was willing to contextualize the gospel for the Hellenistic environs of his churches, he did not want to distort the basic message of the gospel.[23] This approach allows Paul to use both Hellenistic and Jewish terms and images and yet also allows him to be contingent in specific situations. Paul, as a former Pharisee, was steeped in first-century Judaism yet recognized that his message concerning Christ had to be understood by both Jews and Greeks (1 Cor 9:19-23). Therefore, he picked terms and images that were relevant to the situations at hand. In his letters, he takes his basic paradigm of the revelation of Christ and its meaning for believers and applies it to the specific situations that his readers faced. This concept is valid for 1 Corinthians as well, where Paul's language concerning the divine mystery could and should be understood by both Greeks and Jews—at least that is Paul's intention (1:24).

Consequently, this does not invalidate apocalypticism as a useful hermeneutic for understanding Paul's ideology in 1 Corinthians. Apocalypticism was an ideology that could be used and modified by various groups for their own purposes.[24] Paul consciously or unconsciously used apocalyptic concepts to express his understanding of the gospel. He, like many of the hero figures in Jewish apocalyptic, had visionary experiences, but the heavenly figure of his visions was the risen Christ Jesus, Lord and Son of God (Gal 1:11-17). This vision of Christ became the foundation for Paul's preaching activity and message (1 Cor 15:7-11). His perception of the dualism of the two ages, which is a theme present in apocalyptic texts, was significantly modified by his understanding of the Christ-event.[25] He held that the death and resurrection of Christ inaugurated a new age, although there is still a temporary overlap between this present evil age and the glorious age to come. The power of this present evil age, which is symbolized in sin and death, has been conquered by Christ's redemption and resurrection. Only those in fellowship with Christ through the power of the Holy Spirit can live in victory over this evil age (1 Cor 15:23, 51-57).

The revealing of divine mysteries is also common in apocalyptic literature.[26] In this literature, these mysteries were hidden by God and revealed

---

[23] Flemming, "Essence and Adaptation," 102, 533.
[24] See John J. Collins, *The Apocalyptic Imagination: An Introduction to the Jewish Matrix of Christianity* (New York: Crossroads, 1992) 9–32.
[25] Beker, *Paul the Apostle*, 136; cf. Sturm, "Defining the Word 'Apocalyptic,'" 36.
[26] E.g., Dan 2:18-19, 27-30; 1QS 3:23; 4:18; 1QpHab 7:5; 1Q27; *1 Enoch* 103:2; 106:19;

to certain elect people. The content of these mysteries included a key intermediary called by different names including "Son of Man" (*1 Enoch* 46:2), "Chosen One" (40:5), "Lord of the Spirits," "Lord of Wisdom" (63:1-4), "Messiah" (*1 Enoch* 48:10), the "Son of God" (4 Ezra 13:32), and others. He is identified with the "Lord of Glory" in *1 Enoch* 63:2, 11. The "Son of Man" appears at the center of Enoch's vision (48:2-3), providing insight and understanding (49:3), revealing secrets to the worthy (46:3; 48:10; 49:3), but confounding the rulers of the world (46:4-6). He makes known the wisdom of God to the righteous and holy, and salvation is in his name (48:7). The "Elect One" has wisdom, gives thoughtfulness, knowledge, and strength (49:1-4). Another subject disclosed through mystery is the wisdom of God, as seen in Enoch's second vision in *1 Enoch* 37. The third subject of these mysteries is the revelation of future events. There is a paraenetic purpose behind this revelation of future events with emphasis on gaining wisdom which leads to knowledge and understanding and gives meaning to the present time (*2 Bar* 81:4; 85:8; 4 Ezra 6:32-33; 10:38; 13:8; 14:5). The characteristic eschatology in Jewish apocalypticism involves the belief in an early end to the world or this present age which is governed by evil powers. Only the person to whom God has revealed the secrets or mysteries knows about the end, and this knowledge leads to salvation. The unrighteous have not been given the meaning of the mysteries of the end of time and are doomed to judgment and condemnation.

Paul's Ideology of the Christ-Event

Paul uses a concentration of apocalyptic terms and imagery in 1 Corinthians. His ideology is Christ-centered. The goal of human existence is fellowship with Christ. Communion with Christ for Paul becomes the gauge for living. The primary metaphor and description for the new reality brought by the revelation of Christ is being "in Christ" (Col 1:27).[27] Paul succinctly

---

2 Enoch 24:3; 4 Ezra 10:38; 14:5; Rev 10:7. See further, Raymond E. Brown, *The Semitic Background of the Term "Mystery" in the New Testament* (Philadelphia: Fortress, 1968).

[27] "In Christ" occurs in the Pauline corpus (disputed and undisputed letters) at least 161 times. It also occurs outside Paul: John 6:5, 6; 14:20, 30; 15:2-7; 16:33; 17:21; Acts 4:2, 9, 10, 12; 13:39; 1 Pet. 3:16; 5:10, 14; 1 John 2:5, 6, 8, 24, 27, 28; 3:6, 24; 5:11, 20; Rev. 1:9; 14:13. Also it appears in 1 Clem. 32:4; 38:1; Ignatius *Eph*. 1:1; *Trall*. 9:2; and *Rom*. 1:1; 2:2. Other prepositions are used with "Christ" which show fellowship with Christ including "with Christ," "of Christ," "Christ in you," and others. It is beyond the confines of this study to explore the many positions concerning the use of the phrase "in Christ." George Eldon Ladd (*A Theology of the New Testament* [Grand Rapids: Eerdmans, 1974] 481–83), among others, gives a brief history of scholarship. Some of the significant works include G. Adolf Deissmann, *Die Neutestamentliche formel "In Christo Jesu"* (Marburg: Elwert, 1892); Friedrich Büchsel, "'In Christus' bei Paulus," *ZNW* 42 (1949) 141-58; A. Oepke, "*En*," in *TDNT* 2:537–39;

expresses this fellowship with Christ in Galatians 2:20: "I have been crucified with Christ, and I no longer live, but Christ lives in me. The life I live now in the flesh, I live by faith in the son of God who loved me and gave himself in my behalf." The key for experiencing communion with Christ lies with sovereignty—who is in control. Paul realized the futility of living life to please his own desires (cf. Phil 3:4-11). In 2:19 he says that he "died" in regard to the law held under the control of sin. Death symbolizes the cessation of relationship. Paul saw himself moving from the sphere where sin is in control to the sphere of where Christ is in control. For Paul, every thought, word, and deed must come under the control of Christ (Phil 1:21). The death of *self* is not a death of personhood, but a cessation of control. F. F. Bruce comments, "The risen Christ is the operative power in the new order, as sin was in the old."[28] There are two alternatives for Paul: either sin is in control of the self or Christ is in control. Just as Christ gave himself on the cross and received resurrected life, so also believers give up themselves in order to receive a new life (Rom 6:4). Morna D. Hooker writes, "It is not that Christ and the believer change places, but rather that Christ, by his involvement in the human situation, is able to transfer believers from one mode of existence to another."[29] Christ lives within the believer through the Holy Spirit as the sovereign, providing a new spiritual existence free from the condemnation and control of sin (Rom 8:1-2).

When Paul speaks of communion or fellowship with Christ, he is referring to a new eschatological existence inaugurated by the death and resurrection of Christ. One becomes a participant in this existence now by identifying with Christ's death and resurrection through dying to the old way of life controlled by sin and rising to a new way of life controlled by righteousness. He writes in Romans 6:5-8,

> For if we share [with Christ] in the likeness of his death, we will also share in his resurrection. For we know that our old person [*anthrōpos*] was crucified with him, in order that the body of this sin might be destroyed so that we may no longer serve sin. For the one who has died has been freed from sin. So if we die with Christ, we believe that we will also be raised with him.

Ernest Best, *One Body in Christ* (London: SPCK, 1955); Fritz Neugebauer, "Das paulinische 'in Christo,'" *JNTS* 4(1958) 124–38; idem, *In Christus, Untersuchung zum paulinischen Glaubensverstandnis* (Göttingen: Vandenhoek & Ruprecht, 1961); Michel Bouttier, *En Christ: Etude D'Exegese et de Theologie Pauliniennes* (Paris: University of France, 1962); and others.

[28] F. F. Bruce, *The Epistle to the Galatians*, NIGTC (Grand Rapids: Eerdmans, 1982) 144.

[29] Morna D. Hooker, *From Adam to Christ: Essays on Paul* (Cambridge: Cambridge University Press, 1990) 5.

Paul realizes that something must be done to the person in order to find release from the bonds of the present evil age. His answer can be seen in the word *metamorphosis*, "transformation." The new creation involves transformation into the image of Christ through death to the old self and renewal in the image of Christ. New creation in the image of Christ is Paul's most inclusive description of being "in Christ." For Paul, new creation involves a complete transformation of devotion from the objects of the world to the person of Christ. This dying with Christ leads to transformation into the likeness of Christ's glory (2 Cor 3:18). Critical for Paul is that Christ is the agent for this transformation. He writes in 2 Corinthians 5:17, "If anyone is *in Christ*, this one is a new creation" (emphasis added). George Eldon Ladd comments, "The passing of the old does not mean the end of the old age; it continues until the *parousia*. But the old age does not remain intact; the new age has broken in."[30] Thus, Christ creates and is the new life for Paul.

This Christ-ideology stands behind Paul's rhetoric in 1 Corinthians. Paul builds his arguments upon the revelation on the cross and the victory over death in Christ's resurrection (chs. 1–2, 15). His Christ-ideology also serves as his primary conceptual tool to motivate the Corinthians to live according to his example. In other words, the past and future provide the means and motivation for fellowship with Christ *in the present*. Paul criticizes the Corinthians because they had not applied his Christ-ideology in their context and had not allowed it to transform their behavior and form their community in holiness and love. He has to return to the fundamentals, what he terms "milk," because of their lack of maturity (3:1). They were being adversely influenced by their pagan environments and were not following the way of the Christ-event as he modeled it.

Environmental Influences upon the Corinthians' Ideology

Consequently, the adverse religious context of the city of Corinth stands behind many of the passages in 1 Corinthians in which Paul confronts the church. Paul attributes many of the problems that the Corinthians faced to influences from their cultural environment and, most significantly, to their inability to live differently from this environment and live according to the paradigm of the divine mystery. Not every behavior of the unbelieving world is wrong, for example, eating food sacrificed to idols (8:4; 10:15-27). The problem, however, is when such activity contradicts Paul's paradigm of a holy church full of loving people (8:9; 10:28-29).

---

[30] Ladd, *A Theology of the New Testament*, 480.

Paul appears disappointed that the Corinthians had not fully lived out their new life in Christ but still allowed pagan practices to continue to the detriment of the *koinōnia* of the church. Many problems resulted from this continuing influence upon the community, many of which will be discussed in the following chapters. As an example, issues of sexual immorality and eating food sacrificed to idols are the major topics of Paul's second major argument in 5:1-11:1. In the midst of this argument, and after giving a catalogue of vices, Paul writes in 6:11, "And some of you were these things. But you were washed, you were sanctified, you were justified in the name of the Lord Jesus Christ and in the Spirit of our God." Some of the Corinthians acted as if fellowship with Christ made no difference in the way they should live, so Paul calls them to a new way of life.

The Emerging Community

The Corinthian church, like other early churches, functioned as a form of voluntary association which attracted a heterogenous population.[31] Diverse individuals or groups merged in a faith community that lacked a developed self-understanding. Since orthodoxy was regional in nature and not yet defined, the appeal to authority was limited.[32] As a consequence, many of the new believers in Corinth retained elements of their former religions, and these were causing them problems and limiting their new life in Christ. Paul uses his authority and position to define what he considers the true or "orthodox" interpretation of spirituality. If the Corinthian church were like other Pauline churches, it likely included a cross-section of urban society.[33] Religiously, this meant a mix of people from predominantly Greco-Roman religions and a small, but not insignificant, number of Jews. Whatever the religious mix of the Corinthian church, both Jewish and Gentile understandings are implied in Paul's rhetoric (cf. 1:22-24).

---

[31] Wayne A. Meeks, *First Urban Christians: The Social World of the Apostle Paul* (New Haven: Yale University Press, 1983) 75–84.

[32] Walter Bauer noted the regional variations in early Christianity and showed that it is impossible to find any one orthodox position in early Christianity, and early "heresy" was only regional Christianity. These variations become heresy only at a later time when heresy was the loser in a power struggle (*Rechtgläubigkeit und Ketzerei im ältesten Christentum* (Tübingen: Mohr/Siebeck, 1934). Helmut H. Koester has continued Bauer's thesis by arguing that the diversity in early Christianity was caused by two factors: "first, by the several different religious and cultural conditions and traditions of the people who became Christians; and, second, by the bewildering though challenging impact of Jesus' own life, works, words, and death" ("The Structure and Criteria of Early Christian Beliefs," in *Trajectories through Early Christianity*, ed. James M. Robinson and Helmut Koester [Philadelphia: Fortress, 1971] 205).

[33] Meeks, *First Urban Christians*, 73.

It is impossible to determine what portion of the Corinthian church was Jewish and what portion was Gentile, but evidence suggests that both were present.[34] Gordon Fee proposes that the church was a mirror of the city of Corinth and was predominantly Gentile.[35] The phrase "when you were Gentiles" (*hote ethnē ēte*) in 12:2 as well as the mention of issues facing Gentile Christians (particularly those in chs. 6–10) provide strong exegetical support for this view. Paul addresses both the "circumcised" and "uncircumcised" in 7:18-20. A substantial segment of the Corinthian church likely came from a Hellenistic environment where the Greek mysteries, emperor worship, and the Greco-Roman pantheon were the dominant religions and way of life. Roman Corinth was a significant center for the worship of Aphrodite, Apollo, Asklepios, Hera Argaea, the Oracle of Delphi, Tyche, Demeter and Core, and others.[36]

In addition, a small number in this church may have come from a Jewish background. Corinth contained a substantial Jewish population.[37] According to Philo of Alexandria, Jews of the Diaspora came to Corinth as early as the reign of Caligula in 37–41 CE.[38] Philo lists Corinth as one of the three cities in his catalog of geographical regions of the Diaspora, suggesting that it was a place of considerable Jewish population.[39] Internal evidence in the letter also

---

[34] Jerome Murphy-O'Connor says of the sixteen known individuals of this church, six are explicitly Jewish (Aquila, Crispus, Prisca, Sosthenes, Jason, Sosipater) and two are Gentile (Erastus, Justus) (*Paul: A Critical Life* [Oxford: Clarendon, 1996] 273).

[35] Fee, *First Corinthians*, 3-4.

[36] Ben Witherington III, *Conflict and Community in Corinth: A Socio-Rhetorical Commentary on 1 and 2 Corinthians* (Grand Rapids: Eerdmans, 1995) 12–18.

[37] Witherington proposes that "as many as two-thirds of all Jews in Paul's day lived outside Palestine. About seven percent of the empire's population appears to have been Jewish. They ranged from very sectarian and separatist to very Hellenized, and also from rather wealthy to slaves, though there appear to have been fewer Jewish slaves than slaves of any other ethnic group" (*Conflict and Community*, 27).

[38] Philo, *Leg.* 281-82.

[39] Jewish communities resulted from the natural migration of Diaspora Jews to almost every town and city of the Roman empire. Like minded people naturally associated with one another. For the Jews, this meant association at synagogue gatherings (Meeks, *First Urban Christians*, 33–36). The inscription on a broken lintel reading [Sun]agogē Ebr[aiōn], found in 1898 and published in 1903 by Benjamin Power, led some scholars to think that the synagogue of Paul's day had been found (see Benjamin Powell, "Greek Inscriptions from Corinth," *AJA* 7 [1903] 60–61). It was subsequently determined, however, to be from a later period (see Benjamin Merritt, ed., *Greek Inscriptions, 1896–1927;* vol. 8, part 1 of *Corinth: Results of Excavations Conducted by the American School of Classical Studies at Athens* [Cambridge: Harvard University Press, 1931] 79). Not to be discouraged by this later dating, John McRay suggests that this finding still could be important for understanding Paul's time. He writes, "Since it was found on the Lechaion Road at the foot of the marble steps leading to the Propylaea, the synagogue from which it came likely stood north of the Propylaea and the Fountain of Peirene. The synagogue in which Paul preached probably lies under the later one, since Jews in ancient Israel

implies that there was a small percentage of Jews in the church, including the Jewish names mentioned (1:1, 14; 16:19; Rom 16:23; cf. Acts 18:2, 8, 17, 18, 26; and 16:19), visits to Corinth by Cephas and Apollos, the strongly Jewish illustration in 7:18-19 concerning circumcision,[40] allusion to a mixed audience (1 Cor 1:22-24; 9:20-22), appeal to the Mosaic Law (9:8-10; 14:34; 2 Cor 3:4-18), quotations from the Old Testament which assume knowledge of their context (2 Cor 6:2; 9:9; 10:17), and reference to the exodus generation in 10:1-13.[41] Some of these Jewish elements may have come by way of Paul's own experience but still imply that his audience would be somewhat familiar with his terminology.

Cultural Influences

The city of Corinth was a busy center of trade and a temporary stop-over for travelers because of its location, which made it ideal as a melting pot of ideas and religions. According to Dio Chrysostom (40–120 CE), sophists gathered around the temple of Poseidon during the Isthmian games along with writers, poets, jugglers, lawyers, fortune tellers, and peddlers. Then strangers gathered around these people to listen and to spectate, but the Corinthians were so used to such people selling their wares or philosophies that they paid little heed.[42] In the second century CE, Pausanias (d. c. 180 CE) journeyed through the area of Corinth and noted over thirty-seven sacred sites and statues, not including those listed from nearby Cenchreae and Isthmia, more than any other city in the Peloponnese.[43] An earthquake in 77 CE destroyed much in Corinth, so it is difficult to tell which temples and shrines may have existed during Paul's visit and which were newly built or rebuilt after Paul, but there must have been some continuity throughout this period.

Two Ideologies in Conflict

New converts to Paul's Christianity found themselves in the midst of this syncretistic environment. For most, belief in Jesus Christ would have been quite

---

tended to rebuild synagogues over previously destroyed ones" (John McRay, *Archeology and the New Testament* [Grand Rapids: Baker Book House, 1991] 319-20). There is still debate as to the actual importance of this inscription for Paul's time. See also Richard E. Oster, "Use, Misuse and Neglect of Archaeological Evidence in Some Modern Works on 1 Corinthians (1 Cor 7,1-5; 8,10; 11,2-16; 12,14-26)" *ZNW* 83 (1992) 52–73, especially 55–58.

[40] David A. Horrell, *The Social Ethos of the Corinthian Correspondence: Interests and Ideology from 1 Corinthians to 1 Clement* (Edinburgh: T. & T. Clark, 1996) 91–92.

[41] Witherington, *Conflict and Community*, 24–25.

[42] Dio Chrysostom, *Or.* 8.5-10.

[43] See Pausanius, *Desc. Gr.* 2.1.7—2.5.1; Donald Engels, *Roman Corinth: An Alternative Model for the Classical City* (Chicago: University of Chicago, 1990) 43–44.

a new way of looking at the world, though it may have been cloaked in terms with which they were familiar. It was a struggle for them to move from their world to Paul's world. As with all communication, the message Paul preached filtered through the complex religious and cultural experiences of the people of this church. Hans Dieter Betz comments, "The Corinthians did not simply accept the gospel Paul gave them, but went ahead and interpreted that gospel in terms of their hellenistic religiosity."[44]

Consequently, it is evident that some of Paul's views were different from some of the typical beliefs and practices of Hellenistic religions and culture. Although he shared much with Hellenism and Judaism, he had some significant differences. Moreover, both Jewish and Gentile religion and culture proved inadequate to him outside of Christ. Because of this, Paul's letter urges the Corinthians to accept and live by his interpretation of life in Christ. His communication with the Corinthians serves as an attempt to bring the Corinthian church into conformity with his "orthodox" view of how followers of Christ ought to live. There was no such thing as one homogenous church at Corinth. What one finds in Paul's reactions and directions in the letter is a diverse group facing many internal and external challenges.

These different perspectives led to a conflict of ideology over what constitutes spiritual maturity in Christ. Paul writes that the crucifixion of Jesus Christ is a paradox in the minds of those who do not believe in him, in that it is foolishness to the Gentiles and weakness to the Jews, yet in the divine plan, it displays the wisdom and strength of God (1:22-24). This message of the death and resurrection of Christ as the divine "wisdom in mystery" brings righteousness, sanctification, and redemption (1:30), and is revealed by means of the divine Spirit to those who are "spiritual" (2:10, 13). One of Paul's basic problems with the Corinthians is over the definition of "spirituality." His definition of spirituality and theirs differ at some critical points, which resulted in a conflict of ideologies. Spiritual maturity for Paul results from living according to the example of Christ (11:1). His letter, however, implies that the Corinthians attributed their spiritual status to their wisdom, knowledge, spiritual gifts, and speaking abilities (cf. 1:5-7). In other words, they attributed strength and wisdom to their human abilities and achievements and not to divine grace and revelation. Paul reverses this and writes that their wisdom and strength were actually weakness and folly. If the Corinthians would model Paul as he imitated Christ in this paradox, then they too could grow into maturity. Even if they were sincere in their efforts at living out Paul's message, which the letter seems to indicate, they still strayed from the course Paul had intended. They failed to distinguish themselves

---

[44] Betz, "The Problem of Rhetoric and Theology," 24.

adequately from their environment and evidenced a lack of holiness without and love within.

The Corinthian church appears to have had a struggle in its development to maturity. This maturing process involved conflict both within the church and between the church members and its leadership. Bruce Malina states that conflict naturally arises in a community as a result of growth and change.[45] To resolve this group tension, a community will seek to become more organized and centralized often around a key authoritative figure who has the power to command. Wayne A. Meeks writes,

> No group can persist for any appreciable time without developing some patterns of leadership, some differentiation of roles among its members, some means of managing conflict, some ways of articulating shared values and norms, and some sanctions to assure acceptable levels of conformity to those norms.[46]

The church in Corinth was at a significant juncture in its development. The new belief in Jesus as Lord and Christ and joining the new association called "church" may have meant changes for them in a number of areas. These changes brought uncertainty and questions, and in looking for answers they turned to Paul, their founder and mentor. The relationship between Paul and the Corinthians is reciprocal: the Corinthians accept Paul as an authoritative figure, and Paul assumes himself to be in some type of position of authority and leadership over the community.[47] This mutual relationship of dependence becomes the means by which Paul resolves his differences with them. Paul's answer to this conflict comes from his interpretation of the revelation of Jesus Christ.

Paul's Method for Creating Solidarity and Maturity

Paul attempts to resolve his differences with the Corinthians by urging them to accept his views based upon several criteria. First and foremost, he presumes a shared belief in Jesus Christ (1:2). Paul's basic premise is that Christ is the means of salvation and redemption. There is no indication in the letter that the Corinthians disagreed with this or were insincere in their belief in Christ. They only needed to be compelled in the right direction, which was

---

[45] Malina, "The Social Sciences and Biblical Interpretation," 235. Cf. John G. Gager, *Kingdom and Community: The Social World of Early Christianity* (Englewood Cliffs, N.J.: Prentice-Hall, 1975).

[46] Meeks, *First Urban Christians*, 111.

[47] See further Bengt Holmberg, *Paul and Power: The Structure of Authority in the Primitive Church as Reflected in the Pauline Epistles* (Philadelphia: Fortress, 1978); John Schütz, *Paul and the Anatomy of Apostolic Authority*, SNTSMS 23 (Cambridge: Cambridge University Press, 1975); and the discussion in the next section.

essentially Paul's goal in writing the letter. They shared with him the common heritage of a belief in the death and resurrection of Jesus Christ (15:1-11); Paul had no problem with their basic understanding of the gospel. His real problem with them, however, was their lack of growth and maturity as a result of appropriating this basic creed. Where the two parted ways was with their different interpretations of the gospel, which led to a conflict of ideology. Vernon K. Robbins comments, "A person's ideology concerns her or his conscious or unconscious *enactment* of presuppositions, dispositions, and values held in common with other people."[48] How the Corinthians enacted or failed to enact the common presupposition of the gospel is Paul's primary concern in the letter. They had not taken the necessary steps to grow into a community mature in love and holiness. Paul appeals to the core belief as his primary motivational tool. The means by which he makes this appeal, however, is *his own example* because he views himself as the primary steward and interpreter of this message for the Corinthians.

Paul's Authority and Example to the Community

Paul attempts in his letter to persuade the Corinthians to alter their behavior and beliefs into conformity with his own interpretation of life in Christ by offering himself as an example (4:16; 11:1). This imitation is not simply passive. Paul is concerned with influencing social formation by appealing to his authority as apostle.[49] Part of the basis for his ability to serve as an example comes from his authoritative status as the founder of the community (Acts 18).[50] At times he explicitly appeals to his authority in order to add weight to his rhetoric. For example, in 4:14-16 he counsels the Corinthians out of paternal love by calling himself their father and them his beloved children. According to Ernest Best, one of the primary tasks of a good parent is to guide a child into maturity as an adult, which is also how Paul views his task

---

[48] Robbins, *Exploring the Texture of Texts*, 95, emphasis added.
[49] Elizabeth A. Castelli, *Imitating Paul: A Discourse of Power* (Louisville: Westminster John Knox, 1991) 89–117.
[50] See also 1 Cor 3:6, 10; 4:15. One of the uses of "father" can be for generation; see BAGD, 635; 2 Cor 10:14-16; cf. the account in Acts 18:1-17. When Paul founded this church has been a question of debate. Two points in Acts have external evidence. First, the Edict of Claudius, recorded by Suetonius, expelled Jews from Rome who had rioted "at the instigation of Chrestus" (Suetonius, *De vita Caesarum*: Claudius 25; cf. Acts 18:2). Orosius, *Historiae*, a fifth century ecclesiastical historian, dates this to 49 C.E. Second is the reference in Acts 18:12 where Gallio is named proconsul of Achaia. Excavations at Delphi have provided fragments which allow the year in which Gallio held office to be determined as 50–51 or 51–52. Jerome Murphy-O'Connor has provided some challenges to the traditional method of dating but comes to the typical dates of Paul's visit between 49 and 51 CE (*St. Paul's Corinth: Texts and Archeology* [Wilmington, Del.: Glazier, 1983] 129–52, 173–76).

when writing this letter.[51] Not only is Paul a guardian (*paidagōgos*) to the Corinthians, intrusted with caring for them and raising them as children, but he also has the authority of the father who stands behind the guardian. He wants to create community along ideological grounds with himself as "father" or example.[52] Based upon this and other forms of authority, Paul commands the Corinthians to imitate his communion with Jesus Christ. In this regard, he uses his ideology of the divine mystery of Christ to deal with social problems in the community, or as C. K. Barrett offers, he uses "the ideal" to deal with "the actual."[53] Anthony E. Harvey distinguishes the two kinds of problems Paul faced when he wrote his letters: theological controversies and behavioral improprieties. Harvey contends that Paul confronts theological problems straight on with theological terms and addresses behavioral problems by setting them in their theological context.[54] This may explain why Paul begins the letter with an appeal to the theological basis of the kerygma—the revelation of the divine mystery upon the cross (1:18-2:16). This theology provides the foundation for his practical arguments throughout the rest of the letter.

The Reason for the Letter as Spiritual Growth through Imitation

Paul wrote his letters to specific audiences to address specific situations. This occasional impulse is especially apparent in 1 Corinthians where his rhetoric indicates his reason for writing. When he addresses the concerns and questions of the Corinthians, he relies on his authority and rhetoric to spur the church on to growth. He appeals to these two because he can only use his relationship with the Corinthians and the power of his words to accomplish his purpose.

In writing this letter, he reminds the Corinthians of the primary message he preached to them when he was there: Christ crucified and Christ resurrected (2:2; 15:3-4). They should have known this message, and they should have begun to apply it in their situation.[55] Paul's message (*kērygma*, 2:4) was

---

[51] Ernest Best, *Paul and His Converts* (Edinburgh: T. & T. Clark, 1988) 39.
[52] Malina writes, "Formally speaking, community is a set of values, interests and relationships shared by people who are set apart or set off from others on the basis of some shared quality (for example: ethnicity, gender, disability, behavior, ideology) resulting in a sense of oneness, or brotherhood and/or sisterhood, hence of fictive kinship. Community, then, is a social reality rooted in persons whose values, interests, and lifestyle reflect their oneness with others in their group" ("'Religion' in the World of Paul," 98).
[53] C. K. Barrett, *Essays on Paul* (Philadelphia: Fortress, 1982) 1.
[54] Anthony E. Harvey, "The Opposition to St. Paul," in *Studia Evangelica* IV, ed. F. L. Cross (Berlin: Akademie, 1968) 320.
[55] Paul builds upon knowledge the Corinthians already should have had, as can be seen in the

more than simply the preaching of a wandering philosopher so common in Corinth at that time. Rather, he believed his message, though weak in appearance, contained the very power of God and could lead to transformation and growth into a new way of life.

The basic reason Paul writes this letter is that he wants the Corinthians to live up to their potential for which he optimistically and perhaps sarcastically gives thanks in 1:4-9. He contends that a community of believers should be distinguishable from the world around it. When he came to Corinth, he found a dynamic city open to new religions and ideas. Although he was, to some extent, a product of Hellenistic Judaism and shows many similarities with both Jewish and Gentile contexts, he still experienced opposition and even physical persecution from both Jews and Gentiles "for the sake of the gospel" (cf. 2 Cor 11:23-33). The new believers in Corinth may also have begun to experience a clash with their culture as a result of their new faith in Christ. Evidently, some of the Corinthians were slow to leave the influences of their pagan environment and follow Paul's teaching (e.g., 6:9-11). This created tension between them and Paul. Paul wanted the church to be a holy community in an immoral world (5:9-10). John Chow comments, "Since Paul denied that it was his intention to ask the Corinthians to withdraw totally from the world (1 Cor 5:10), this implies that the relationship between the Corinthians and the pagan world was a point at issue."[56] According to Paul's assessment in chapter 5, the immoral "brother" had gone beyond even the pagans in his immorality (5:1). Having the immoral "brother" in their midst and accepting his behavior caused the Corinthians to succumb to the influence of their pagan context. Therefore, Paul's answer for them is to expel the "brother" and with him, the influence of the flesh (*sarx*) and thereby allow the new life in Christ to penetrate their lives (5:6-8).

There are some positive signs of growth in Corinth, so at least Paul has some basis upon which to build his appeal. For example, he is thankful for the spiritual gifts (*charismata*) given to the Corinthians. But lest the Corinthians feel too self-confident, he gives the basis for his thanksgiving as *God's grace in Christ Jesus* (1:4).[57] Paul attempts to make clear throughout the letter that what the Corinthians received from God came as a *gift* and not by their own effort (4:7), and in this section he reminds them of this very fact. Worthy of note is that he does not give thanks for any quality in the commu-

---

repeated phrase, "do you not know" (3:16; 5:6; 6:2, 3, 9, 15, 16, 19; 9:13, 24). The kerygma should have transformed their outlook. Their behavior and beliefs should have been changed because of Paul's preaching activity and continuing correspondence with them.

[56] Chow, *Patronage and Power*, 113.

[57] Paul mentions grace (*charis*) and gifts (*charisma*) together in Rom 12:6. The root *char-* has the connotation in Paul of a gift offered undeservingly by God. The concept of *charisma* was uniquely developed by Paul (Dunn, *Jesus and the Spirit*, 205–7).

nity but only for God's grace.[58] Fee comments, "The whole of the thanksgiving is God-oriented and Christ-centered. Everything comes *from God* and is given *in Christ Jesus*."[59] Paul gives thanks for some of the very things for which he is in contention with the Corinthians (e.g., speaking, knowledge, and spiritual gifts). He assumes that seeds with the potential to grow had been sown in them; the seeds only needed to sprout and produce. The Corinthians were only "infants" and had to grow into spiritual "adulthood" (3:1-3). Paul attempts to remind the Corinthians of the goal of being like Christ and in fellowship with him, and Paul sees himself as a good example of Christ for them to follow.

Paul's Use of Authority to Resolve His Differences with the Corinthians

Paul's fellowship with the resurrected Christ provided him with authority over his churches. As he writes to the Corinthians, he appeals to this authority in order to conform them to his ways. The work of Bengt Holmberg is a useful tool in understanding how Paul uses his authority in 1 Corinthians. Holmberg utilizes the model of sociologist Max Weber to demonstrate that Paul uses what Weber calls "charismatic authority" in dealing with his churches. Weber does not intend by "charismatic" the New Testament use of the term *charisma*, especially as found in 1 Corinthians. According to Weber's model, this type of authority comes from a prophet's immediate contact with the supernatural or sacred. Charismatic authority disrupts previous routines or institutions and can only be sustained by itself being routinized or institutionalized. Paul's letter to the Corinthians shows early steps in this process of institutionalizing Paul's position by his very attempts to provide a model for imitation. The charismatic leader holds a special position in relation to God that provides him or her with authority over a group. This authority comes not from an office but by virtue of her or his encounter with and subsequent mission from the divine. Weber describes charismatic authority in the following way:

> The term "charisma" will be applied to a certain quality of an individual personality by virtue of which he is considered extraordinary and treated as endowed with supernatural, superhuman, or at least specifically exceptional powers or qualities. These are such as are not accessible to the ordinary person, but are regarded as of divine origin

---

[58] Cf. Rom 1:8; Phil 1:3-5; 1 Thess 1:2-3; Phlm 4-5; Reimund Bieringer, "Paul's Divine Jealousy: The Apostle and His Community in Relationship," in *Studies on 2 Corinthians*, by Reimund Bieringer and Jan Lambrecht (Leuven: Leuven University Press, 1994) 244.
[59] Fee, *First Corinthians*, 36.

or as exemplary, and on the basis of them the individual concerned is treated as a "leader."[60]

Holmberg summarizes his own model of "pure charismatic authority in a religious context" under five headings: (1) the leader's person and way of life, (2) the leader's mission, (3) the relation of the followers to the leader, (4) the behavior of the charismatic group, and (5) the differentiation within the charismatic group. Holmberg's model is useful for illustrating Paul's appeal to the Corinthians to imitate his position because Paul viewed himself as specially endowed as a steward of the divine mysteries of God (4:1).[61]

The first heading of Holmberg's model helps explore Paul's person and way of life in special relationship with the divine. Paul understood his own charismatic authority as having come through a special and direct call from Christ and his position as apostle (Gal 1:1, 11-12; 1 Cor 9:1-2). He saw himself on the same level of authority as the other apostles precisely because of his vision of and direct commission from the risen Jesus Christ (9:1; 15:9-11). Paul also had super-human powers especially endowed from God. The primary manifestation of charisma for him came through the preaching of the gospel received directly from the Lord, a task which he viewed as his primary purpose in life (14:18-19; Gal 1:13). Furthermore, he functioned in a special position between Jesus and his converts. Most notably this position was fulfilled in his serving as the father-figure or founder of various churches. Unlike a "pure" charismatic authority such as Jesus, Paul was only an instrument for bringing people to Jesus, not a savior figure.[62] He could only plant the seeds; it was God who actually produced the harvest (1 Cor 3:5-7). Paul showed no attempt to pre-empt Christ's position as Lord. There was a definite order of authority for him: God, Christ, and then, on his own level, other apostles (11:1, 3).[63] Even with this awareness, however, Paul saw himself standing in a special position as mediator of the ways of Christ as 11:1 implies: "Become imitators of me as I [have become an imitator] of Christ."

Paul's mission falls under Holmberg's second heading. The mission of a "pure" charismatic authority is the founding of a new social order. Unlike a "pure" charismatic leader, Paul stood in a tradition in his identification of the gospel as an independent authority. His charisma was balanced by the higher

---

[60] Max Weber, *Economy and Society. An Outline of the Interpretive Sociology*, ed. by Guenther Roth and Claus Wittich (New York: Bedminster, 1968) 241; quoted by Holmberg, *Paul and Power*, 137.

[61] The following is based on Holmberg, *Paul and Power*, 149–58.

[62] According to Gager, a pure charismatic authority is a theoretical impossibility and historical fiction (*Kingdom and Community*, 70).

[63] Holmberg, *Paul and Power*, 157.

authority of the gospel to which he was subject as an apostle.[64] His message presupposed ethical living consistent with developed Jewish and Gentile traditions and emerging early Christian traditions. However, he at times appealed to his own authority in moral issues. Because of his authority over the church, he could provide his "opinion" (7:12), sometimes with the force of the word of the Lord (14:37).

The third heading proposes that Paul expected and received the respect, imitation, and trust due a founder or father-figure.[65] He expected that his churches would listen to him and obey his commands based on a relationship of love.[66] When he calls himself the father of the Corinthian church in 4:15, he shows a style not of an overbearing authoritarian, but one of teaching, exhorting, explaining, and appealing.[67] He sees himself as an ambassador of Christ. The words he writes carry divine authority and should be obeyed as the very words of Christ (14:37; cf. 2 Cor 5:18-20; 1 Thess 2:13). Paul can also call for imitation of himself precisely because he himself imitates Christ (1 Cor 11:1).

This imitation of Christ is made possible through the indwelling Spirit of Christ. What does Paul want the Corinthians to imitate? Simply stated, Paul wants the Corinthians to experience the charismatic power of the Spirit which, in his understanding, comes through a relationship with the risen Christ. Paul preached to the Corinthians with power from the Spirit *in order that* (cf. the *hina* clause in 2:5) they too might experience the power of God. His charismatic authority as apostle must be distinguished from the potential for charisma in the Corinthian church.[68] The Corinthians, like Paul, could experience the divine presence through the Spirit, but they could not supplant his position as apostle. This would become more of a problem in 2 Corinthians where he had to confront "charismatic" type opponents who threatened his position as apostle (2 Cor 11:13).

The fourth heading of Holmberg's model relates to the Corinthians' obedience to Paul's leadership and their experience of new life according to Paul's perspective. This new life provided an awareness of being elect and holy. The Corinthians would be different from their neighbors if indeed they modeled Paul's life (1 Cor 1:2). John H. Schütz comments that Paul could assert power over his churches because they had a power vacuum in them which could be filled by their appropriating the power of the gospel like Paul

---

[64] Schütz, *Paul and the Anatomy*, 284.
[65] Passages where Paul calls himself a father are 1 Thess 2:5-12; Gal 4:19; 1 Cor 3:1-3a; 4:14-16; 2 Cor 6:11-13; and 12:14. Imitation is connected with fatherhood in Isocrates, *Philip.* 113; *Ad. Dem.* 9.11.
[66] Holmberg, *Paul and Power*, 81.
[67] Ibid., 79.
[68] See Schütz, *Paul and the Anatomy*, 275.

had done.[69] The Corinthians had begun to appropriate Paul's interpretation of the divine mystery of Christ but had not gone the full course; some still held onto their old way of life and had failed to cross-over to Paul's new way of life. Schütz also points out that the gospel, and not some personal attribute, was the source of power for Paul. He adds, "The apostle may preach the gospel, he may thereby make power available but he does not himself provide it or control it."[70] In Paul's view, the fundamental problem with the Corinthians was that they remained tied to their pagan environment and old way of life and had not fully appropriated and accepted his interpretation of the new life in Christ.

Finally, the fifth heading articulates the Corinthians' desire to differentiate between those who had prominent charismatic gifts (e.g., prophecy, tongues, miracle working) and those who had less celebrated gifts or no apparent gifts at all. Paul would have none of that but rather sets limits to the use of such extraordinary gifts (cf. 1 Cor 14:29-32). The use of *charisma* within the group had to be used for the edification of the group and not for the glorification of the individual. The ultimate authority for Paul is the gospel, and its proclamation is the greatest outcome of the endowing of the Holy Spirit (14:1, 3, 5, 19).

Conclusion

Paul's concern for the Corinthian church appears in his effort to persuade them to follow his example. This concern was influenced to some degree by the different backgrounds and experiences of Paul and the Corinthians. Paul's outlook was significantly influenced by his experience of the risen Jesus Christ. His apocalyptic hopes were altered with his belief that a new age had begun with the death and resurrection of Christ which also offered him a new paradigm. The Corinthians, however, were not meeting Paul's standard but were living like the world around them. They had failed to shift paradigms and continued to be adversely influenced by a religious context dominated by a world view different than his. Their pattern of behavior showed him that they had not matured in their spirituality to the point where their ideology was likewise influenced by the Christ-event. Their immature behavior followed the pattern of the world around them and not the divine mystery of the cross.

The letter suggests a collision between these two perspectives. Paul intentionally creates conflict with the Corinthians out of his concern for them as their spiritual mentor. He views the problems in Corinth significant

---

[69] Ibid., 282.
[70] Ibid., 285.

enough to write a letter in response. He contextualizes his gospel and uses his words, example, and authority to accomplish his goal of persuading the Corinthians to accept his answer of appropriating the divine mystery and to grow into maturity. He attempts to create solidarity and maturity by offering a paradigm shift for the Corinthians with specific and expected responses based upon the indicative of communion with Christ. The "mystery of God" is both the subject and object of this paradigm for Paul (2:1, 7). The power of the divine mystery for Paul is that he and those who put their faith in the death and resurrection of Christ (Rom 10:9) have available to them the opportunity to experience restored relationship with God through redemption, justification, and sanctification because of Christ's sacrificial death on their behalf (1 Cor 1:30).

Paul found the solutions to these problems in having fellowship with Jesus Christ through the Holy Spirit. This new existence in Christ is made possible because of the Christ-event (the indicative). Paul's hope is for the future completion of the divine plan with the resurrection of those "in Christ" who have identified with Christ's death and resurrection. Those who have put their faith in Christ should live (the imperative) in the present moment as holy people of love.

3

Revealing the Mystery in the Paradox of the Cross *(1 Corinthians 1–4)*

THE way Paul attempts to solve the problems in Corinth is full of *irony*. On the one hand, he speaks of coming to Corinth with a rod of correction (4:21). Yet, he also speaks with the tenderness of a father concerned for the welfare of his children (4:15). He appears weak (2:1), yet possesses the mind of Christ (2:16). He calls himself a fool (4:10), yet speaks a message of wisdom (2:6). The *paradox* of his demeanor embodies the paradox of his theme in chapters 1–4. He could use his authority as apostle to persuade the Corinthians to follow his example, but chooses, in weakness, to forfeit his apostolic rights in order that some might be saved (9:1, 15; cf. 4:1-13). Instead of an ethos of power and wisdom, he chooses one of weakness and folly.

His status before the Corinthians is not what one might expect in the ancient world for one who intends to impress and persuade. Quintillian wrote,

> But what really carries the greatest weight in deliberative speeches is the authority of the speaker. For he, who would have all men trust his judgment as to what is expedient and honourable, should both possess and be regarded as possessing genuine wisdom and excellence of character.[1]

Paul chooses to live according to a model where power and honor come in being weak and foolish from the world's perspective. He has a different qualification for authority—one based upon the gospel. Instead of beginning his letter on the topic of authority and power, he chooses the themes of weakness and foolishness. He then attempts to convince the Corinthians to follow this ironic way of life!

---

[1] Quintillian, *Inst. Or.* 3.8.12-13.

The way he does this is by appealing to the past revelation of divine wisdom in Christ's death upon the cross. This revelation engenders Paul's solution for the Corinthian community. He uses the paradigm of the cross as his basis for assessing the Corinthians as immature in chapters 3–4. He assumes by the end of chapter 4 that the Corinthians would accept his position and make the necessary changes to conform to his views.

Paul begins by immediately setting up several contrasts which control the remainder of his argument.[2] According to 1:17, his primary task during his first stay in Corinth was to preach the gospel.[3] He clarifies this by stating that he did not preach with clever "words of wisdom" in order that he might not render the message of the cross "powerless" or "meaningless" because of his outstanding wisdom or rhetorical ability. This thought introduces the basic comparison that he deals with in 1:18-4:21 and undergirds much of his argument in the rest of the letter. Simply stated, he puts the best that humanity has to offer—"in wisdom of word" (v. 17), against the best God has to offer—"the word of the cross" (v. 18). His basic message to the Corinthians is that living a life of folly and weakness according to the model of the cross could lead them to spiritual maturity and communal solidarity. How this is actually to be worked out in the community is where the maturity will take place.

This paradox is based on the event of the death and resurrection of Jesus Christ which also serves as the central topic of Paul's preaching. The divine paradox for Paul is that the very power and wisdom of God have been shown in the apparently foolish and weak act of death on a Roman cross. In this paradox is revealed the *divine mystery* which transformed Paul's life and offered a new way of life for the Corinthians (2 Cor 5:17). Christ inaugurated a new way of life in relationship with God by becoming the means of righteousness, sanctification, and redemption for those who put their faith in him (1 Cor 1:30).

Paul references this *past* event as his model for the *present* situation at Corinth. This event was hidden for long ages and prophesied about in the scriptures (Rom 16:25–26) but was revealed at a specific moment *in time*. This moment transformed history and human existence because through death and resurrection, Jesus Christ conquered two of humanity's worst enemies: sin and its consequence of death (1 Cor 15:26; Rom 1:2-4; 5:17). Paul

---

[2] This letter has four major rhetorical arguments or "proofs" in it: 1:18-4:21; 5:1-11:1, 11:2-14:40; and 15:1-57. See Mitchell, *Rhetoric of Reconciliation*, 192–290.

[3] The "cross" is Paul's rhetorical shorthand for the gospel (Margaret M. Mitchell, "Rhetorical Shorthand in Pauline Argumentation: The Functions of the 'The Gospel' in the Corinthian Correspondence," in *Gospel in Paul: Studies in Corinthians, Galatians and Romans for Richard N. Longenecker*, ed. L. Ann Jervis and Peter Richardson, JSNTSup 108 [Sheffield: Sheffield Academic, 1994] 65).

based his own life on this moment of time and the consequences of joining in the death and resurrection of Christ through personal commitment (Gal 2:20). When he faced the problems and questions from Corinth, he returned to his foundation in the preached message. He saw in Christ's submission to death on the cross the model by which the Corinthians could grow into maturity, both spiritually and communally. Christ's death was much more than simply a model of self-less love. His death also offered the potential for a new existence in the sphere of his lordship, a sphere where the Holy Spirit communes with believers in intimate fellowship, empowering them to "have the mind of Christ" (1 Cor 2:16; cf. Phil 2:1-5).

Paul articulates his Christ-ideology in the context of the needs at Corinth by way of a paradox. The Corinthians' ideology must be read through Paul's ironic and sarcastic letter. His letter invites them to accept his evaluation of them and provides opportunity for social and spiritual growth. He also uses the power of his words to demonstrate his own orientation to the paradox of the cross. His authority comes from his demeanor relative to the cross and is his primary tool for motivating the Corinthians to accept his views.

Revealing the Mystery of Christ

The "word of the cross" serves as a dynamic event of eternal significance for Paul. God's recreative power works through the cross-event for those who are *being* saved (1:18). The cross makes new creation possible *now* (cf. Gal 6:14-15) and is the apocalyptic turning point of history. It reverses human expectation in a decisive and dynamic way and establishes new relationship between God and humanity. The significance of the cross as the symbol of the divine paradox is important to Paul's purpose in the letter because it offers the Corinthians the possibility of transformation. Alexandra R. Brown comments that "by this power to dislocate, the Word begins to create the conditions under which readers may be transformed and transferred into a new world."[4] Paul views the word of the cross as the divine "mystery" which has been hidden for long ages and is finally revealed in Christ (cf. Rom 16:25-26). The revelation of this mystery begins a new age and brings new life to those, both Jew and Gentile, who put their faith in Christ (Rom 11:25; Col 1:27; cf. Eph 3:1-11). Paul considered this revelation the key to solving the problems in Corinth and uses himself as an example of how to live out this mystery. His letter *raises* his own position while *razing* the views of the Corinthians.

---

[4] Alexandra R. Brown, *The Cross and Human Transformation: Paul's Apocalyptic Word in 1 Corinthians* (Minneapolis: Fortress, 1995) 76.

The Structure and Purpose of Paul's Argument

The section which begins with 1:18 and ends with 4:21 forms one rhetorical unit. Paul gives an *enumeratio* or recapitulation of his main point in 3:23 when he reminds the Corinthians that they cannot boast because they are dependent on Christ ("you are of Christ," 3:23a). Chapter 4 continues the themes of the previous chapters and provides Paul the opportunity to appeal to his authority in relation to the cross and his example of being "in Christ." Paul uses 1:17 as a transition from the letter's *propositio* or basic topic (1:10) to the first proof and introduces several key terms or concepts which will be repeated throughout the entire unit: wisdom, word, cross and empty or powerless. Ironically, after Paul appeals in 1:17 and other places throughout the argument to a position of weakness based upon the paradigm of the cross, he then reverses this in 4:20 by saying that the kingdom of God consists not in meaningless words but in power.

Paul begins the *probatio* or body of his letter in 1:18. The *probatio* is the heart of a rhetorical speech or letter and lays out the basic arguments using proofs that give the reasons or benefits for the suggested action.[5] Paul begins the body of his letter with reference to the divine paradox of the cross, a paradox that condemns human wisdom and power. He uses the message of the cross to shame and condemn the Corinthians and to alert them to which paradigm they were living by. According to Isocrates,

> It is not, however, possible to turn men from their errors, or to inspire in them the desire for a different course of action without first roundly condemning their present conduct; and a distinction must be made between accusation, when one denounces with intent to injure, and admonition, when one uses like words with intent to benefit.[6]

Paul uses blame or censure against the Corinthians because their behavior revealed that they had not built upon his message and grown spiritually and communally (cf. 4:14), but instead, remained mere "infants" in Christ (3:2). The real issue for Paul is this lack of maturity and not any division which was only one of the *results* of spiritual immaturity. The divisive attitudes and potential rifts could be solved by growing in the divine wisdom about which Paul had preached (cf. 3:1-3).

---

[5] See Mitchell, *Rhetoric of Reconciliation*, 202.
[6] Isocrates, *Or.* 4.130, quoted by Mitchell, *Rhetoric of Reconciliation*, 214, who argues that Paul uses this same type of strategy.

The Cross as Divine Wisdom and Power

Paul's basic ideology can be seen in his message about the cross. He writes in 2:1-2 that he came to Corinth with the sole purpose of preaching Jesus Christ and him crucified. Paul's message to the Corinthians in this letter is contingent upon his interpretation of the problems in Corinth. He expresses his gospel differently in 1 Corinthians than he does in other letters. For example, the legal language of Romans and the experiential language of Philippians correspond to the sapiential language of 1 Corinthians. A clear theme that appears in these and other Pauline letters is the event of the death and resurrection of Jesus Christ and its affects upon humanity.[7] In 1 Corinthians 1–4 Paul begins with this theme and contextualizes it by using terms that were relevant to the situation at Corinth.

Paul and his readers share a basic knowledge of the crucifixion of Jesus, or what Paul terms, the "cross of Christ" (1:17). This tradition is fundamental to his preaching and was indispensable to his early mission and message at Corinth. He opens his argument with his thesis statement in verse 18: the cross, although representing human weakness and foolishness, is the very power of God. Antithetic parallelism in this verse shows the uneven comparison between the foolishness of the world and the power of God by using terms from different semantic fields:

> For the word of the cross
> to those who are perishing is foolishness,
> but to you who are being saved is the power of God.

One would expect "foolishness" to be compared with "wisdom," and "power" to be compared with "weakness." This surprising aporia is intentional on Paul's part because it leads to a tension in the text which is not resolved until verse 25. The final resolution of this illogical comparison allows the wisdom and power of God to stand in complete contrast to human folly and weakness. After verse 25 and until the conclusion and application of the argument in 4:13, Paul expands this illogical idea and uses it to claim a position of authority (cf. 4:14-17). This paradox creates anticipation for transformation.[8] Paul gives two alternatives in verse 18: one leads to destruction ("to those who are perishing") and the other to salvation ("to those who are being saved"). Brown comments,

---

[7] Christopher A. Davis finds four main themes that remain constant in Paul's writings: (1) Christ's death, (2) Christ's resurrection or "eschatological life," (3) the believer's "death" with Christ, and (4) the believer's resurrection or "eschatological life" with Christ ("'The Trust which is the Gospel': The Coherent Center of Paul's Theology" (Ph. D. diss., Union Theological Seminary, 1992) 41.

[8] Cf. Isa 43:19; 65:17-25; Jer 31:31-34; and Ezek 37:4.

Paul has said something new and epistemologically offensive about salvation. It is now not the wisdom of the wise that "saves," despite the high value of wisdom in the traditions of both Jews and Greeks; in fact, this wisdom is equated with "emptiness." Rather, what saves is the "power of the cross," a formulation that is nonsensical in the perspective of worldly wisdom.[9]

As Paul begins to explain the divine paradox, he uses scriptural support from Isaiah 29:14 in 1:19 in order to show God's sovereign freedom to reverse accepted human perceptions. In this quotation, Paul changes the word "hide" (*krypsō*) to "reject" (*athetēsō*) in order to intensify "the divine negation of human wisdom."[10] In the original context of Isaiah, the prophet criticizes superficial traditionalism. Gordon Fee comments,

> In its original context this passage belongs to that grand series of texts that regularly warn Israel, or someone in Israel, not to try to match wits with God (cf. Isa. 40:12-14, 25; Job 38-42). Yet it is the folly of our human machinations that we think we can outwit God, or that lets us think that God ought to be at least as smart as we are.[11]

In 1:20 Paul asks the same question as Isaiah 19:12 in the form of an anaphora: "Where is the wise man?" His second question echoes Isaiah 33:18: "Where is the expert at law?" The third question has Hellenistic connotations: "Where is the debater of this age?" Brown writes, "The three 'occupations' mentioned—sage, scribe, debater—may be meant to cover the bases of both Jewish and Greek intellectual pride."[12] Isaiah 44:25 may stand behind the fourth question of the series which foreshadows the discussion to follow: "Has God not made foolish the wisdom of the world?"

Paul continues his argument in the next four verses (vv. 21-25) by clarifying the paradox he has created. In verse 21, he lays out in explicit terms what he means in verse 18 with "foolishness" and "power." "Foolishness" ironically refers to the supposed wisdom of the world seen in Jews who demand miracles and Greeks who seek wisdom. "Power" ironically refers to the cross of Christ which, from the human perspective, is both a scandal and foolishness. Only to the "called" does this paradox make sense (v. 24). Paul uses two expressions to show the remarkable contrast involved in the "foolishness" of the cross: Christ who is the "power of God" and the "wisdom of God" (v. 24). Through crucifixion God chose one of the most foolish and weak ways during the first century to show his wisdom and power, and Paul

---

[9] Brown, *The Cross and Human Transformation*, 75.
[10] Ibid., 81.
[11] Fee, *First Corinthians*, 70.
[12] Brown, *Cross and Human Transformation*, 82.

invites the Corinthians to join in with this folly. The message of a crucified Christ or Lord was a scandal to Jews and an absurdity to Greeks. Paul states in verse 22 that Jews expected the messiah to come with powerful signs—not to be scandalized by being executed on a cross. Furthermore, the very concept of death by crucifixion was appalling to Jews because of the law given in Deuteronomy 21:23, "Cursed is the one who is hung on a tree" (cf. Gal 3:13). Crucifixion was the penalty for state criminals and slaves in the Roman empire.[13] It was not even proper in Roman society to mention a cross.[14] How could the Lord be a common criminal? This was foolishness to Greeks who sought wisdom.[15] Paul turns these perceptions around and condemns those who accept them.[16] Ernst Käsemann writes,

> The cross always remains scandal and foolishness for Jew and Gentile, inasmuch as it exposes man's illusion that he can transcend himself and effect his own salvation, that he can all by himself maintain his own strength, his own wisdom, his own piety and his own self-praise even towards God.[17]

Paul concludes this part of his argument in verse 25 with a series of reversals: human wisdom is revealed for what it is—foolishness in God's eyes; and the foolishness of the cross is revealed for what it is—beyond human wisdom. John Painter comments, "This reversal is characteristic of Paul's apologetic method (1 Cor 9:19-23) because the preaching of the cross as the saving event is the reversal of human values."[18] In verse 25 Paul uses a method called *expolitio* in rhetoric to clarify his thought given in verse 18. *Expolitio* is a form of refining or embellishing. The ancient rhetorical handbook, *Rhetorica ad Herennium*, describes it as

> dwelling on the same topic and yet seeming to say something ever new. It is accomplished in two ways: by merely repeating the same idea, or by descanting upon it. We shall not repeat the same thing precisely–for that, to be sure, would weary the hearer and not refine

---

[13] For texts and discussion on ancient crucifixion, see Martin Hengel, *Crucifixion: In the Ancient World and the Folly of the Message of the Cross*, trans. John Bowden (Philadelphia: Fortress, 1977).
[14] Cicero, *Rab. Post.* 16.
[15] The pursuit of wisdom was characteristic of the Greeks according to Herodotus, *History* 4.77: "All Greeks were zealous for every kind of learning."
[16] According to Justin, *Apology* I.13.4, the cross was known as the madness of Christians. A negative evaluation of adherence to the cross by unbelievers can be found in Pliny (the Younger) *Ep.* 10.96.4-8. An anti-Christian polemic can be seen in Minucius Felix, *Oct.* 9.4.
[17] Ernst Käsemann, *Perspectives on Paul*, trans. Margaret Kohl (Philadelphia: Fortress, 1971) 40.
[18] John Painter, "Paul and the *Pneumatikoi* at Corinth," in *Paul and Paulinism: Essays in honour of C. K. Barrett*, ed. Morna D. Hooker and Stephen G. Wilson (London: SPCK, 1982) 242.

the idea—but with changes. . . . Our changes will be verbal when, having expressed the idea once, we repeat it once again or oftener in other, equivalent terms.[19]

In this verse, Paul finally resolves the mismatched pairs of v. 18 through synonymous parallelism:

because
<u>the foolishness of God</u> <u>is wiser than people</u>,
and
<u>the weakness of God</u> <u>is stronger than people</u>.

Although this verse makes better semantic sense than verse 18, the paradox of the foolishness of the divine plan remains. This seeming absurdity is part of Paul's rhetorical effort to force his readers to examine their own claims of power and wisdom. By judging God's plan of the cross as foolish, at the same time they are judging their supposed wisdom and strength.

Paul moves on to apply this to Corinthians in verse 26 by addressing their immaturity and lack of understanding of God's plan. Since most of them would not be considered wise, influential, or of noble birth, they would find themselves in a position of weakness or foolishness from a human perspective (v. 26, cf. v. 20). Paul corners the boasters in Corinth by making his comparison explicit: God chose the foolish things of the world in order to shame the wise things, and the weak things of the world to shame the strong (v. 27). In emphasizing God's choice of the lowest things of human existence, Paul exalts the grace and election of God as a theological foundation while setting the stage for condemning the Corinthians in their self-exalted state.[20]

As Paul dismantles the common misconceptions about the cross, he focuses upon the clearest evidence of problems in Corinth—boasting. The Corinthians boasted in their own wisdom, which showed their immaturity (3:18-23). Paul tells them that there is no place for boasting before Christ who defines wisdom and provides justification, sanctification, and redemption (1:30). To add authority to this thought, Paul quotes Jeremiah 9:24 in verse 31. It is possible that behind all of Paul's rhetoric in the paragraph of 1:26-31 stands Jeremiah 9:23-24:

> Thus says the Lord, "Let not the wise one glory in his wisdom, let not the strong glory in his might, let not the rich glory in his riches; but let the one who glories glory in this, that he understands and knows me, that I am the Lord who practices mercy, justice, and righteousness upon the earth; for in these things is my will," says the Lord.

---

[19] *Rhet. Her.* 4.54; quoted by Kennedy, *New Testament Interpretation*, 29.
[20] Fee, *First Corinthians*, 82.

Jeremiah proves to be very useful for Paul. Gail O'Day writes, "Jeremiah's critique of wisdom, power, and wealth as false sources of identity that violate the covenant are re-imaged by Paul as a critique of wisdom, power and wealth that impede God's saving acts in Jesus Christ."[21] James Davis comments, "Paul has deliberately chosen to focus attention on what he considers to be the most crucial and relevant element of Jeremiah's polemic, namely the boastful confidence which has been produced as a result of a reliance upon wisdom."[22] Paul makes one significant change in his quote in verse 31 by switching Jeremiah's "in this" to "in the Lord." The "in this" in Jeremiah 9:23 refers to understanding and knowing the nature of God. If Paul had not modified Jeremiah's statement, or perhaps clarified it from his point of view, the Corinthians could have misunderstood the intent of the prophet and used this passage as support for their own position because, after all, they thought they had "the mind of the Lord" and possessed knowledge and understanding (cf. 2:16; 13:2). Moreover, it is noteworthy that Paul attributes to Christ the attributes of Jeremiah's Yahweh: love, justice, and righteousness. Consequently, Paul shows that the object of boasting is not human knowledge but relationship with Christ (1:31).

The Divine Mystery in Context

Paul chooses his words carefully in the context of 1 Corinthians 1–4. Even if he uses terms from the world of the Corinthians, his grounding in the gospel is still evident. Particularly significant is his use of apocalyptic themes and words. One such theme is the possible allusion to the throne figure of apocalyptic visions and expectations. When Paul had his vision of the risen Jesus Christ described in Galatians 1 (cf. 2 Corinthians 12), he saw (or heard) the risen Jesus. Paul, as an apocalyptic Jew, may have identified Jesus as the throne figure of apocalyptic expectations who was called, among other names, "the Lord of glory."[23] The revelation of the power and position of this figure in the event of the crucifixion and resurrection lies at the heart of Paul's gospel. Paul then appeals to this revelation as the basis for change and growth in the Corinthian community.

The question might be asked, why did Paul choose the cross as the central theme in chapters 1–4 and the resurrection in chapter 15? Part of the

---

[21] Gail O'Day, "Jeremiah 9:22 and 1 Corinthians 1:26-31: A Study in Intertextuality," *JBL* 109 (1990) 267.

[22] James A. Davis, *Wisdom and Spirit: An Investigation of 1 Corinthians 1.18-3.20 against the Background of Jewish Sapiential Traditions in the Greco-Roman Period* (Lanham, Md.: University Press of America, 1984) 75.

[23] See especially *1 Enoch* 40:3; 63:2. Also worthy of note are 22:14; 25:3; 27:3, 5; 36:4; and 83:8.

answer may be that the reference to the cross for Paul implied also the resurrection; both were part of his message (2:2; 15:1-11). The cross served also as a metonymy of the gospel itself; it symbolized the saving power of the death of Christ.[24] But, the cross also represents reality from two different perspectives. From the human perspective it symbolizes weakness, but from the divine, it represents submission in strength. If the Corinthians wanted to be spiritually mature according to Paul's view, they needed to submit in humility to the divine prerogative. Paul's apocalyptic hermeneutic appears again when he says that the "rulers of this age" crucified the "Lord of glory" (2:8).[25] He does not attempt to identify these "rulers" with any specific group. Rather, as Richard B. Gaffin suggests,

> The rulers of this age are representative; in them we see the most impressive achievements of the present world-order, measured by the standards of human rebellion and unbelief; within the creation, as presently subject to the curse on sin (cf. Rom 8:18-22), they exemplify the most that it has to offer and is capable of attaining.[26]

The text is clearer about this "age" and this "world" standing in opposition to the ways of God (1:20, 21, 27, 28; 2:12). It was due to their *ignorance* that the rulers crucified Jesus. Paul is essentially saying that it was human wisdom at its best that actually was the cause, but this wisdom was only a symbol of human foolishness before God. The Corinthians were in the same position as the rulers because they knew about the crucifixion (2:2; cf. 15:1-3) yet did not know how to appropriate it in their situation. God reveals in the cross what the rulers misunderstood. With the revelation of the cross, a shift of power over human destiny took place from this "world" or "age" to the sovereignty of God in Christ (cf. 15:24).

❖ A New Wisdom from God

Paul relates the theme of the cross-event to divine wisdom specifically in 2:6. This wisdom for Paul is not simply wisdom in the general sense of elevated human intellect, but the specific, revealed will of God in line with Jewish tradition. Obedience and knowledge of the Law were central concerns of the Jewish Wisdom tradition in the centuries before Paul.[27] Paul interpreted divine wisdom not through the Law but through Christ (cf. Phil 3:4-7). When

---

[24] Robert G. Hammerton-Kelly, *Sacred Violence: Paul's Hermeneutic of the Cross* (Minneapolis: Fortress, 1992) 65.
[25] E.g., 4 Ezra 7:50, 113; 8:1.
[26] Richard B. Gaffin, "Some Epistemological Reflections on 1 Cor 2:6-16," *WTJ* 57 (1995) 110.
[27] Prov 4:4-5; Wis 7; Bar 3:9-4:1; Sir 1:26; 39:1-11; 51:35-36.

God revealed his highest wisdom, he chose to do it on the cross and not in the Law. James Davis writes that "for Paul, the Christ-event is the place where all of God's mysteries, past, present, and future, converge; the place from which all of them must now be interpreted."[28] Denys E. H. Whiteley states,

> When St. Paul speaks of Christ in terms of Wisdom, his intention is not to identify him with an hypostatisation of Wisdom, but to ascribe to him the function of being God's agent in creation, revelation and redemption. In fact, the "Wisdom Christology" of St. Paul may be summed up in these words: What Wisdom meant to the Jews was part of what Jesus Christ meant for Paul.[29]

Paul's emphasis appears in the repeated words in 2:6-16. He begins verse 6 with his theme word "wisdom" (*sophia*) which he uses 16 times in chapters 1-3. The frequency of this word suggests that its meaning is one of the central concerns of the letter. Another frequent word is "humanity" (*anthrōpos*) which Paul contrasts with "God" (*theos*) in 1:25. The rather concentrated use of this word implies that Paul is concerned with the status of humanity in relation to God. Paul also draws out words that have "spirit" in them, especially in his play on words in verse 13 where he gives three "spirit" words together: "the *Spirit* reveals to *spiritual* people *spiritual* things." This indicates Paul's concern with spiritual matters and matters of the Spirit which, if the Corinthians would only agree with him about, would solve most if not all of their problems. Finally, an important theme related to wisdom occurs with the dense use of apocalyptic words in verses 6-8: "perfect," "mystery," "revelation," "glory," and "this age."

In verses 6-10a Paul expands his association of God's wisdom with Jesus Christ by using relative clauses and scriptural quotation. He defines wisdom in a chiastic pattern that establishes what it is and is not, as the following paraphrase suggests:

    A It is spoken to the mature or initiated (6a).
        B It is not the temporal wisdom of this age or the rulers of this age (6b).
            C It is revealed as a mystery (7a).
            C' It is part of God's eternal plan (7b).
        B' No one from this temporal age can understand it (8a-9).
    A' God has revealed it to "us" by the Spirit (10a).

Paul is comparing human wisdom with divine wisdom. He appeals to scripture in verse 9 to support his distinction: "Things which no eye has seen and no ear has heard, and which have not entered into the human heart,

---

[28] Davis, *Wisdom and Spirit*, 93.
[29] Denys E. H. Whiteley, *Theology of St. Paul* (Philadelphia: Fortress, 1964) 112.

things which God has prepared for the ones who love him."[30] This quotation also helps Paul confirm that the mystery of Christ is beyond human comprehension and needs to be revealed by God. This wisdom from God is what no human can see, hear, or understand.

Significant in the context of the letter is the last phrase, "things which God has prepared for those who love him." Only those in the special relationship of love will be given the mystery of the divine wisdom. Only those who allow the Holy Spirit to teach them the implications of the cross in their lives will grow to have the mind of Christ within them. The question left to the Corinthians is, are they part of this special group who have this wisdom from God and are they showing their love for God by how they love one another? The unspiritual of the world hinder the love of God from flowing through them. Some of the Corinthians were acting like these unspiritual people and their immaturity was causing major problems in the church.

Next, Paul shows how this wisdom is revealed (10b-13). His logic can be seen in a syllogism:

> **Thesis**: God has revealed to "us" the divine mystery through the Spirit (10a).
>
> **Supporting premises**: Only the Spirit of God knows the things of God (11).
> The Spirit discloses these to spiritual people (12).
> "We" are spiritual people (12).
>
> **Conclusion**: Therefore, "we" can interpret the mystery of God (13).

He accomplishes two things in this sequence. First, this assertion is based on his claim that he and the Corinthians have received the Holy Spirit who enables knowledge of God's grace. Second, this establishes once again his position regarding the divine mystery of the cross (2:1-5) and also reminds the Corinthians of their own standing in complete dependence upon God for their spiritual status.

---

[30] The source of this quotation is questionable because no passage from the Old Testament matches it exactly. The first two lines are close to Isaiah 64:4 and the third is close to 65:17. It is also similar to Judith 8:14: "For you cannot find the depth of the human heart, neither can you perceive the things that one thinks; then how can you search out God who has made all these things and know his mind or comprehend his thought?" Other similar passages include Ps 31:20; Wis 9:13; Sir 1:10; and Pseudo-Philo, *Bib. Ant.* 26:13. E. Earle Ellis asserts that Paul considers the quotation to be scripture because of the introductory formula "it is written" (*Paul's Use of the Old Testament* [Grand Rapids: Baker, 1957] 22–23).

The supreme wisdom of God revealed on the cross remains a mystery to those on the outside because of unbelief. Knowing the mystery of God's supreme wisdom is not meant to remain hidden but to be disclosed to both Jew and Greek (12:13). Paul addresses both Jews and Greeks in this section because both had the same basic problem with their perception of wisdom.[31] The reason the Corinthians had failed to understand God's mystery was because of their living as "fleshly" (*sarkinoi*) people (3:1). Robert Funk appropriately writes,

> Paul cannot give them the "mysteries" (which they thought they possessed) because they have been and are "fleshly" (which they thought they were not) until they become "spiritual" (which they believed themselves to be) when they become "spiritual" they will see that the "mysteries" are nothing other than the word of the cross, which is foolishness, and the strife among them is the sign of this fleshliness (3:3).[32]

What is noteworthy about Paul's position is that God's supreme wisdom does not come through contemplation upon the Law (Jew) nor upon knowing the true self (Greek), but in the simple preaching of the cross. According to Johan S. Vos, Paul adds new definition to the term "wisdom" by using the device called "persuasive definition" to dissociate the Corinthians' concept of wisdom from his own. By giving his own definition of wisdom as the divine mystery, Paul reverses the role of the "strong" and "wise" Corinthians. He shows the futility of their position compared to his own which is as an example of what it means to be a mature, spiritual (*pneumatikos*) person.[33]

❖ Revealed by the Spirit

Paul writes in 2:10 that God has revealed his wisdom by means of the Holy Spirit. This revelation is more than simply a way of thinking (2:16) but involves also a way of living. The Spirit becomes the eschatological power for the morality demanded in accepting the gospel. This eschatological gift impacts mind, body, and community. The Spirit as divine agent and power of life is universally available to all who are "in Christ" (the "spiritual" or *pneuma-*

---

[31] Veronica Koperski, "Knowledge of Christ and Knowledge of God in the Corinthian Correspondence," in *The Corinthian Correspondence*, ed. Reimund Bieringer (Leuven: Leuven University Press, 1996) 381.

[32] Robert W. Funk, "Word and Word in 1 Corinthians 2:6-16," in *Language, Hermeneutic, and the Word of God: The Problem of Language in the New Testament and Contemporary Theology* (New York: Harper and Row, 1966) 300. See also James A. Francis, "'As Babes in Christ'–Some Proposals Regarding 1 Corinthians 3.1-3," *JSNT* 7 (1980) 41–60.

[33] Johan S. Vos, "Die Argumentation des Paulus in 1 Kor 1,10—3,4," in *The Corinthian Correspondence*, ed. Reimund Bieringer (Leuven: Leuven University Press, 1996) 87–119.

tikoi). Paul's reasoning is quite logical in 2:10b-12: only the Holy Spirit can know divine thoughts and present divine "gifts." The divine thoughts in the context refer to the mystery of the wisdom of God revealed through the cross. The "gifts" should be understood in the general sense of divine grace and not with any specific "spiritual gifts" to which Paul refers later in chapters 12–14, since he is not concerned at this point about any specific manifestations of God's gracing. The divine mystery in Christ involves more than simply initial salvation, which the Corinthians apparently had experienced. Their problem, however, was that they had not allowed this mystery to impact all of their life, especially their attitudes and behaviors within the community.

There is no hidden secret to Paul's *mystery* like with the mystery religions of his day. When he writes that only the spiritual can understand the words of the Spirit, he is not speaking of some secret only for the initiated (Greek *teleioi*). Rather, he views the Spirit as God's primary means of disclosing the message of the cross through the human agency of preachers such as himself. He implies that he has more to share with the Corinthians about the significance of the cross-event and its eternal implications but has been stopped because of their worldly (Greek *sarkikos*) attitudes and behaviors (3:1). They could not understand because they had hindered the Spirit from speaking to them, just as the worldly (Greek *psychikos*) person does. Hence, there are two types of receptions of the divine mystery: the *psychikos* person who cannot understand the mystery because of unbelief that hinders one from hearing the voice of the Spirit, and the *pneumatikos* person who can grow in understanding and live out the mystery. Brown comments,

> The *psychikos*, for Paul, is one whose experience of spirit is informed neither by the cross event in the past nor by God's new creative activity in the present. The dislocation that the psychic experiences does not bring him into the transforming reality of new creation. Rather, it catapults him out of the created world in a retrogressive plunge toward his origins (which perhaps he calls the "depths of God"). The mystery he knows moves him, not to ministry *in* the world, but to withdrawal *from* it.[34]

The problem with the Corinthians was not so much an unbelief in the event of the cross and resurrection but a failure to grow in that revelation. They did not have the mind of Christ because they were relying on their own wisdom and power. Because of this, Paul has to address them as infants and remind them of the basic elements of their faith in Christ. They could not understand the deeper things of the divine mystery because of their human (*sarkikos*) mind-set. Because they were relying on their own way of thinking,

---

[34] Brown, *The Cross and Human Transformation*, 137.

their community was also suffering. Paul must believe that their minds could be transformed by the power of the divine mystery in Christ otherwise his rhetoric would be in vain. His message was not in the typical format of human wisdom nor with rhetorical excellence; it was only effective because of the power of the Spirit. God's recreative powers in Christ had been stopped by the Corinthians' spiritual immaturity. As Fee writes, "Spiritual people are to walk in the Spirit. If they do otherwise, they are 'worldly' and are called upon to desist. *Remaining worldly* is not one of the options."[35]

❖ New Eschatological Existence

The divine mystery brings a new eschatological existence to those who allow the Spirit to transform them. As James Dunn states, "The most important event of revelation for Paul is the eschatological event of Christ, unveiling the mystery of God's final purposes."[36] History made a decisive shift with the cross-event when God's eternal plan for human recreation was revealed. Through Christ, death and condemnation—the effects of Adam's disobedience—are reversed and new life is promised (15:21-22; cf. Rom 5:17; 6:4; Phil 2:5-11). God's actions in Christ demonstrate for Paul that the end is near and that the present world is passing away (1 Cor 7:31). Paul wanted to know the transforming power in the cross and resurrection (Phil 3:10). Jesus Christ's death and resurrection had inaugurated the new age which would be completely consummated at Jesus' *parousia*.

The revealing of the divine plan in the cross-event brought about the destruction of "the rulers of this age" (2:6). By causing the death of Christ, these rulers had actually brought about their own destruction, symbolizing also the end of the reign of the power of adamic existence. Death is the primary symbol of existence in Adam, but through Christ's resurrection, death has been swallowed up and its power forever destroyed (15:54-56). The Holy Spirit is the sign of this new age (2:4; 6:11). Paul stands in the tradition of Jewish apocalypticism where God's Spirit reveals his plan (mystery) of the end of the ages.[37] For Paul, however, this plan has already been revealed in part and most significantly with Christ's death and resurrection and will be fully seen at Christ's *parousia*. Paul holds a special position as mediator of this divine mystery (4:1; 1 Thess 5:1-11), some of which may have been revealed to him in one of his visions (e.g., Gal 1:11-16; 1 Cor 15:51).

---

[35] Ibid., 128.
[36] Dunn, *Jesus and the Spirit*, 213. Beker says, "The Christ-event is the turning point in time that announces the end of time" (*Paul the Apostle*, 362). Cf. William D. Dennison, *Paul's Two-Age Construction and Apologetics* (Lanham, Md.: University Press of America, 1985) 55–85.
[37] 1QS 4:3; 9:18; 11:19; 1QH 12:11; 13:19.

Not everyone, however, gains access to this divine mystery. Paul is explicit yet also subtle in describing those who are not transformed through the power of the Spirit. He lucidly writes that those who cannot see God's wisdom in the cross cannot gain access to the transforming mystery of God (2:6b). The "rulers of this age who crucified the Lord of glory" (v. 8a-9) serve as ready examples of the type of approach to the divine paradox that the Corinthians should *not* have. Thus, in a more subtle way, Paul exhorts the Corinthians not to treat the wisdom of the cross as folly by living as if the new reality in Christ makes no impact on temporal experience.

Consequently, Paul emphasizes that the eschatological transformation through the Spirit (cf. 2 Cor 3:18) impacts the present situation. The Corinthians had not allowed the Spirit to change their behavior to a point that convinced Paul that they were actually growing spiritually. They may have believed that they had already received the promises of the Spirit (1 Cor 4:8). With their spiritual enthusiasm, they gloried in what they had already received from God (1:4-7). Their "transformation" was not like the one Paul had envisioned. His paradigm was one of humility and reliance upon God. They may have thought that they had obtained a special position of power, wisdom, and enhanced human ability. Paul demonstrates that this position is actually one of weakness because it is based on the faulty foundation of human existence devoid of the Spirit. C. K. Barrett writes that "for them there is no 'not yet' to qualify the 'already' of realized eschatology."[38] The Holy Spirit brings a new way of living to those who are "in Christ" and who have the "the mind of Christ" (2:16).

❖ The Mind of Christ

Before calling the Corinthians to account for their immaturity, Paul describes how one can actually pursue divine wisdom. In verse 14 he introduces the difficult word *psychikos*, roughly translated as "unspiritual." He uses this word only in 1 Corinthians and only here and in 15:44. As far as argumentation goes, his purpose here is to continue his comparison between pursuing spiritual maturity through self-reliance or through divine assistance. He compares the *psychikos* person with the *pneumatikos* or "spiritual" person. The main point of comparison is how a person receives, understands, and discerns spiri-

---

[38] Barrett, *First Corinthians*, 109. See also Hans Conzelmann, *1 Corinthians: A Commentary on the First Epistle to the Corinthians*, trans. James W. Leitch, Hermeneia (Philadelphia: Fortress, 1975) 88–89; Fee, *First Corinthians*, 172, who writes, "Paul's perspective . . . is one of 'already but not yet' held in tension: theirs is one of 'already' with little room for 'not yet.'" Cf. Chael Goulder, "Already?" in *To Tell the Mystery: Essays on New Testament Eschatology in Honor of Robert H. Gundry*, ed. Thomas E. Schmidt and Moisés Silva, JSNT 100 (Sheffield: JSOT Press, 1994) 21–33.

tual truths related to the word of the cross. These truths are foolishness to the *psychikos* person in the same way that the cross is foolishness to those who do not believe in a crucified Christ (cf. 1:22-25). The *pneumatikos* person, however, is able to "discern all things," which in this context probably refers to "the depths of God" (2:10) where the cross is at the center of the divine will and plan.[39]

In 2:16 Paul asks a rhetorical question based on Isaiah 40:13: "Who knows the mind of the Lord, so as to instruct him?"[40] Paul uses this quotation to support his contrast between the person (*pneumatikos*) who relies upon the Spirit to know the Wisdom from God and the person (*psychikos*) who relies upon human ability for the inferior human wisdom. He uses this question in such a way that demands the negative response, "No one can know the mind of the Lord." It is impossible to know the divine mind without the divine Spirit. But Paul knows a way that makes it possible—by knowing the mystery of God. This way of knowledge comes by experiencing and being filled with the Holy Spirit and leads to a new way of life in Christ. The impossible is made possible by the grace of the revelation of the eternal plan of God. This revelation is conditioned upon a person agreeing with the divine paradox. Fee comments, "Indeed, whoever would pursue wisdom so as to avoid the story of the cross fares no better than the person who would commit the ultimate folly of thinking he or she could instruct the Lord himself."[41]

According to other letters of Paul, a person's "mind" can be controlled by sin (Rom 1:28) or be transformed by God (12:3). It can be controlled by the flesh (*sarx*) or by the Spirit (8:5-8; see 2 Cor 2:11; 4:4; 10:3-5). The mind expresses the focus of a person, or as Brown states, "The mind reflects the orientation of the whole self toward or away from God. Noetic disposition determines one's relationships with God and with others in body, mind, and spirit."[42] To know the mind of Christ, one must experience and receive the mind of Christ through the mediation of the Spirit (1 Cor 2:12). In 1:10 Paul urges the Corinthians to be united in "thought," a word similar in meaning to "mind." This unity in mind occurs also in Philippians 2:2, 5, but with a near synonym (*phronēma*). The concept in Philippians is similar to 1 Corinthians 2:16. The mind-set to which Paul refers is the one Christ demonstrated on the cross. It is based on the divine paradox of weakness and folly. Christ's submission on the cross meant humiliation and death (Phil 2:5-11). In 1

---

[39] Cf. Eccl 7:24; Job 11:8; *2 Bar* 24:8; 54:12; *1 Enoch* 63:2; 1QS 11:18-19; 4 Ezra 4:10, 21; 10:35; *2 Bar* 14:8.

[40] In this verse from Isaiah, the Septuagint uses the word "mind" (Greek *nous*) for the Hebrew "spirit" (*ruach*). It is impossible to know if Paul knew of this difference, but he does link the divine mind to the divine Spirit.

[41] Fee, *First Corinthians*, 119.

[42] Brown, *The Cross and Human Transformation*, 146.

Corinthians Christ's submission meant weakness and foolishness from the world's perspective. Both of these are inverted with the weakness and folly of the cross actually being a demonstration of God's power and wisdom, and Christ's humiliation resulting in his exaltation. Thus, those who have the mind of Christ have associated themselves with the divine paradox. They have had their outlook shaped by an awareness of Christ who has become the norm for the community.[43]

The opposite of the "mind of Christ" in verse 16 is implicit: the wisdom of the world. Paul ends this section by drawing attention to the source of his ability to discern spiritual truths—the mind of Christ. The reader by this point must be able to compare a number of terms and concepts:

mind of Christ	wisdom of the world
pneumatikos	*psychikos*
discern	not able to know
divine wisdom	human wisdom
"spirit" word group	human
divine Spirit	spirit of the world
mature	infant
wisdom	foolishness

This comparison offers the Corinthians a clear choice. He has shown that they had been given the Holy Spirit but their actions demonstrate that they had not experienced their full potential in Christ because of their attitudes and behaviors. They had preempted the position of the Spirit by replacing the gift of Christ-likeness with human struggle for spiritual wholeness. Paul makes this comparison explicit in the following section.

The Immaturity of the Corinthians

Paul provides a select image of himself and his ministry in order to counter the claims of the Corinthians. His rhetoric is full of irony for the purpose of motivating them to grow into spiritual adulthood which would then resolve their fractious fellowship. After providing the indisputable foundation of the cross of Christ, Paul attempts to convict the Corinthians of their errors. If something were not done, the church would be divided and their fellowship with Christ would be incomplete, if not destroyed. Their basic problem was that they were not united in self-surrendered fellowship with Christ through the Holy Spirit. Paul uses his rhetoric to trap them and convince them to accept his paradigm of the divine mystery.

---

[43] Wendell Willis, "The 'Mind of Christ' in 1 Corinthians 2:16," *Bib* 70 (1989) 118.

The Corinthians' Behavior Relative to the Divine Mystery (3:1—4:31)

Beginning with chapter 3, Paul makes a significant shift in mood and again writes directly to his readers in the form of a diatribe using a series of vivid images with penetrating irony. After the rather abstract logic and thought of chapter 2, he allows the Corinthians a breath of fresh air in chapter 3 through the use of concrete images, but with each breath, they find themselves further trapped by his pointed rhetoric. He tersely puts them in the word group listed in the right column on the previous page. As J. Reiling points out, "Paul drops the term *psychikos* immediately; when he comes to the application of his argument to the Corinthian situation it is no longer *psychikos* that is the counterpart of *pneumatikos* but *sarkinos* and *sarkikos* (3:1, 3)."[44] Paul cannot call the Corinthians mature (*teleoi*) but infants (*nepioi*) because of their fleshly (*sarkinoi*) behavior. They were acting immature, as if the cross of Christ made no difference in the way they lived. Paul is not willing to call them *psychikos* with its connotations of being devoid of the divine Spirit. They had the Holy Spirit (2:14-16) but were living as "fleshly" people (*sarkinos*), without any regard for God, relying only on human ability. Their nutrition was like that of a baby who must rely on milk and not the solid food of the more mature. In 3:3 Paul repeats the key word "human," thereby associating the Corinthians with the other terms of immaturity.

Paul uses imagery familiar in the ancient world when he describes the Corinthians in 3:1-2 as "infants" and not "mature." Epictetus wrote, "Are you not willing, at this late date, like children, to be weaned and to partake of more solid food?"[45] Philo uses similar imagery:

> But seeing that for babes [*nepioi*] milk [*gala*] is food, but for grown men [*teleioi*] wheaten bread, there must also be soul-nourishment, such as is milk-like suited to the time of childhood, in the shape of the preliminary stages of school-learning, and such as is adapted to grown men [*teleioi*] in the shape of instructions leading the way through wisdom and temperance and all virtue.[46]

For Philo, one becomes mature (*teleioi*) by "school-learning," but for Paul, one becomes mature by faith in Christ. Paul wanted the Corinthians to realize that their maturity came by faith and submission to what the Holy Spirit

---

[44] J. Reiling, "Wisdom and the Spirit: An Exegesis of 1 Corinthians 2, 6-16," in *Text and Testimony: Essays on NT and Apocryphal Literature in Honor of A. F. J. Klijn*, ed. T. Baarda et al. (Kampen: Kok, 1988) 208.
[45] Epictetus, *Diss.* 3.19.1 and 2.16.25. For a list of ancient sources using this imagery, see Wilfred L. Knox, *St. Paul and the Church of the Gentiles* (Cambridge: Cambridge University Press, 1939) 111.
[46] Philo, *Abr.* 9.

wanted to teach them in response to the crucified Christ. Spiritual maturity cannot come by human effort, especially the effort to make oneself look better than another brother or sister in Christ. The Corinthians could experience the deeper truths of the mystery of the cross if they would open themselves to the Spirit and walk in the ways of the Spirit as Paul directs. But they were "not yet ready," a phrase Paul repeats twice in 3:2. Morna Hooker writes, "The Corinthians' failure to understand the wisdom spoken in a mystery is not due to the fact that Paul is withholding it from them, but is the result of their own inability to digest what he is offering them."[47]

The rhetorical question in 3:3, "Are you not fleshly and behaving only as a human?" allows the Corinthians a moment of introspection. Paul has proved his point and they have to respond in the affirmative. If in doubt, he presents more evidence in another question in verse 4 where he uses the problem of factions under the phantom leadership of himself and Apollos to verify his assessment of the Corinthians, again repeating the idea: "Are you not being merely human?" The very idea that they would split apart the servant leadership of Paul and Apollos proves to Paul that they were relying on their own power and judgment. The biggest evidence in Paul's argument at this point for the Corinthians' worldly (*sarkikos*) behavior was their lack of unity, to which Paul next turns his attention. They may have had the Spirit but were not acting like people of the Spirit. This is a matter that goes beyond simply respectable living but involves fundamental spirituality. Morality (the imperative) should be a result of spirituality (the indicative), and not the reverse.

Paul faces a two-sided challenge. He must prove the faultiness of the Corinthians' position *and* still preserve his own apostolic integrity and authority. To meet this challenge, he uses two analogies to illustrate his relationship with Apollos in order to prove that the supposed division of the two in the minds of the Corinthians was unfounded. His first analogy from agriculture (3:6-7) shows how he and Apollos were involved in the same overall task and would be rewarded by God for their work. Both he and Apollos were involved in the same mission and were coworkers for God (v. 9). Like farmers, he and Apollos could do nothing to produce growth in the church. They could not make the Corinthians mature (*teleioi*); only God could grow the community. Paul and Apollos were only God's agents or servants working the field by planting and watering. Everything is dependent upon God. There is no reason why they should be compared to one another or be leaders of two separate factions.

Apollos is not explicitly involved in the second analogy taken from architecture. Paul leaves Apollos behind in the discussion and refers to those who

---

[47] Morna D. Hooker, "Hard Sayings, I Corinthians 3:2," *Theology* 69 (1966) 20.

follow them in building up the church. He is still concerned here with the fundamental problem of how the Corinthians received the gospel, as verse 11 suggests: the only real foundation is Jesus Christ. The temple Paul describes can be built out of two types of materials. One type is made of wood, hay, and straw—perishable, inexpensive materials that can be easily destroyed. The other type, made of gold, silver, and precious stones, can withstand the test of purifying fire.

In verse 16 Paul draws the Corinthians into the discussion again by pointing out that they are the temple to which he has been referring. He uses a question common in diatribe, "Do you not know?" suggesting that they should already know the answer.[48] This subtle and frequent question recalls the authority of Paul's apostolic word. Had not his preaching of the cross to them, his presence among them, and his continued correspondence with them made any impact on the way they lived as a community? Does he still need to remind them of matters of conduct about which only an immature community should be concerned (3:1)? In his view, the church as a temple is threatened with destruction because of the use of the lesser materials in its foundation. He shows through analogy that the real problem for the Corinthians involves the basic issue of living out the message of the cross, and that the only thing that lasts is that which has been built upon new existence in Christ.

In verse 17, this temple is described as "holy." In the Old Testament, the holy of holies in the temple was the special dwelling place of God because it was holy. Likewise, the Corinthian "temple" must be holy in order for the Holy Spirit to dwell there.[49] Paul is careful in his order: since God's Spirit is in the temple, the temple must be holy. In other words, the moral imperative (v. 17) follows from the statement of fact (v. 16). With these various images, Paul reminds the Corinthians that they as the temple of God were different from the many pagan temples in Corinth where false gods made by human hands by definition excluded the Spirit of God (8:4-6). Paul also addresses misunderstandings about the nature of being "church." Being church does

---

[48] Epictetus, *Diss.* 1.4.16. Paul uses this question also in 5:6, 6:2, 3, 9, 15, 16, 19; 9:13, 24; and Rom 6:16.

[49] The use of temple imagery and the presence of God with his people is an important theme in the Old Testament. Psalm 114:2 alludes to the tradition of God's presence dwelling in the midst of his people: "Judah became his sanctuary, Israel his dominion." The presence of God with his people was a critical factor in the national life of ancient Israel. The new temple described in Ezekiel 40–48 provides helpful background to Paul's thought. At the end of Ezekiel's vision of the restored temple are the words, "The Lord is there." This eschatological temple is spiritualized by Paul who believes the church in Corinth is God's temple. What makes this temple significant is that God's presence dwells there in the Spirit just as in the temples in scripture.

not mean boasting in one's leader or one's ability to understand, but in being and acting as a temple fit for the Spirit of holiness.

If the Corinthians would act according to the message of the cross as spiritual people and not as fleshly people, they could possess all for which they longed: world, life, death, *present*, and future—everything which confines humanity. This suggests that Paul's labeling of them as fleshly and human was for the rhetorical purpose of arousing them to the dangerous direction to which they were heading which, if not corrected, could ultimately lead to the destruction of the community. Evidence of this appears in Paul's admonition to stop boasting (v. 21). He expands the views of the Corinthians by offering them glimpses of what life in Christ is like. The answer to growth in Christ lies in the ownership or lordship of Christ: "you are of Christ" (vv. 22-23).

It may appear that with chapter 4 Paul begins a new argument since he changes topics. Under close examination, however, it is apparent that he establishes his reliability as a messenger of the message he laboriously lays out in 1:18-2:16. In this way, chapter 4 is also dependent upon the theological foundation given in 1:18-2:16. Paul's tone is apologetic and his rhetoric judicial as he defends himself while skillfully condemning the Corinthians for their faulty ideology. The imagery shifts to the courtroom where Paul is accused of a lack of stewardship. Before he is through, however, he is vindicated and the Corinthians have been judged and condemned. They had judged him on the very issues he discusses. Therefore, he must defend his position—not for the sake of himself but for the sake of the gospel—in order that they might see the folly of their ways. He begins by reminding his readers of his position as a steward of the divine mysteries, linking his ministry back to the kerygma (4:1). The term for steward, *oikonomos*, describes the duty of a household slave and implies responsibility, accountability, authority, trust, and faithfulness. With the rank of apostle with direct accountability to Christ, Paul is responsible for handing on the divine mystery of the revelation of Christ. He then moves from the courtroom in Corinth to the heavenly court before God's throne (vv. 3-5). He calls God as his first and only witness thereby leaving the Corinthians defenseless. He wins his case without a trial because he aligns himself with the divine paradox of the gospel.[50]

Beginning in verse 6, Paul reverses his position from defender to prosecutor by using the rhetorical device called "covert allusion" in order to work certain effects on his readers. Rollin Ramsaran defines covert allusion as an "argument for reproach or correction in veiled form, using figurative exam-

---

[50] Paul again mentions Apollos in 4:6 implying that Apollos was in the background of his defense. His positive assessment of Apollos here frees Apollos from later accusation from the Corinthians.

ples that do not directly implicate the offenders. The audience is invited to learn from these examples and amend their own behavior."[51] Benjamin Fiore comments that Paul's tone "rises to sharpness, but carries a paternal concern not to be expected in a controversy."[52] Where Paul successfully defends himself, the Corinthians are left defenseless after he finishes his argument. He begins to undermine their position in verse 7 with a series of rhetorical questions by which he chooses words that describe their actual attitudes.[53] They mistakenly assumed that what they possessed came by their own efforts and not as a divine gift. Basically, their problem was spiritual pride resulting from boasting in their human abilities. After this questioning, Paul gives three short clauses in verse 8 which pinpoint the problem: they thought they had been filled up, had become rich, and even were reigning in some sense as kings, thus suggesting that they thought they had arrived at the eschaton and were indeed mature (*teleioi*; cf. 1:7-8). With this Paul reaches the height of his irony.

Paul has one final move as prosecutor and that is to appeal to the divine paradox of the gospel. By contrasting the weakness of "us apostles" to the strength of "you" Corinthians, he is able to disarm the Corinthians of their last defense (vv. 9-13). By aligning himself (and other apostles) with the paradox of the cross, he dispels any hopes of defense by the Corinthians. If the Corinthians truly believed the message of the cross, which the letter does not doubt, then they are left defenseless and Paul's rhetoric has been completely successful.

Paul changes imagery one final time in his conclusion to this first section of his letter. For a moment he becomes conciliatory by calling the Corinthians his children and himself their father. He has much more to say about specific issues that the Corinthians were facing, but because they stood defenseless before the divine paradox, they had no other alternative but to accept Paul's view. He claims that he has not meant to shame the Corinthians, but that has been the result (v. 14). His single passion emerges in verse 17 when he invites the Corinthians to follow Timothy who would remind them of his "ways in Christ."[54] The solution to the whole problem is orienting one's life according to the gospel of the cross. Paul's final question of this section leaves the decision to the Corinthian church: "Shall I come to you with a rod of discipline or in the love of a gentle spirit?"

---

[51] Rollin A. Ramsaran, *Liberating Words: Paul's Use of Rhetorical Maxims in 1 Corinthians 1–10* (Harrisburg, Pa.: Trinity, 1996) 30–31.
[52] Benjamin Fiore, "'Covert Allusion' in 1 Corinthians 1–4," *CBQ* 47 (1985) 93.
[53] Conzelmann, *1 Corinthians*, 87.
[54] Fee, *First Corinthians*, 186.

Paul's argument attempts to shame the Corinthians and leave them defenseless. Their problems prove to him that they had missed the target of applying the gospel in their lives. He has removed every grounds for boasting in *purely human means* (*sarx*). He has shown that the way to spiritual maturity comes not in relying upon human ability but in relying upon the Holy Spirit to guide and reveal God's plan in the mystery of Christ. To be mature (*teleios*) involves opening one's self to God's way in complete submission. From the outside, this way looks foolish and weak. These may have been hard words for the self-sufficient Corinthians to hear.

Debates on the Sources of this Errant Ideology

Since Paul's language is rather unique and direct in the first section of his letter, is it possible that he is specifically reacting against a certain ideology in Corinth? In other words, how much does Paul contextualize his argument for the contingent situation at Corinth? A significant amount of scholarship has attempted to solve this issue. The debate has focused upon three possible backgrounds for the language and thought structure behind the letter, especially 2:6-16: so-called "Gnosticism," Greek Rhetoric, and Hellenistic-Judaism.

✣ Gnosticism

Some scholars such as Rudolf Bultmann, Walter Schmithals, Ulrich Wilckens, and Gerd Theissen have argued that Paul reacts in these chapters against a form of pre-Christian Gnosticism.[55] Evidence for this is deduced from the terms Paul uses that are also found in later Gnostic literature. The contention is that Paul took over these terms from his Gnostic opponents in Corinth. For example, the Corinthian's self-sufficiency and claims to wisdom can be found in Gnosticism.[56] Knowledge for Gnostics consists of being "on the road to perfection."[57] The argument is that a certain group of Corinthians believed they had reached a higher level of gnosis and possessed superior knowledge. That is why they had no qualms about eating meat sacrificed to

---

[55] Rudolf Bultmann, *Existence and Faith: Shorter Writings of Rudolf Bultmann*, trans. Schubert M. Ogden (New York: Meridian, 1960); Walter Schmithals, *Gnosticism in Corinth: An Investigation of the Letters to the Corinthians*, trans. John E. Steely (Nashville: Abingdon, 1971); Ulrich Wilckens, *Weisheit und Torheit* (Tübingen: Mohr/Siebeck, 1959); Gerd Theissen, *The Social Setting of Pauline Christianity: Essays on Corinth*, trans. and ed. John H. Schütz (Philadelphia: Fortress, 1982) 134–36.

[56] *Corp. Herm.* 10:9; Irenaeus, *Adv. Her.* 1.23.5; *Gos. Heb.* 4b; *Gos. Thom.* 60, 3, 29, 85; 20. Conzelmann, *1 Corinthians*, 88, n. 30: "Thus it is plain that we have here a set combination of language and motifs which express the self-consciousness of the Gnostic."

[57] Hippolytus, *Haer.* 5.24.2; *Gos. Phil.* 40.

idols (1 Corinthians 8). Likewise, the over-realized eschatology evident in 4:8 and chapter 15 suggests that they believed the resurrection had already taken place. The Corinthians' "wisdom" led them to the resurrected Christ and not to the crucified Christ. In addition, later Gnostics appealed to Paul's letters for authority, suggesting that he used terms or concepts which lent themselves to Gnosticism.[58]

This position has been severely criticized by many scholars. R. McL. Wilson, for example, argues that there is no real evidence of a "pre-Christian Gnosticism" in Corinth but rather projections of second century categories upon the first century. He writes,

> The Sophia of the gnostic systems is an aeon, a figure of the supra-mundane world, whose fault is ultimately responsible for the creation of the world and consequently for the woes that afflict mankind. There is no grounds whatever for seeing any such Sophia-myth in the background to 1 Corinthians. Paul's concern is to set on the one side a merely human wisdom of this world, and over against it Christ as the wisdom of God.[59]

He cautions, "It is not enough to label something as 'Jewish' or 'gnostic' and have done with it. We must ask in what sense, to what tradition does the element belong, to what extent it has been modified in the transition from one tradition to another." He concludes with a safer assumption: "What we have at Corinth, then, is not yet Gnosticism, but a kind of *gnosis*."[60] The basic problem inherent in the Gnostic approach is with definitions.[61] Many of the words and concepts used in 1 Corinthians were common in the general religious milieu of the period. Some of the elements common between Gnosticism and 1 Corinthians were also shared with Hellenistic Judaism.

✢ Rhetoric

Another solution to issues of background has been to pinpoint the Corinthian problem with Greek rhetoric. A. Duane Litfin argues that chapters 1–4 show a clash over rhetoric.[62] Paul sets the wisdom of the cross against the wisdom of rhetoric. Paul's goal is to defend his way of proclaiming the gospel against

---

[58] See Elaine Pagels, *The Gnostic Paul: Gnostic Exegesis of the Pauline Letters* (Philadelphia: Fortress, 1975) who discusses how a Valentinian Gnostic might interpret Paul's letters.
[59] R. McL. Wilson, "Gnosis at Corinth," in *Paul and Paulinism: Essays in Honour of C. K. Barrett*, ed. Morna D. Hooker and Stephen G. Wilson (London: SPCK, 1982) 105.
[60] Wilson, "Gnosis at Corinth," 109, 111, 112.
[61] Michael Williams, *Rethinking "Gnosticism": An Argument for Dismantling a Dubious Category* (Princeton: Princeton University Press, 1996).
[62] A. Duane Litfin, *St. Paul's Theology of Acclamation: 1 Corinthians 1–4 and Greco-Roman Rhetoric* (Cambridge: Cambridge University Press, 1994).

the empty appeal of rhetoric. The average person in first-century Corinth would have understood wisdom in the context of rhetoric which was held in high regard in educated circles. To be eloquent was to be considered wise. Paul knew the message was deeper than one's ability to proclaim it. Timothy H. Lim suggests that Paul does not simply reject all rhetoric but the rhetoric *of the Corinthians* which was based on human wisdom.[63] Stephen Pogoloff has shown that there was a close relation between status and eloquence in the Roman Empire. Wisdom as rhetoric implied far more than just technical skill but a whole world of social status; it was the socially or politically powerful who had been trained in the art of rhetoric.[64] Ernest Best contends that Paul is concerned with the form of rhetoric rather than the content of the gospel in his discussion in 1:18—2:5.[65] When Paul came to Corinth, he did not want to appear as one of the sophists who used their rhetorical skills to further their own agenda (2:4). Cicero wrote, "From eloquence those who have acquired it obtain glory and honour and high esteem. From eloquence comes the surest and safest protection of one's friends."[66]

The Corinthians honored those skilled in rhetoric—those whom they considered wise. Paul counters this by ironically demonstrating his so-called rhetorical inferiority (2:1). He rejects wisdom connected with speech many times in this passage (1:17; 2:1, 4, 13; 4:19-20). Some in Corinth may have believed that eloquent speech was a sign of spiritual maturity (1:19). Paul shows that the power resides in the apocalyptic message of the mystery of God's wisdom and not in the so-called power of the messengers.[67] It is also ironic that Paul seems to discount rhetorical skill in 1:20; 2:1, 4, yet uses sophisticated rhetoric throughout his letter. He was not against the power of words to persuade (1:21; 2:4), but against speech used to edify human status rather than the gospel (e.g., tongues and prophecy in chapter 14). Some of his opponents, who may have been skilled in spoken rhetoric, later recognized his rhetorical skills in writing (2 Cor 10:9-11).

---

[63] Timothy H. Lim, "'Not in Persuasive Words of Wisdom, but in the Demonstration of the Spirit and Power,'" *NovT* 29 (1987) 137–49.
[64] Stephen M. Pogoloff, *Logos and Sophia: The Rhetorical Situation of 1 Corinthians*, SBLDS 143 (Atlanta: Scholars, 1992); cf. Welborn, "On the Discord in Corinth," 85–111.
[65] Ernest Best, "The Power and the Wisdom of God, 1 Corinthians 1:18—2:5," in *Paolo a Una Chiesa Divisa (1 Cor. 1–4)*, ed. L. De Lorenzi (Rome: St. Paul Abbey, 1980) 9–41.
[66] Cicero, *Inv. Rhet.* 1.5.
[67] E. Elizabeth Johnson, "The Wisdom of God as Apocalyptic Power," in *Faith and History: Essays in Honor of Paul W. Meyer*, ed. John T. Carroll, Charles H. Cosgrove, E. Elizabeth Johnson (Atlanta: Scholars, 1990) 137–48.

❖ Hellenistic Judaism

A third approach locates the background for Paul's language in a mixture of Judaism and Hellenism. Richard A. Horsley contends that the problems in Corinth can be explained from "a Hellenistic Jewish religion of enlightenment" documented in the Wisdom of Solomon and Philo.[68] Horsley builds upon an earlier argument by Birger Pearson who contends that the immediate background of the Corinthians comes from Hellenistic Diaspora Judaism represented by Philo and from the larger context of Hellenistic philosophical paraenetic usage, particularly that of Stoicism.[69] According to Pearson, Paul's *pneumatikos-psychikos* terminology derives from Hellenistic Jewish exegesis of Genesis 2:7, such as can be seen in Philo. In interpreting this verse, Philo distinguishes between the earthly (*psychikos*) and heavenly (*pneumatikos*) person. Paul uses this same type of terminology in 1 Corinthians 2-3 to show two levels of spiritual experience, status or achievement. The *pneumatikos* person is described as being *teleios* ("mature"), which in Philo denotes "one who has achieved the highest religious attainments, including especially 'wisdom.'" Receiving wisdom leads to this higher plane of being *teleios*. Philo says that the *teleioi* are those who have achieved *sophia* ("wisdom," *Mig.* 28) and have been created according to the image (*eikona*) of God (*Leg. All.* I.94).[70] Pearson writes,

> The opponents of Paul in Corinth were teaching that they had the potentiality of becoming *pneumatikoi* within themselves by virtue of the *pneumatikos* nature given them by God, and that by a cultivation of Wisdom they could rise above the earthly and "psychic" level of existence and anticipate heavenly glory.[71]

Paul battles against this misperception of wisdom as the means of salvation and develops a different criteria for evaluating spiritual maturity.

Building on Pearson's approach, Horsley proposes that Paul is reacting against two aspects of wisdom speculation: wisdom as eloquence in speech and wisdom as the means of salvation.[72] Both of these are important elements in the Jewish wisdom tradition. Philo criticizes the abuse of empty eloquence

---

[68] Richard A. Horsley, "Gnosis in Corinth: 1 Corinthians 8:1-6," *NTS* 27 (1980) 32–51. Wis 4:24 reads, "For wisdom is known through speech, and education through the words of the tongue."

[69] Birger A. Pearson, *The Pneumatikos-psychikos Terminology in 1 Corinthians: A Study in the Theology of the Corinthian Opponents and Its Relation to Gnosticism*, SBLDS 12 (Missoula, Mont.: Society of Biblical Literature, 1973) 28.

[70] Ibid., 28–39.

[71] Ibid., 39.

[72] Richard A. Horsley, "Wisdom of Word and Words of Wisdom in Corinth," *CBQ* 39 (1977) 224.

when it is not consistent with action, but values its proper use with true wisdom.[73] Horsley writes that for Philo,

> eloquence used properly as the integral mode of communicating *sophia* is the expression appropriate to the mind which possesses knowledge of the divine. Thus coupled with its "brother," mind, speech is one of the endowments necessary for becoming perfect (*teleios*) and wise (*sophos*).[74]

Apollos as an Alexandrian Jew provides a possible but not necessary link between Philonic thought and the Corinthians.[75] The tradition given in Acts 18:24 and 26 is that Apollos was an eloquent man who knew the scriptures and who spoke with boldness when preaching. Where Paul fell short in eloquence and intellectual teaching from the Corinthians' perspective, Apollos fulfilled that need.[76] It is difficult to determine Paul's attitude towards Apollos behind his rhetoric of irony in 1 Corinthians. He could be positive towards Apollos because Apollos was not the real problem with the Corinthians, or he could be sarcastic by uniting himself with Apollos against the Corinthians' arrogance. Horsley comments,

> If anyone had cultivated a wisdom-school, in Corinth at least, it was not Paul but Apollos. Through the latter's ministry some of the Corinthians apparently had come to regard the (Christian) gospel as wisdom, the leaders as teachers of wisdom, and themselves as wise. This wisdom was, to be sure, "like that of the Greeks," a mixture of philosophy, religion and rhetoric. But this was understood by Apollos and others as Sophia, the Divine Teaching to be contemplated in the Scriptures.[77]

The Corinthians may have been using terms common in Philo's teaching to distinguish between the wise or eloquent and the weak of the church.[78] Paul turns these terms around and uses them on the Corinthians, some of whom thought

---

[73] Philo, *Vita* 31; *Det.* 69–78; *Leg.* 1.74–78; *Migr.* 70-85; *Her.* 14-21.
[74] Horsley, "Wisdom of Word," 229.
[75] See Birger Pearson, "Hellenistic-Jewish Wisdom Speculation and Paul," in *Aspects of Wisdom in Judaism and Early Christianity*, ed. Robert L. Wilken (Notre Dame: University of Notre Dame Press, 1975) 46, 59; N. Hyldahl, "The Corinthian 'Parties' and the Corinthian Crisis," *Studia Theologica* 45 (1991) 20–23; Richard A. Horsley, "'How Can Some of You Say That There Is No Resurrection of the Dead?' Spiritual Elitism in Corinth," *NovT* 20 (1978) 207. Murphy-O'Connor comments, "Given that Jews were an alienated minority in the Corinthian church, the Diaspora synagogue is most unlikely to have been the source of Philonic influence at Corinth. The obvious channel by which Philo's philosophical framework entered the community was Apollos" (*Paul: A Critical Life*, 282).
[76] Murphy-O'Connor, *Paul: A Critical Life*, 275–76.
[77] Horsley, "Wisdom of Word," 232.
[78] See Philo, *Sobr.* 9-11; 55–57.

they had gained possession of divine wisdom and felt exalted in their spiritual maturity.

A similar view to that of Horsley and Pearson has been offered by James A. Davis who argues that the view of the Corinthians is similar to the link between wisdom and Torah in Jewish thought. Davis sees a strong Jewish element in Corinth. The Corinthians had a Torah-centered wisdom similar to Philo's that contributed to their christology. Paul offers a corrective from a Torah-centered wisdom to a Christ-centered wisdom. Davis writes that for Paul, "The Christ-event has displaced the Torah as the most complete source for a knowledge of the divine design and intention."[79] "Christ, cross, and kerygma have replaced Torah as the definitive loci of divine wisdom.... The kind of wisdom upon which the Corinthians were now relying had proved itself, in the final analysis, to be incomplete and inadequate in the light of the cross (cf. Deut 21:22-23)."[80] If the Philonic influences upon Corinth, by the possible agency of Apollos, do indeed lie behind the problems within the community, then Davis' argument adds considerable weight to that of Horsley and Pearson. Philonic-like teachings may not be the only negative influence in Corinth, but may have been at least present.

In summary, these three approaches share a common assumption: Paul uses language either from his own experience and world-view and/or from the experience and environment of Corinth. It is impossible to determine the exact source of the language. The evidence of his rhetoric suggests that the Corinthians had an interpretation of wisdom and power that was a mix of both Hellenistic and Jewish elements.[81] Paul appears in the letter to be familiar with the language of Hellenistic Judaism similar to Philo's and is able to challenge this mixture with his own interpretation. Although some of the terms he uses were current in Hellenistic and Jewish contexts, his words were carefully chosen to address the needs in Corinth and to correct the Corinthians' misunderstanding of God's plan of the cross. This language suggests a church struggling with the issues of pride and power which were dividing fellowship and hindering spiritual growth. Paul turns the slogans of the Corinthians upside down by his rhetoric.[82] Brown writes,

---

[79] Davis, *Wisdom and Spirit*, 94.
[80] Ibid., 74.
[81] Brown, *The Cross and Human Transformation*, 33.
[82] Lincoln writes, "The apostle employs these terms with no explanation, evidently expecting his readers to be familiar with them" (*Paradise Now and Not Yet*, 40). Pearson remarks, "What is decisive in this passage is that Paul is dependent upon the opponents' terminology, but uses this terminology to express his own radically different theological point of view" (*Pneumatikos-psychikos Terminology*, 31).

> No other Pauline letter displays such interest in *what* and *how* one "knows," and none other brings so prominently and polemically into play the epistemologies of the wisdom and apocalyptic traditions. In his effort to effect a perceptual reorientation at Corinth, Paul must take account of those conventional structures of knowing that will determine how his Word of the Cross is heard and appropriated.[83]

Paul is not concerned about what religious or cultural influences may have lain behind the Corinthians' boasting and claims to power, but about the underlying cause of their not following the way of the cross and how this affects community formation. As Reiling comments, Paul offers them new definitions for old words, new interpretations of familiar texts, and new authority to events that seemed insignificant to them. He shows them a wisdom that cannot be found or gained by human effort but which comes only through divine revelation.[84] He challenges their misguided perceptions and uses his own hermeneutic, filled with apocalyptic terms and imagery, to interpret the kerygma for a contingent situation.

Conflict with Paul's Map of Reality

How does Paul want the Corinthians to live out his message of new life in Christ? Throughout the letter and significantly in chapters 1–4, his primary means is by an appeal to his authority. In chapters 1–4 he accomplishes his goal of convincing the Corinthians of his views by claiming a position in agreement with the divine paradox of the cross. His rhetoric serves as the articulation of existing conflict between himself and the Corinthians with the intended result of shaming them for the way they were acting. There are several forces that allow Paul to influence the beliefs and behaviors of the Corinthians. One is the power of his persuasion, that is, the ability of his words to shame the Corinthians. This rhetoric can only go so far; after all, the Corinthians could ignore his letter. Another is the power of established relationship. Paul assumes that his authority would add support to his argument. Through both means Paul attempts to re-socialize the church into a stronger community based on fellowship with Jesus Christ. The Corinthians were called to a new way of life as holy ones (1:2), to be set apart from their pagan environment. This new way should begin with the divine paradox, what Jerome Neyrey calls "a principle of divine reversal that establishes a

---

[83] Brown, *The Cross and Human Transformation*, 35.
[84] Reiling, "Wisdom and the Spirit," 203. Gaffin comments, "The necessity of revelation appears from the side of the recipients . . . in their absolute dependence. But, further, the revealer is under no outside compulsion to reveal; no claim arising from the (potential) recipients necessitates revelation. Rather, the act of revealing is free, sovereign, of entirely uncoerced divine initiative. . ." ("Epistemological Reflections," 105).

new order."[85] Paul challenges his readers to shift paradigms and to follow his example as he follows the example of Christ (11:1).

Mapping Paul's Way in Christ

According to Neyrey, one way to establish the relationship between Paul and his readers is to examine the social "maps" drawn in Paul's letters. Neyrey borrows from anthropologist Mary T. Douglas in his investigation of the social world behind Paul's letters. In anthropology, maps are patterns that describe a person's "symbolic universe" or "cosmos" and how a person attempts to make sense of it. A symbolic universe consists of

1. *Purity*: patterns of order and classification
2. *Rites*: either rituals of making and maintaining boundaries or ceremonies confirming values and institutions
3. *Body*: the social perception of the human physical body
4. *Sin*: the social definition of sin and deviance
5. *Cosmology*: who is in the world, and who is doing what?
6. *Evil and Misfortune*: how are they explained?[86]

Paul as a Jew had a sense of order in the cosmos in which everything had its place, including persons, things, places, and time. The map that is particularly important in this section of the letter is Paul's map of people. Paul appeals to his own map, which he believes is modeled after the map of Christ, as the new map for the Corinthians. In his letter, he is in the process of creating a map of people which the Corinthians could model. His goal is to show the Corinthians in what map their actions showed they remained and to offer to them a new map modeled after his own, which is really not his own but of Christ. In chapters 1–4 he is not concerned about any specific social issue like what occupies much of the rest of the letter. His primary concern is to remind the Corinthians of his own map. He then uses *shame* to motivate them to live in this right map.

Where does Paul locate himself? What does the map look like in which he places himself? There are several answers to these questions. The most significant map indicator for Paul is the kerygma and the response to it. He reminds the Corinthians in clear terms of what his kerygma consists. In its simplest, the kerygma consists of *the death and resurrection of Jesus Christ and the inauguration of a new reality which believers of Jesus Christ can experience in the present moment*. The Corinthians had no problem with that basic state-

---

[85] Jerome H. Neyrey, *Paul in Other Words: A Cultural Reading of His Letters* (Louisville: Westminster John Knox, 1990) 61.
[86] Ibid., 15.

ment of faith. The problem arises when the kerygma is expanded, explained, and allowed to influence behavior and belief. Paul feels he must explain his kerygma more fully in order for his readers to understand its implications. He had hoped that they would have caught on, but he ends up assessing them as immature.

According to Neyrey, Paul uses dualistic terms to describe those who belong to Christ and those who do not.[87] These terms surface specifically in 1:18-2:16. Paul's distinctions are not just theoretical or theological, but practical. He lays out the ideal and compares it to the present situation. This is not just a theoretical ideal but a *present* possibility, chiefly because he himself models it in his ministry. Neyrey provides an outline, similar to the division given above, which illustrates on the left the "ideal" map of Paul, and on the right the actual map of the Corinthians as Paul evaluates them:

in the know	vs.	not in the know
pneumatikoi	vs.	non-*pneumatikoi*
strong	vs.	weak
wise	vs.	foolish
honorable	vs.	dishonorable
presentable	vs.	unpresentable
superior	vs.	inferior
adults	vs.	babes[88]

In chapters 3 and 4 Paul makes his mapping an explicit part of his argument. He makes it clear in 3:1 that he would place the Corinthians in the map on the right, pinpointing their fundamental spiritual problem. They were mature (*teleioi*) when they were able to define the term in their own way. But Paul has a different paradigm in mind, and in this paradigm, they were clearly acting as immature (*nepioi*). In spite of this critical assessment, Paul can still call them the temple of God (3:16), which suggests he has in his mind a map of sacred space; he is concerned about issues of purity. God's presence can only dwell in holy places. If the Corinthians defile the sacred temple, they make it unfit for the presence of the holy God. Neyrey writes,

> The perception is spatial; something unclean has crossed the boundary meant to protect pure space, and pollution occurs. In the case of 1 Corinthians 3:16-17, the space is not just any mapped territory, but the holiest of spaces, a temple where God's Spirit dwells. *Corruptio optimi est pessima!*[89]

---

[87] Ibid., 41–43.
[88] Ibid., 43.
[89] Ibid., 97. He also notes that the verb for "destroy" (*phtheiro*) in v. 17 can also mean

Paul's underlying purpose is to protect the integrity and viability of the church as believers who exist in the realm of Christ. This is a reciprocal relationship whereby being in Christ allows the Spirit to be in the church. Adolf Deissmann comments, "Paul is most fond of regarding the community of believers under three aspects—as a family, as a body, as a temple. Each of these metaphors has its centre in the living Christ."[90]

Paul's Map of Apostolic Authority

One social map in which Paul places himself repeatedly in this letter is with the select group called apostles. What allows him this special classification is his association with the weakness of the cross (cf. 4:1-13). Paul's map is defined by one's position relative to Christ and the cross and whether or not one lives by the divine power and wisdom revealed through the weakness and folly of the cross. Paul describes his map in these terms: "one should regard us as servants of Christ and stewards of the mysteries of God" (4:1). According to Elizabeth Castelli, since Paul claims no other authority except the simple truth of the gospel, he is removed from any of the problems or criticisms at Corinth.[91] Chapter 4 has an interesting chiastic thought pattern:

> **A** Paul begins by claiming authority (4:1-5).
>
> > **B** He then assumes a position of weakness (4:8-13).
>
> **A'** Finally, he ends by reclaiming and using his authority (4:14-21).

The middle of this chiasm is full of irony, as has already been noted, which invites the reader to reverse what is stated. Paul's position of weakness is actually the position of power because he aligns himself with the gospel.[92] He assumes that his relationship with the Corinthians as their founder and apostle would provide him with some basis of authority. His rhetoric is based on this assumed position of authority. He writes, "For in Christ Jesus through the gospel I became your [father]. Therefore, I urge you, become imitators of me" (4:15-16). The sequence here is significant. Christ functions here as agent, content, and goal, and forms the basis of Paul's appeal of authority. John Schütz argues that authority is an interpretation of power and that power is

---

"defile."

[90] Adolf Deissmann, *Paul: A Study in Social and Religious History*, trans. William E. Wilson (New York: Harper, 1957) 208.

[91] Castelli, *Imitating Paul*, 98–99. Castelli goes on to argue that imitation of Paul is in political terms of community and that the content of his imitation is vague (4:17). She misses the power of Paul's position "in Christ" and the implications of this for the community.

[92] Schütz, *Paul and the Anatomy*, 229.

the source of authority for Paul. Paul mediates divine power to the world and appeals to his readers' sense of commitment to the power that he claims.[93]

The Corinthians should adhere to his position because it is the right one and coheres with the gospel. For example, Paul can pass judgement on the immoral "brother" in 5:3-5 and urges the Corinthians to implement this judgement when they and his spirit gather "in the name of the Lord Jesus, with the power of the Lord Jesus" (v. 4). It is difficult to determine what Paul means by his use of "in the name" in verse 3 and "with the spirit" in verse 4, but more relevant here is his ability to pass judgement and give direction to a confessing community gathered in the name of Jesus (v. 4a). Paul gives directions to the church based on his authority, which is directly linked to the power of Jesus. The source of Paul's authority comes directly from Jesus and can even be substituted for Jesus' authority (cf. 11:16; 14:37-38). Paul begins from the basic assumption of similar experience "in Christ" and works out the implications of this experience for the community.

In the ironical passage of 4:8-13, Paul describes the position he assumes relevant to the gospel. The maps in this passage are revealing.

Paul	**The Corinthians**
Last, sentenced to death a spectacle to all	Filled, rich kings, sovereign of all
Fools	Wise
Weak	Strong
Despised	Honored
Hungry, thirsty, ill-clad, mistreated, homeless, labor with own hands, reviled, persecuted, slandered, refuse of the world	

There is nothing appealing about Paul's position of dishonor. Moreover, he may have appeared unassuming to the Corinthians as a Jew, a manual laborer, and a supposedly inferior speaker.[94] What affect could such a position have upon the community?

A sense of guilt or shame could result if the Corinthians were sincere in their belief in Jesus Christ, especially since they adhered to the belief of a crucified Lord.[95] Aristotle provides some important insights about the concept of

---
[93] Ibid., 19.
[94] Stanley K. Stowers, "Social Status, Public Speaking and Private Teaching: The Circumstances of Paul's Preaching Activity," *NovT* 26 (1984) 74.
[95] One of the purposes of crucifixion was to shame the victim by public exposure, often in the nude, with the possibility of the indignity of mockery.

shame in the ancient world which are relevant for understanding this passage. He defines shame as "a kind of pain or uneasiness in respect of misdeeds, past, present, or future, which seem to tend to bring dishonour and shamelessness as contempt and indifference in and to these same things."[96] Paul has gone through great lengths to show the folly and weakness of the "powerful" and "wise" position of humanity. By associating the Corinthians with this position in 4:8-13 he has exposed them to the possibility of shame. Aristotle further says that shame also results when one lacks "a share in the honorable things which all men, or all who resemble us, or the majority of them, have a share in. By those who resemble us I mean those of the same race, of the same city, of the same age, of the same family, and, generally speaking, those who are on an equality."[97] One of Paul's primary methods of social integration is through the use of terms of fictive kinship or familial terms such as "brothers" (3:1), "beloved children" (4:14), and "father" (4:15).[98] Furthermore, according to Aristotle, "people feel shame before those whom they esteem."[99] At this point in the Corinthian correspondence, there is no indicator that the Corinthians did not hold Paul in some type of esteem.[100] Shame results when one realizes that eyes are watching.[101] Paul reminds the Corinthians that God is watching them when he quotes from Job 5:13 and Psalm 94:11 in 3:19-20, which essentially says that the Lord knows what is really behind the Corinthians' so-called wisdom. Likewise, shame intensifies when people "have to be seen and to associate openly with those who are aware of their disgrace."[102] Paul's threat of a promised visit intensifies the shame of the Corinthians (4:18-21). A face to face confrontation is much less pleasant than a second-hand encounter through written letter or emissary.

In his appeal for the Corinthians to come over to his map of weakness, Paul creates social dissonance between them and their environment. The very concept of worshiping a crucified messiah or lord may have had adverse social effects upon them. To be associated with slave punishment, public disgrace, the humiliation of exposure, or divine curse created an unpleasant barrier for many people to cross, even those who were in a position of human weakness when Paul preached (1:26).[103] The appeal to experience the foolishness of the

---

[96] Aristotle, *Rh.* 2.6.1.
[97] Aristotle, *Rh.* 2.6.12.
[98] See Meeks, *First Urban Christians*, 86–88.
[99] Aristotle, *Rh.* 2.6.15.
[100] This notion may have changed by the time Paul wrote 2 Corinthians as Paul's apology and defense in 2 Corinthians 10–13 suggest.
[101] Aristotle, *Rh.* 2.6.18.
[102] Aristotle, *Rh.* 2.6.27.
[103] Cf. Stephen C. Barton, "Paul and the Cross: A Sociological Approach," *Theology* 85 (1982) 13–19.

cross also called the Corinthians to leave the social norms of Corinth. Corinth was known for being a center of learning in antiquity. Aelius Aristides writes in his *Orations*,

> While traveling about the city, you would find wisdom and you would learn and hear it from its inanimate objects. So numerous are the treasures of paintings all about it, wherever one would simply look, throughout the streets themselves and the porticos. And further the gymnasiums and schools are in themselves instruction and stories.[104]

When it comes down to essentials, Paul is asking the Corinthians to make a choice between honor before God or honor before their world.

The Effects of the Divine Mystery upon the Corinthian Church

Paul addresses the Corinthians with sarcasm and irony in order that they might see the folly of their ways. He is deeply concerned about their spiritual immaturity because he knows that it could lead to the destruction of the church. If they continued to live as "fleshly" people, they would become an unfit dwelling for the Spirit of God (3:16-17). The threat of this exists with the presence of the immoral "brother," in whom the Corinthians seemed to boast (5:1-13). They failed, at a basic level, to grow in their understanding of being "in Christ." Their actions betrayed their morality as inconsistent with their claims. They believed that they had reached the pinnacle of spiritual experience, but Paul says that they had only begun and there was more for them to experience; they were living only at an elementary level. Paul does not want them to think that spirituality leads to asceticism or liberality. Fee comments, "Being human is not a bad thing in itself, any more than being *sarkinoi* is (v. 1). What is intolerable is to have received the Spirit, which makes one more than merely human, and to continue to live as though one were nothing more."[105] For the Corinthians to accept Paul's ideology would mean replacing their human wisdom and strength with divine wisdom and strength. They would have to allow themselves to be taught the meaning of the divine mystery by the Spirit. Davis writes, "The intended, or expected result of our possession of the Spirit is that we might come to know the whole wisdom of God, but such knowledge is only progressively realized by the one who is maturing in the Spirit as he takes part in the speaking and sharing of spiritual insights."[106] The result for the community would be unity in mind and purpose (1:10).

---

[104] Aelius Aristides, *Or.* 46.28.
[105] Fee, *First Corinthians*, 127.
[106] Davis, *Wisdom and Spirit*, 109–10.

Paul's Call to Imitate

Paul's call to imitate forms one of the basic strategies for persuading the Corinthians to change their behavior and grow in their faith in Christ. He views his own ideology—which he considers not *his* own but revealed from God (2:10)—as the solution to the problems of the Corinthians. When Paul urges them to be imitators of him in 4:16, he has a specific model in mind, the context and structure of which imply submission in weakness to the way of the cross and to the lordship of Christ. What Paul means in verse 16 is described in verse 17 with the phrase, "my ways in Christ, just as I teach everywhere and in every church." These ways are linked to Paul's teaching which included the kerygma and its ethical implications (cf. Rom 14:1-15:7).

One cannot stop only with this general interpretation. Paul has gone through great rhetorical effort up to this point in the letter to describe what exactly he wants the Corinthians to imitate. The comparison between his and the other apostles' experience and that of the Corinthians described in 4:8-13 recalls his paradigmatic contrast in 1:18-25 between divine foolishness and weakness in the cross and human ability and wisdom. Especially noteworthy is the repetition in 4:10 of the key words "fool," "wise," "weak," and "strong." What Paul has essentially done in this passage is to align himself with the divine paradox and the Corinthians with the world. What should come to the readers' mind when the call to imitate is given is Paul's association of himself with God's eternal plan in Christ. Paul opened himself to allowing the Spirit to teach him the depths of divine grace, and he humbled himself in order to experience divine strength. Boykin Sanders writes, "Just as the weakness of the cross reveals the power of God, his own weakness gives an opportunity for the presence of God's power (2 Cor 12:7-10)."[107] Paul expresses this differently in 2 Corinthians 3:18: "And we with unveiled faces, while beholding the glory of the Lord, are being transformed into his image from one degree of glory to another which is all from the Lord who is the Spirit." Paul's authority comes as an authority of association. The Corinthians also could experience God's power and wisdom with Paul by their own association with the way of Christ.

Conclusion

Paul's answer for the Corinthian problem lies with the divine paradox seen in the cross of Christ. The main way Paul attempts to correct the behavior and beliefs of the Corinthians is by looking *backwards* to the first major moment in his scheme of time: the death and resurrection of Jesus Christ. By looking back, Paul reminds the Corinthians of the way they should act in the *pres-*

---

[107] Boykin Sanders, "Imitating Paul: 1 Cor 4:16," *HTR* 74 (1981) 358.

ent. If they did not live in a manner consistent with the Christ-event then they could not grow into spiritual maturity. The Holy Spirit could not teach them the deeper truths of the gospel nor could the Spirit reside within them because of their unholiness and identification with the ways of the world. The immature spiritual condition of the Corinthians resulted in boasting and divisiveness within the community.

Paul creates a world view in his letter which contradicts typical perceptions: power from weakness and wisdom from folly. If the Corinthians wanted to be in this map of true power and wisdom, they had to begin living according to this view. Paul seeks to *shame* them into accepting this position of weakness in order that they might experience the power of God. They needed to live according to the absurdity and foolishness of the gospel so that they might be empowered by the Spirit. Living according to the paradox of the cross is the true position of strength for Paul because it is where the power of God's Spirit is allowed to work. The position of humility, submission, and reliance upon God, though seen as weakness from the world's perspective, opens the way for the believer to experience the very power of God. In the cross God creates a radical new map of the cosmos that alters human perceptions and experiences.

Misunderstandings over spirituality were the basic cause of the breakdown of fellowship in the Corinthian church. The potential for divisions in this church and the ethical and theological issues with which Paul deals later in the letter were the result of a basic error on the part of the Corinthians. Social cohesion could occur only if the community united in purpose and shifted to Paul's map. The problems could be resolved if the Corinthians grew in their relationship with Christ by allowing the Spirit to teach them "the mind of Christ." Paul attempts to provide the community a new sense of identity. Paul, as a leader and individual, remains somewhat vague at this point in the letter because he attempts to stand behind the kerygma. By doing this, he offers the Corinthians the best example he possibly can. He may say at this point, "Imitate me" (4:17), but he actually means, "Imitate me as I imitate Christ" (11:1).

4

Completing the Mystery with the Resurrection of Believers *(1 Corinthians 15)*

Fellowship with Jesus Christ was Paul's primarily motivation and hermeneutic. The cross-event provided him the primary model for life, and the immanent appearance (*parousia*) of Christ provided him the hope. The mystery of God revealed on the cross will be completed with the parousia (15:24-28). Paul looked back to the cross and forward to the parousia as the basis for dealing with the problems in Corinth. The full-gospel of new life in Christ necessitates these two focal points. Paul's letters indicate in many places that he kept this memory and hope in his mind as he dealt with the present problems in his churches. The same holds true in 1 Corinthians.

Paul appears reactionary in chapter 15 because he considers the situation critical. He continues to use God's revelation in Christ as his answer to the situations in this church. He refers to the *future completion* of God's plan in order to affect the *present* attitudes, beliefs, and behaviors of the Corinthians. He urges them to make a paradigm shift in their pursuit of becoming "spiritual" by living the new existence "in Christ." He attempts to redefine their spirituality according to the model of the Christ-event and the fellowship with Christ that comes through the Holy Spirit.

Apparently some of the Corinthians denied the resurrection of the body (15:12-34) and misunderstood the transforming power that comes in Christ (15:35-58). Significantly, Paul ties the concept of resurrection to spiritual maturity. He weds his concept of identification with Christ's death and resurrection in baptism and the new life that follows (Rom 6:4) to his understanding of the future resurrection and transformation of the body. To divorce these two concepts leads to a denial of the kerygma. His objective is to create dissonance in the thinking of the Corinthians, or as Richard B. Hays writes, "he is not trying to reassure believers who have anxiety over the ultimate fate of their loved ones. Instead, he is trying to *induce* some anxiety among the

Corinthians about this point!"[1] Paul's ultimate paradigm for the Corinthians is the new eschatological existence in Christ inaugurated by Christ's resurrection. The basic, soteriological process for Paul is that Christ died and rose from the dead, making redemption from sin and death possible for believers. Because of Christ, believers can then experience freedom from the grip of sin and death through faith in Christ. Christ's resurrection and believers' union with him guarantee believers' future resurrection and eternal life with him. This assertion is critical to Paul's argument in chapter 15. This chapter is the climax of the letter and discloses Paul's understanding of the full revelation of the mystery of Christ.[2]

Paul's Problem with the Corinthians

Paul's knowledge of the situation in Corinth prompts him to respond by pointing the Corinthians back to the basic enthymeme or premise he shares with them. This basic premise is the theme of the kerygma: that Christ died, rose, appeared alive, and will come again (15:3-5, 58). Paul is concerned about some of the beliefs of the Corinthians that threatened the validity of this premise. He can assess these people as being in a dangerous position because their attitudes towards resurrection contradicted the gospel of Christ's own resurrection.

The Rhetorical Situation of Paul's Argument

Paul writes this chapter in reply to a situation that calls for a response, which, in rhetorical theory, is called the "rhetorical situation." An author's response to a rhetorical situation is guided by what effects he or she wishes to have upon an audience.[3] It is difficult to assess the exact situation in Corinth that prompted Paul to write about the resurrection of Christ and believers. It is possible that Paul heard about the situation by word of mouth. From a methodological perspective, it is difficult to determine the views of the Corinthians represented in Paul's rhetoric. Johannes N. Vorster cautions that a rhetorical situation is always a construct of reality. He writes that "a rhetorical situation is constituted by a need, an identification of that need and the possibility of responding to that need." Furthermore, the only way to know the opposite

---

[1] Richard B. Hays, *First Corinthians,* IBC (Louisville: Westminster John Knox, 1997) 261.
[2] Karl Barth, *The Resurrection of the Dead*, trans. by H. J. Stenning (London: Hodder and Stoughton, 1933) 13–124, held that ch. 15 was the climax of the whole letter and all the issues with which Paul deals are solved in ch. 15. I argue that it is the climax of the letter because in this chapter Paul articulates his understanding of the complete divine plan begun on the cross and the significance of this completion for believers in the present time.
[3] Cf. Lloyd F. Bitzer, "The Rhetorical Situation," *Philosophy and Rhetoric* 1 (1968) 1–14.

view is by reconstruction from the author's perspective. Thus, the views represented in the text are Paul's reconstruction of the problems in Corinth.[4]

In this chapter, as in the rest of the letter, Paul addresses the Corinthians' misperceptions about the gospel message he preached to them. To what problem does Paul seem to respond in this chapter? He does not mention any disagreement with the Corinthians until verse 12 when he writes, "Now if it is preached that Christ rose from the dead, how can some of you say that there is no resurrection of the dead?" Whom does Paul have in mind when he speaks about "some of you"? According to Duane F. Watson, two views seem to be present in Corinth: those who were loyal to the apostolic tradition given in verse 3-11 but whose degree of loyalty was in doubt, and those who challenged the tradition by denying bodily resurrection of the dead.[5] Paul does not single out this last group, the "some of you," but speaks to the community as a whole (vv. 12, 32-34, 35, 52, 58). Just as with the immoral "brother" in chapter 5, this also is a community-wide problem. The community was allowing itself to be influenced more by those who deny the resurrection than by the apostolic tradition represented by Paul.

Paul deals with two alternatives and attempts to show which is more advantageous to the community. On the one hand, from his perspective, some of the Corinthians misunderstood what resurrection of the body entails (15:35-36). Gerhard Sellin has identified three possible positions for the Corinthians: they denied post-mortal existence, they denied bodily nature of resurrection, or they denied the futurity of resurrection.[6] Their position has sometimes been identified as an "over-realized" eschatology.[7] C. K. Barrett writes that the Corinthians were "behaving as if the age to come were already consummated."[8] Gordon Fee offers, "Their outlook was that of having arrived (see 4:8)—not in an eschatological sense, but in a 'spiritual' sense."[9] They did not consider that the body must die in order to be transformed, that resurrection involves a transformation *after* physical death. This view may have led

---

[4] Johannes N. Vorster, "Resurrection Faith in 1 Corinthians 15," *Neot* 23 (1989) 287.
[5] Duane F. Watson, "Paul's Rhetorical Strategy in 1 Corinthians 15," in *Rhetoric and the New Testament*, ed. Stanley E. Porter and Thomas H. Olbricht, JSNTSup 90 (Sheffield: JSOT Press, 1993) 233. For the various positions on the situation in Corinth, see Alexander J. M. Wedderburn, *Baptism and Resurrection: Studies in Pauline Theology Against Its Greaeco-Roman Background*, WUNT 144 (Tübingen: Mohr/Siebeck, 1987) 6–37.
[6] Gerhard Sellin, *Der Streit um die Auferstehung der Toten: Eine religionsgeschichtliche und exegetische untersuchung von 1. Korinther 15,* FRLANT 138 (Göttingen: Vandenhoeck & Ruprecht, 1986) 17; cf. Christopher M. Tuckett, "'No Resurrection of the Dead' (1 Cor 15:12)" in *The Corinthian Correspondence*, ed. Reimund Bieringer (Leuven: Leuven University Press, 1996) 251–61.
[7] Anthony C. Thiselton, "Realized Eschatology at Corinth," *NTS* 24 (1978) 510–26.
[8] Barrett, *First Corinthians*, 109.
[9] Fee, *First Corinthians*, 339.

to a devaluation of the body, which the letter suggests the Corinthians had done (6:12-14). Their concept of resurrection involved a spiritual resurrection but not a bodily one. They may have thought of themselves as "spiritual" (*pneumatikos*) and in possession of great gifts of the Holy Spirit (3:1; 4:8; 12:1; cf. 2 Tim 2:17-18; Acts 17:32). The body was unnecessary for them since they had already been given the Holy Spirit and were only awaiting the opportunity to discard the body so that they could be *pneumatikos* without hindrance.[10]

Paul, on the other hand, stresses the futurity of bodily resurrection. He builds his position on the tradition and kerygma of Christ's death and resurrection, the new existence this brings to believers, and his own preaching and experience. He also has a form of realized eschatology, but he stresses the reality of death while emphasizing the power of the resurrection. Martinus de Boer suggests that the fundamental issue in chapter 15 is over what to do with death.[11] There are thirteen references to "resurrection of the dead" in the chapter.[12] There is also a significant concentration of two key words: the verb "to raise up" and the noun "resurrection."[13] Paul's problem with the Corinthians focuses upon their views of the resurrection of the dead and the reality of death.[14] He takes very seriously the creed concerning the resurrection of Christ and the promise this holds for believers. His seriousness can be seen in his claim that the very foundations of the faith of the Corinthians rested upon the belief in resurrection (vv. 12-19). No resurrection meant no redemption and no forgiveness of sins, and hence, condemnation with "the world" (cf. 11:32).

Paul's *propositio* or thesis for the argument is rather simple: since Christ has been raised, so will believers (vv. 12, 20). Paul's argument is not designed to prove the first half of the thesis but the last half. Burton Mack comments, "This means that the kerygma is not only the point of departure for, but the ultimate ground of Paul's persuasion. None of the arguments are introduced in support of the kerygma, but in support of Paul's contention that the kerygma guarantees the resurrection of the dead."[15] Paul and the Corinthians agree over the basic confession that Jesus Christ rose from the dead, but the Corinthians had failed to see the important implications of this resurrection

---

[10] Ibid., 778.
[11] Martinus de Boer, *The Defeat of Death: Apocalyptic Eschatology in 1 Corinthians 15 and Romans 5* (Sheffield: JSOT Press, 1988) 105.
[12] 15:4, 12 (twice), 13, 15, 16, 20, 21, 29, 32, 35, 42, 52.
[13] The verb "to raise up" (*egeirō*) appears in 6:14; 15:4, 12, 13, 14, 15 (twice), 16 (twice), 17, 20, 29, 32, 35, 42, 43 (twice), and 52; the noun "resurrection" (*anastasis*) appears in 15:12, 13, 21, and 42.
[14] Note 15:20-28, 29, 30-32, 35-49, 36, 42, 50-58.
[15] Mack, *Rhetoric and the New Testament*, 58.

for their faith, behavior, present, and future (15:34, 58). Mack adds that Paul's argument with them involves thesis and antithesis by which he defines the issue with positive points and counters objections to the issue through refuting the opposite view.[16] Paul attempts to persuade the Corinthians of the futility of the view that denies the future bodily resurrection of believers. He is adamant about this point in his last argument possibly because the eschatological resurrection of believers is the completion of God's mystery in Christ. The future resurrection completes the old story prophesied by the prophets and revealed in Jesus Christ (Rom 16:25-26). If the Corinthians denied the end of the story, they also invalidated the beginning of the story.

Paul proves this thesis by using deliberative rhetoric to convince the Corinthians to accept what was advantageous and honorable to them in consideration of future consequences they faced if they failed to adhere to his interpretation of the gospel.[17] He is concerned with the *present* behavior of the Corinthians but argues for changes that would impact the *future* of both individuals and the community. Deliberative rhetoric often uses examples to support a thesis.[18] Paul uses a number of examples and analogies to confirm his thesis. He expects his rhetoric to be effective and is confident that the Corinthians would respond to his letter. His choice of words and his style of writing are carefully and intentionally chosen.

The Corinthians and Death

The Corinthians may have been influenced in their attitude towards death and resurrection by the views present in their culture. Delineating these views can suggest the possible ideology or ideologies of the Corinthian church. The topics of death and resurrection were important to many people in the first century. There were many different beliefs in the ancient world about what happens to a person after death. The Greeks generally did not hold to the resurrection of the body, while some Jews did, especially those with apocalyptic interests or with Pharisaic backgrounds.

❖ Death and Greco-Roman Religions

Paul deals with a common first-century idea when he counters the claims of some in the community that there is no resurrection of the body. Most Greeks believed in the immortality of the soul but not in the resurrection

---

[16] Ibid., 56.
[17] Watson, "Paul's Rhetorical Strategy," 232; Mack, *Rhetoric and the New Testament;* Mitchell, *Rhetoric of Reconciliation,* 286; Insawn Saw, *Paul's Rhetoric in 1 Corinthians 15: An Analysis Utilizing the Theories of Classical Rhetoric* (Macon, Ga.: Mellen, 1995) 183–98.
[18] See Aristotle, *Rh.* 1.9.40; *Rhet. Her.* 3.5.9.

of the body. In addition, as Ben Witherington comments, "Greco-Roman paganism did not place much stress on a blessed afterlife. Religion was to be practiced for its present benefits, such as health and safety."[19] There are many well-known examples from Greek literature of a denial of the resurrection of the body. For example, Aeschylus (c. 525–456 BCE) has Apollo say, "When the dust hath drained the blood of a man, once he is slain, there is no resurrection."[20] In Aeschylus' play *Agamemnon*, a member of the chorus says, "I know no way how by mere words to bring the dead back to life."[21] Herodotus (c. 484–425 BCE) reports that Presaspes told Cambyses, "If the dead can rise, you may look to see Astyages the Mede rise up against you; if nature's order be not changed, assuredly no harm to you will arise from Smerdis."[22] The chorus in Sophocles's *Electra* says, "Yet him, they sire, from Acheron's dark shore; by prayers or cries thou never can'st restore; No, never more."[23]

The Greeks generally thought that resurrection was impossible because the body and soul could not be rejoined. The soul was seen as immortal and the body as part of mortal existence. According to this view, it is impossible for the body to exist in a post-mortem existence. Philo, as a Hellenistic Jew, also espoused this view.[24] The belief in the immortality of the soul can be traced back to Platonism which had infiltrated much of Greco-Roman thought by the first century,[25] and even further back into ancient Greek epics where death was conquered in various journeys and heroic feats. The significant difference with the latter is that, often, the hero did not die but escaped death in order to live in the Elysian fields or the Isles of the Blessed.[26] For Plato and many who followed him, the goal of the soul was migration from the world of the senses to the realm of the real. Plutarch later wrote that the soul could reach the realm of the gods only by becoming free from the senses, that is, the world of mortality.[27] There are many divergent views on whether or not this concept speaks of resurrection in the sense that the Corinthians or Paul would have understood it, and how far scholars should take the parallels. A lot of the discussion hinges upon the definition of "resurrection."[28] These major currents of thought were present to some degree or another at every

---

[19] Witherington, *Conflict and Community*, 293.
[20] Aeschylus, *Eum.* 647–48.
[21] Aeschylus, *Ag.* 1360–61.
[22] Herodotus, *History* 3.62.
[23] Sophocles, *El.* 137–39.
[24] Wedderburn, *Baptism and Resurrection*, 183, referring to Philo, *Cher.* 114; *QE* 2.46.
[25] See Plato, *Phdr.* 64–95.
[26] E.g., Proteus in Homer, *Od.* 4.561–569; see Wedderburn, *Baptism and Resurrection*, 185.
[27] Plutarch, *Rom.* 28.6.
[28] For a discussion of this difficult topic, see Wedderburn, *Baptism and Resurrection*, 190–211.

level in the ancient world, and the Corinthian church likely did not escape their influence.

Yet, as John Schütz contends, there is nothing in the text that indicates that the Corinthians held to the belief of the immortality of the soul. The basic problem the Corinthians had was with the resurrection of the body. Their doubts about the resurrection of the body could have been influenced by Greek philosophy, such as the skepticism of Epicureanism.[29] It is possible that, as Hays writes, "Rather than correcting the 'ignorance of God' of their pagan neighbors, the 'knowing' Corinthian Christians [were] trying to tailor their faith to the intellectual standards of pagan philosophy, with the result that they [were] surrendering the heart of the gospel and being drawn into idolatrous and immoral behavior."[30]

❖ Preoccupation with Death in Corinth

In addition, first-century Corinth may have had a preoccupation with death. Richard E. DeMaris argues that archeological evidence suggests that those who lived in Corinth around the first century CE paid high regard to burial practices. It was believed by both Greeks and Romans that the dead benefitted from actions performed on their behalf. After burial, the dead would be remembered by grave-side feasts and annual festivals. The Panhellenic games, held near Corinth, honored the dead hero Palaimon, also called Melikertes, and were funerary in nature; the worship of Palaimon involved offerings to the dead. These games probably took place while Paul was in Corinth.[31] DeMaris writes, "Thus, the rise of the Palaimon cult in Roman times indicates that the Corinthia's religious center, Isthmia, represented not only Poseidon but more and more that side of religion having to do with the dead and the gods of the dead."[32]

Demeter worship was also important in and around Corinth. Demeter was often associated with the gods of the dead and the underworld since her daughter, Kore, spent half the year with Hades in the underworld. Evidence suggests that the Demeter sanctuary of first-century Corinth was dedicated to Kore rather than Demeter, thus giving it a chthonic appearance. Further evidence suggests that both cremation and inhumation were practiced in Corinth, which may show a concern for burial practices. In the Eleusinian mysteries, which took place near Corinth, on the last day of the initiations

---

[29] Dale B. Martin, *The Corinthian Body* (New Haven: Yale University Press, 1995) 275, n. 79.
[30] Hays, *First Corinthians*, 269.
[31] Richard E. DeMaris, "Corinthian Religion and Baptism for the Dead (1 Corinthians 15:29) Insights from Archeology and Anthropology," *JBL* 114 (1995) 663–66.
[32] DeMaris, "Corinthian Religion," 666.

libations and rites were given for the dead.[33] It was believed that Demeter bestowed two gifts through these ceremonies: grain, the basis of civilized life, and the mysteries, which promised a better hope for a happy afterlife.[34]

The Corinthian Christians were not immune to these practices and some may have even taken part in them.[35] Often the case for this is made with respect to the difficult reference to baptism for the dead in 15:29. Paul mentions baptism for the dead in this letter for some reason, possibly because of the influences of the pagan environment upon the Corinthian church. Although this reference in 15:29 remains obscure, it is still apparent that the Corinthians' lack of belief in a bodily resurrection was paramount in Paul's mind because such a belief undermined the foundations of faith in Christ. To Paul this type of thinking threatened the kerygma and showed spiritual immaturity. The Corinthians had a new definition of spirituality based upon edification of individual abilities, including wisdom and speech. It is possible that they thought that they had begun some type of new spiritual existence in which the body was unnecessary and unwanted since they could speak in tongues like angels (13:1; 4:9; 7:1-7).[36]

❖ Resurrection and Judaism

Furthermore, the Corinthians could have been influenced by some of the Jewish views of the time. Resurrection from the dead was a much debated topic in Judaism before and during Paul's day, with no dominant orthodox position.[37] Belief in bodily resurrection was a late development in Jewish writings, with only a few places in the Old Testament suggesting resurrection. Ancient Israelite religion tended to be concerned with existence in the present world, and the only future concern was the fate of the nation as a whole. The Elijah and Elisha narratives provide the earliest antecedents to a later belief in resurrection. Elijah was able to revive or resurrect the son of the widow of Zarephath so that the boy's soul (Hebrew *nephesh*) could return to him (1 Kgs 17:17-24). A parallel account is given of Elisha reviving the dead son of a Shunammite woman (2 Kgs 4:18-37). A dead man was revived when he was thrown into the grave of Elisha and touched Elisha's bones (13:20-21).

Ancient Israel believed that Yahweh is the God of the living. Life after death is spoken of as a shadowy existence in Sheol, the place of the dead or

---

[33] George E. Mylonas, *Eleusis and the Eleusinian Mysteries* (Princeton: Princeton University Press, 1961) 239–80.
[34] Walter Burkert, *Ancient Mystery Cults* (Cambridge: Harvard University, 1987) 4–5.
[35] DeMaris, "Corinthian Religion," 671.
[36] Fee, *First Corinthians*, 715.
[37] Christopher Francis Evans, *Resurrection and the New Testament* (Naperville, Ill.: Allenson, 1970) 27.

the grave (Eccl 9:10). It is where a person is cut off from Yahweh (Ps 6:5; 115:17), yet Yahweh is not hidden from that person (139:8; Prov 15:11). God has power over death—most significantly in a national sense (Ps 16:10). Ezekiel's vision of the valley of dry bones becoming living soldiers shows this power over the death of a nation (Ezek 37:1-14; cf. Hos 6:1-2). These national hopes easily lent themselves to the individualistic interpretation picked up in later Judaism and the New Testament. Two passages imply reference to bodily resurrection. Isaiah 26:19 refers to the dead as living and their bodies as rising from the dust. Daniel 12:2-3 gives the most developed understanding of resurrection in the Old Testament. The context is the eschaton when Israel and, specifically, those whose names are written in "the book," will be finally delivered. Then, "those who sleep in the dust of the earth will awake, some going to everlasting life and others to everlasting shame."

Daniel provides a good transition into the apocalyptic thought of the first few centuries before Christ. The fate of the individual begins to be separated to some degree from the fate of the nation, and this fate involved reward or punishment for acts done in this life. During the intertestamental period, people became more interested in the question of life after death in an eschatological sense. In the face of martyrdom, 2 Maccabees asserts bodily resurrection as the hope of the righteous (7:9, 11, 14; 12:43-45; 14:46). The *Sibilene Oracles* 4:18 refers to God refashioning bodies to their original forms. Slovanic Baruch 21:13 says, "For if there were this life only, which belongs to all men, nothing would be more bitter than this." According to *2 Baruch* 50-51, both the evil and righteous will arise in the last day; the righteous will be transformed into the glory of heaven and the evil will experience torment in Gehenna (cf. 85:13). The earth will give back the dead in the same form as it took them (49:2-3). At the end of time, the corruptible also ends and the incorruptible begins (74:2; 44:9; cf. 1 Cor 15:53-54). Bodily resurrection is suggested in the *Apocalypse of Moses* 40-41 where God reunites Adam's soul in the third heaven with his body still on earth.

Yet not all Jews were in agreement that there would be a resurrection of the body or about how to interpret resurrection. Before the fall of Jerusalem there were two opposing views in first-century Judaism concerning death and resurrection represented in the two parties, the Sadducees and Pharisees. The Pharisees believed in a resurrection of the body but the Sadducees denied it (cf. Acts 4:2; 23:7-8; 24:21). R. J. Sider writes, "As a good first-century Pharisee, Paul could not conceive of the resurrection of the dead in purely immaterial terms."[38] Paul's apocalyptic convictions may have come from his

---

[38] R. J. Sider, "The Pauline Conception of the Resurrection Body in 1 Corinthians XV.35-54," *NTS* 21 (1974–75) 438.

Pharisaic world view.[39] The significant difference between Paul and other apocalypticists is that the Christ-event altered his apocalyptic views. His vision and experience of the risen Christ convinced him that the destiny of humanity had shifted and a new hope had come with Christ.

Paul's Ideology of Resurrection

Paul attempts to cultivate the correct perspective in Corinth by a thorough and convincing argument. His ideology appears in this chapter in his reaction to the troubling news that some doubted the resurrection of the body. To combat this errant view, he turns the attention of the Corinthians to the *future* moment in his scheme of time when Christ will come and those in fellowship with him will be raised from the dead. Paul references this future moment in order to motivate them to act and believe in a certain way *in the present*.

The Structure of Paul's Argument

Chapter 15 is Paul's fourth and last major argument in the letter. Many scholars have recognized the rhetorical character of the chapter, how it has its own rhetorical arrangement and strategy, and how it contains all the parts of a concise rhetorical speech.[40] This chapter is not isolated from Paul's larger concern over spirituality but in many respects is the summation and completion of the argument of the entire letter. The basic structure of the chapter can be divided into three topical units: (1) the tradition of the resurrection of Jesus from the dead (vv. 1-11), (2) proofs for resurrection of believers (vv. 12-34), and (3) a description of the nature of the resurrection body (vv. 35-58). Paul uses the first section as the basis for his argument in the last two sections. There is a rather abrupt change of topic from communication with tongues and prophecy in chapter 14 to the gospel tradition and resurrection from the dead in chapter 15. Underlying both chapters, as well as the entire letter, is the topic of spiritual maturity. Paul wants to inform the Corinthians of the implications of the gospel in 15:1, just as he wants to inform them about spiritual matters in 12:1. The topic of discussion is the gospel and the Corinthians' interpretation of the gospel. Paul wants them to stand firm in the tradition they received and to see the meaning of this tradition for their present conduct and future hopes.

---

[39] Beker, *Paul the Apostle*, 144.
[40] E.g., Conzelmann, *1 Corinthians*, 249; Mack, *Rhetoric and the New Testament*, 56.

❖ Exordium, vv. 1-2

Paul gives the *exordium* or statement of purpose for his argument in verses 1-2. The purpose of an *exordium* is to capture the attention and good will of the audience and to introduce the topic of the speech.[41] Paul does that here by recalling the gospel he preached to the Corinthians. In 2:1-5 he writes that the content of this gospel was "Jesus Christ and him crucified." In chapter 15 he expands this content and gives the other side of the "cross-event," namely the resurrection of Christ. Paul's *exordium* consists of three parts: the message of the gospel, the reception of it by the Corinthians, and the potential of hearing it in vain.[42] "In vain" is a theme that surfaces several times in the argument (vv. 2, 10, 14, 17, 58) and serves as a motivational strategy for Paul. The last thing the Corinthians should want is to miss out in the promises of the gospel. Therefore, it would be to their advantage to agree with Paul's interpretation of the gospel tradition lest their faith be for nothing. There is no indication that they disagreed with the basic creed given in verses 3-5. Nowhere in the letter is Paul in disagreement with them because they did not believe the message of the death and resurrection of Christ. His basic problem with them is over the interpretation and appropriation of the *terms* of this message for their spiritual maturity. In this part of the letter, he wants to show them that by their denying the bodily resurrection of believers, they were, in essence, undermining the terms of the gospel and showing their unbelief in the death and resurrection of Christ. By not accepting the implications of the gospel, they were acting as unbelieving people of the world (*psychikos*; 2:14).

❖ Narratio, vv. 3-11

After his brief introduction to the issue, Paul moves on to give the *narratio* for the *exordium* in verses 3-11. The purpose of a *narratio* is to provide the basis of proof or background for the argument.[43] Paul's basis of proof for the two-part argument which follows is his citation of the tradition of Christ' death and resurrection in verses 3b-5.[44] He restates the basic terms of his kerygma possibly to emphasize the totality of the cross-event. The creed is short and concise, and contains four parts:

---

[41] Aristotle, *Rh.* 3.13; Cicero, *Part. Or.* 4.13.
[42] Watson, "Paul's Rhetorical Strategy," 235.
[43] Cicero, *Part. Or.* 4.13; *Inv. Rhet.* 1.19.27; Quintillian, *Inst.* 4.2.
[44] See Jerome Murphy-O'Connor, "Tradition and Redaction in 1 Cor 15:3-7," *CBQ* (1981) 582–89; Helmut Koester, *Ancient Christian Gospels* (Philadelphia: Trinity, 1990) 6–7.

Christ **died**
> in behalf of our sins
> *according to the scriptures,*

he **was buried**,

he **was raised**
> on the third day
> *according to the scriptures,*

he **appeared**.

The creed emphasizes the death of Christ by affirming his burial and emphasizes his resurrection by providing news of eye-witness reports of his post-resurrection appearances. The verb tenses used in the creed are noteworthy. Three verbs are historical aorists ("died," "was buried," and "was raised"), but the verb for "raised" is a perfect passive. The death and burial of Christ are *past* historical events which have been completed, but his resurrection is an *ongoing* reality. Paul uses the same tense throughout the chapter to speak of Christ standing in a resurrected state (vv. 12, 13, 14, 16, 17, 20). The verb is also a divine passive with God being the implied subject. This was all done "according to the scriptures," which is a significant point for Paul who believed that Jesus as the Christ was the fulfillment of ancient prophecy (Rom 1:2; 16:26).

Paul expands the creed with a long list of witnesses, including himself at the end, and by doing this, provides a link from the *past* (Jesus) to the *present* (Corinth) and on into the *future* (the eschaton). He considers his vision a resurrection appearance on par with the other apostles. This appearance of the risen Christ was foundational to his apostleship and message. He attempts in this section to build up his *ethos* as messenger of the gospel by claiming his position as apostle.[45] *Ethos* shows the qualities of the speaker and provides a significant basis for persuasion, or according to Aristotle, "the most effective means of proof."[46] The audience gives more confidence in a person of worth. Paul is a credible witness to Christ's resurrection and the Corinthians' link to the tradition and past.

❖ Partitio I, vv. 12-34

Paul's argument can be divided into two *partitio*'s. The first gives the proofs for the resurrection of believers from the dead, and the second discusses the nature of the resurrected body. Both sections begin with rhetorical questions (vv. 12, 35) and end with exhortations (vv. 34, 58).

---

[45] Watson, "Paul's Rhetorical Strategy," 238.
[46] Aristotle, *Rh.* 1.2.4.

Refutatio, vv. 12-19

Paul begins the first *partitio* with a *refutatio* of the view opposite of his own, a view presumably present among the Corinthians. A *refutatio* tries to disprove or weaken the contrary view of the speaker/author by showing the opposite view in the least favorable way possible.[47] Paul starts by quoting, in a rhetorical question, the thesis of his opponents in Corinth, which also suggests the rhetorical situation: "How can some of you say, 'There is no resurrection of the dead'?" The rest of the *partitio* focuses upon this statement by refuting the opposite view and confirming the proper view. Paul begins with the common claim of the gospel in verse 13 and then, by a cumulative effect of interlocking phrases in verses 14-19 (called *sorites*), ends with the futility of a gospel without the resurrection. Basic to his argument is the common enthymeme of the tradition, just quoted in verses 3-5, that Christ has been raised from the dead (vv. 13, 16). The Corinthians apparently did not recognize the logical consequences of the claim that the dead are not raised. Paul concedes to this position for the moment only to refute it by giving the logical consequences of claiming it.

Paul repeats the phrase twice, that if the dead are not raised, then Christ could not have been raised. He gives three distinct but related consequences of Christ not being raised. The first consequence, given in verses 13-15, is the futility of Paul's preaching and the Corinthians' acceptance of it. If they did not want their believing to be "in vain," then they had to believe in the resurrection of the dead.

The second consequence is given in verses 16-17 and builds upon and adds intensity to the first. Paul repeats the thought of the first but adds the important phrase, "you are still in your sins." The Corinthians' belief in their salvation could be undermined by their claim that the dead are not raised. To deny the resurrection from the dead was to deny the gospel message and, ultimately, new existence in Christ. Apparently the Corinthians missed this logic. If there is no resurrection of the dead, then death, the consequence of sin, remains victor (15:26, 54b-56). If death wins, then the power of sin has not been broken, and, therefore, Christ died for nothing. This leaves the Corinthians without eternal hope.

The third consequence is a result of the second and is that believers have hope only for this life (v. 19). If this view is accepted, then there is no resurrected bodily existence nor even spiritual existence after death. The Corinthians may have understood resurrection in only a spiritual sense, similar to what Paul writes the Romans about in Romans 6. Through baptism, believers emerge from the water as new, spiritually resurrected persons with

---

[47] Cicero, *Inv.* 1.42.78.

the gift of eternal life. Paul moves beyond simply a spiritual reality and links this *present* gift in Christ with the *future* gift of bodily resurrection in Christ. This is an important step in accomplishing his goal for the second half of the argument: that there will be a resurrection of the body and that such a resurrection is a necessary part to God's overall plan in Christ. Resurrection for Paul is more than simply a metaphor for a new spiritual existence (cf. Rom 6:4) but is a reality for those in fellowship with Christ. In this *refutatio* of denying the resurrection of the dead, Paul ends with absurdity and shows the utter futility and disadvantage of claiming that the dead are not raised. The ultimate disadvantage is "pity" (v. 19) because of the utter hopelessness that results if the dead are not raised.

Confirmatio, vv. 20-28

Paul next answers the hopeless situation resulting from the claims in verses 12-19 by confirming his thesis that since Christ has been raised from the dead, so will those in Christ be raised. This part of an argument is called a *confirmatio* and provides proof or lends support to the case.[48] After discounting denial of resurrection, Paul moves on to give support to the tradition and his own belief that the dead will indeed be raised. In verse 20 he counters the hypothetical assumption made in verses 14 and 17, that Christ has not been raised from the dead, with a bold, "But now the case is that Christ has been raised." Paul's concern is not with proving Christ's resurrection because it is the necessary given in the argument. His concern, rather, is with the remainder of verse 20: "the first-fruits of those who have fallen asleep," an idiom referring to those who have died. The idea of "first-fruits" is critical to his argument because it is the essential tie between the resurrection of Christ and the resurrection of those in Christ. The term "first fruits" is a metaphor used to designate the first part of the harvest that guarantees the quality of the rest of the harvest.[49] The resurrection of Christ guarantees that resurrection is an eschatological possibility for those who are identified with him. In this case, God is understood to be the guarantor of the rest of the harvest.

Paul's basic point is that Christ's death and resurrection impacts others. He links, by analogy, identification with Adam and identification with Christ. Similar to Romans 5, Paul sees two basic spheres of existence: the realm or sphere symbolized by Adam, who represents the power of sin and death, and the realm or sphere of Christ, who represents salvation and life. Because of Christ's victory over sin, the reign of the Adamic sphere is limited

---

[48] Cicero, *Inv.* 1.24.34.
[49] See Exod 22:29; 23:19; Lev 2:12; 23:10; Num 15:20; 18:12, 30; and others. See also G. Delling, "*Archē*," *TDNT* 1:484–86.

and will end when Christ appears. Believers, however, can participate in this sphere of Christ *in the present*.

Paul makes the contrast between these two spheres explicit by his parallelism:

> A For through a man came death
> > B and through a man came the resurrection of the dead;
> A' for just as in Adam all have died,
> > B' so also in Christ all shall be made alive (vv. 21-22).

Identification with Adam leads to death, and identification with Christ leads to life. This analogy is incomplete and its parallelism breaks down in that "in Adam" is universal but "in Christ" is conditional.[50] Everyone is cursed with death because of the transgression of Adam (Rom 3:23; 5:12). But those in union with Christ are promised eternal life (3:24; 6:23). Fee paraphrases the last clause, "in Christ *all who are in Christ* will be made alive."[51] The curse of death is universal, but the gift of life is provisional for all who are "in Christ" (1 Thess 4:16). Paul's emphasis in this analogy is to show how one condition, death, is replaced by another condition, resurrection life. By identifying with Christ's death and resurrection symbolized in baptism, believers are guaranteed future resurrection of the body because of their corporate solidarity with Christ. There are two alternatives for Paul. The first is the unconscious and universal choice of death in Adam. The other is the conscious decision and identification with Christ in life. In the context of this letter, according to C. E. Hill, "The Corinthians [had] not worked out the implications of Paul's fundamental notion of incorporation into Christ, whereby the merits and resultant glorification of Christ, may, in the unsearchable wisdom and benevolence of God, accrue to believers."[52]

In verse 23 Paul makes his analogy and use of the "first-fruits" metaphor explicit for the Corinthians. Because Christ was raised from the dead, those who identify with him will also be raised. Paul then gives his view of how the reign of death will be replaced by the reign of Christ and ultimately of God.[53]

---

[50] The datives in the prepositional phrases, *en tō Adam* and *en tō Christo* may be more than simply instrumental, "by Adam" and "by Christ," but may also be locatives of sphere.

[51] Fee, *First Corinthians*, 750, his italics.

[52] C. E. Hill, "Paul's Understanding of Christ's Kingdom in 1 Corinthians 15:20-28," *NovT* 4 (1988) 305–6.

[53] Paul appears unconcerned with giving a systematic representation of his apocalyptic chronology but, rather, points to the power of Christ over death (Fee, *First Corinthians*, 747, 752). Nevertheless, his apocalyptic eschatology is apparent in this passage in that he sees the revelation of Christ at the eschaton as paramount to the completion of the divine plan and directly relevant to the situation in Corinth. Paul takes the kerygmatic assertions about the resurrection and coming again of Jesus, puts them through the filter of his apocalyptic eschatology, and demonstrates the need for believing in the resurrection of the body. Since

God's hidden plan in Christ will be completed when death as the last enemy is conquered. The divine mystery of Christ will be finally fulfilled when the dead in Christ are raised. This will signify that Christ reigns supreme and that there is nothing, not even death, he has not conquered. When this happens, Paul writes, then Christ will hand over the conquered kingdom to God so that God can be "all in all" (v. 28).

Christ's resurrection as the "first-fruits" guarantees the outcome of this great eschatological battle between him and all the "rulers, authorities, and powers" (v. 24), of which death is representative. His reign is incomplete in the present age because death still has force over those in fellowship with him.[54] He will reign completely when death is destroyed (v. 26). The "end" or "completion" (*teleios*, v. 24) of the divine plan will occur at Christ's *parousia* after he hands over the conquered kingdom to God once and for all. Fee comments, "Therefore, the inevitable chain of events set in motion by Christ's resurrection has ultimately to do with God's own absolute authority over *all things*, especially death."[55] God stands as the supreme power responsible for the destruction of the power of death. Fee adds,

> God himself stands as both the source and goal of all that is; and since he has set in motion the final destruction of death, when that occurs he will be "all in all." Christ's role is to bring about this destruction through the resurrection, which is inherently tied to his own. When that occurs, all of God's enemies will be subjected to Christ, so that in turn he may be made subject to God, who, it turns out, has been the one who subjected all things to him in any case.[56]

For Paul, the eschatological kingdom has already come in Christ, which is proven by his resurrection. Hill writes, "Paul understands the kingdom of Christ in 1 Cor 15:24-28 to be Christ's present, cosmic lordship which he exercises from heaven. It does not await the *parousia* for its inauguration, it is not a kingdom of this world . . . but began with the resurrection of and acquisition of life-giving prerogatives by the Last Adam."[57] This *interim* period has been marked by the paradigm of the cross-event,[58] of Christ's subjection to the power of death only to take away its power in this age by his own resurrection and to take away its reign in the age to come with the resurrection of those in union with him.

---

the Corinthians accept these kerygmatic assertions, they then must accept Paul's apocalyptic eschatology.

[54] Paul personifies death also in Rom 5:12, 14, 17; 6:9; and 8:2.
[55] Fee, *First Corinthians*, 747.
[56] Ibid., 755.
[57] Hill, "Paul's Understanding," 317.
[58] Conzelmann, *1 Corinthians*, 270.

Examples, vv. 29-34

Paul next gives several examples *ad hominem* in order to prove the validity of the thesis he has just expressed. According to Mack, Paul uses *pathos* (appeal to shame) to bolster a weak argument with loose examples.[59] The examples are not as loose as Mack implies, but all revolve around the notion that there must be something beyond this life that motivates one to live as one does. With these examples Paul continues to prove the absurdity of the position that there is no resurrection of the dead. The examples are based on the assumption that the described activities are meaningless without the hope of resurrection.[60] The examples can be assorted into three. The first is the very obscure reference to baptism for the dead (v. 29). The second example includes scenes in which Paul, presumably other apostles (cf. 4:8-13), and possibly even the Corinthians expose themselves to dangerous and possibly life-threatening situations (vv. 30-32). Paul would not willingly expose himself to the threat of death unless there was a hope of resurrection. According to Fee, the word "human" (*anthrōpon*) in verse 32 has the same connotations as in 3:3 and refers to being devoid of the divine Spirit and relying on purely human means.[61] Such a life devoid of the Holy Spirit lacks the essential motivation of hope in Christ, and such a life, according to Paul, is to be pitied (v. 11). Paul supports his argument with a quotation from Isaiah 22:13 which demonstrates the futility of no hope: "Let us eat and drink for tomorrow we die"—and the understood thought is, "we die and stay dead." The third example moves from this statement of apathetic morality to one of the greatest concern over sinning (vv. 33-34). Paul concludes the first part of his argument with exhortation: the indicative of the *future* hope of resurrection leads to the imperative of concern over *present* conduct. Some of the Corinthians showed a lack of concern for ethical behavior because they lacked an adequate eschatology. Paul ends with the ethical consequences of bad theology.[62] One of the underlying problems with the Corinthians, according to Paul's assessment, is that "some [were] ignorant of God" (v. 34). It is Paul's purpose in this chapter to *inform* (v. 1) them of the importance of the gospel. They should have known better, especially since Paul (and presumably others) preached Christ crucified and raised.

---

[59] Mack, *Rhetoric and the New Testament*, 58.
[60] On this, see also 2 Macc 12:43-45.
[61] Fee, *First Corinthians*, 771.
[62] Ibid., 762.

❖ Partitio II, vv. 35-58

After a strong argument showing the logical, theological, and experiential necessity of resurrection from the dead, Paul turns his attention to discussing the specifics of the resurrection hope. He uses the diatribe style of posing hypothetical questions the audience is invited to answer. He anticipates the question one might ask after being shown the necessity of the resurrection, and he asks it in verse 35: "How then are the dead raised and what kind of body will they have?" This is the subject of the second *partitio* of the argument. The central theme in this *partitio* can be seen in the word "body" (*sōma*) which is repeated nine times in the passage.[63]

The Analogy of Seeds, vv. 35-38

In answering the question posed by a hypothetical "someone," Paul turns to an analogy from the life-cycle of a seed. The answer to the question should be obvious because new life must come from something *already* dead. The proof for this thesis is the God-ordained life of a seed which is sown dead but is raised as a new, living plant. Paul makes the important point in verses 37-38 that there is continuity and transformation in the life of a seed and, by analogy, in the resurrection body.[64] The dead grain seed becomes a living grain plant; it has the same essential body but two types of existence. The *sōma* body is the same body but also has two types of existence.

Two Types of Bodies, vv. 39-44

In verses 39-41 Paul adds support to his seed analogy by describing three different levels of existence. First, he mentions the obvious difference in the physical (*sarx*) construction of various creatures (v. 39). This diversity then allows him to demonstrate the contrast between earthly and heavenly bodies (*sōmati*) (v. 40). He finally substantiates this with the claim that diversity of glory (*doxa*) occurs even within the various cosmic entities of heaven (v. 41). He uses these differences to demonstrate that there are distinct levels of existence: earthly and heavenly. He only needs to show, then, how a person can move from one sphere of existence to another.

He begins to do this in verse 42a where he applies the continuity and transformation from the seed analogy to the resurrected body. Yet, in verses

---

[63] 15:35, 37, 38 (twice), 40 (twice), 44 (thrice).
[64] Ibid., 777. E. Earl Ellis writes, "Paul portrays the relationship between this age and the age to come as one of both continuity and discontinuity, a discontinuity as sharp as 'a new creation' and a continuity so firm that the individual body raised at the last day of this age is the same (although transformed) body that is buried" ("*Soma* in First Corinthians," *Int* 44 [1990] 142).

42b-44a he stresses the discontinuity between the two stages of existence by using antithetical parallelism:

The Earthly Body	Resurrected Heavenly Body
sown perishable	raised imperishable
sown in dishonor	raised in glory
sown in weakness	raised in power
sown a natural (*psychikon*) body	raised a spiritual (*pneumatikon*) body

Several times in this passage he repeats the significant apocalyptic term "glory" (*doxa*). This term is often used to refer to the state of the righteous in the eschaton (Dan 12:3; 1 Enoch 62:15; 105:11, 12; 2 Bar 51:10). The concept of the divine glory in the Old Testament is linked to the divine presence (Exod 16:10; 24:17; 33:22-23; 34:29-35). The eschatological hope was for God's glory to fill the earth (Hab 2:14). Paul links the divine glory to the glorification of those in Christ (Rom 3:23-24; 1 Cor 2:7; 2 Cor 3:18). The glory of God was lost in Adam's fall and in the continuing sin of humanity (Rom 1:21-23). Christ reverses this curse by his death and resurrection and opens the way for us to be remade into God's glory (2 Cor 3:18).

In verse 44 Paul uses two important terms he also uses in 2:6-16: *psychikos* and *pneumatikos*. As with much of the dualism of this chapter, Paul sets these two terms in contrast:

> It is sown a *psychikos* body,
>   it is raised a *pneumatikos* body.
> If there is a *psychikos* body,
>   there is also a *pneumatikos* one.

The term *psychikos* has the connotation as in 2:14 of being devoid of the divine Spirit. It refers to living as earth-bound with no access to the mind of Christ. The word *pneumatikos* refers to the state in which the divine Spirit can reveal God's wisdom and instruct one in the ways of Christ. It can be translated as "spiritual" and is used for those who allow the Holy Spirit to grow them in Christ. *Psychikos* can be translated as "earth-bound" or "unspiritual" because there is no access to the divine mystery of Christ. Paul uses these terms in chapter 15 in a way consistent with 2:6-16. The body is sown lacking the Holy Spirit in the sense that it is bound by the curse of Adam. It is relegated to exist on the earth since it is part of the earth ("dust," v. 47; cf. Gen 3:19; Eccl 3:20). The body transformed by resurrection is no longer bound to the earth but is completely open to the ways of the Spirit and can see "face to face" (13:12). It is the promise of those in Christ who make being *pneumatikos* possible (15:45-46). Paul may be subtly linking *pneumatikos* with belief in resurrection, and *psychikos* with denial of resurrection, and thereby confining those who deny the resurrection to the category of *psychikos*. This, like 2:14, may be another example of Paul's effort to shame the Corinthians into accepting his views about mature spirituality.

Adam and Christ in Comparison, vv. 45-49

Paul turns to scriptural support and a comparison between Adam and Christ for his distinction between the stages and types of bodily existence. He loosely quotes Genesis 2:7 in verse 45a and adds "first Adam"; the second clause, "the last Adam became a life-giving spirit," is not found in Genesis.[65] Paul's comparison between Adam and Christ and what they represent can be seen in the following chart:

Adam	Christ
the first Adam	the last Adam
living being	life-giving spirit
first	second
from dust of the earth	from heaven
those in Adam are only dust	those in Christ are of heaven
psychikon	*pneumatikon*

Adam and those who remain in his sphere are bound to earthly existence. They lack the filling of the Holy Spirit and the spirituality which comes from union with Christ. Christ and those in his sphere have a heavenly nature and are spiritual because of the resurrection life made real in their lives by God. Just as in 2:6-16, here there are different animating forces between the two spheres. Hays comments that

> our mortal bodies embody the *psyche* ("soul"), the animating force of our present existence, but the resurrection body will embody the divine given *pneuma* ("spirit"). It is to be a "spiritual body" not in the sense that it is somehow made out of spirit and vapors, but in the sense that it is determined by the spirit and gives the spirit form and local habitation.[66]

Paul's argument gives a stark contrast between the fate of those *in Adam* and those *in Christ*. If the Corinthians believed only in this life and that there is no resurrection of the dead, then they aligned themselves with Adam whose fate was to return to dust. Belief in the resurrection of the dead is tied

---

[65] Fee calls this citation a "midrash pesher," "a quotation that is at once citation and interpretation" (*First Corinthians*, 788). Ellis and others suggest that the verse could have been an early Christian *testimonia* (*Paul's Use of the Old Testament*, 97).

[66] Hays, *First Corinthians*, 272.

in with being *pneumatikos* with its destiny of heavenly existence with Christ. It is noteworthy that Paul calls both Adam and Christ *anthrōpos* ("human") in verse 47. Both were human like the Corinthians, but each had a different fate. In a subtle way, Paul is offering the Corinthians a choice between two alternatives: existence in Adam as *psychikos*, or existence in Christ as *pneumatikos*. This corporate solidarity can be seen in verses 48-49. The fate of the type is also the fate of the antitype. Paul restates the goal of the divine mystery in verse 49: to bear the image of Christ, which in this context is the resurrected and glorified existence as *pneumatikon* people.

Finally, for believers to experience their full potential as transformed beings, they must undergo a resurrection like Christ did in order to enter heavenly existence since "flesh and blood [i.e., "dust," v. 47] cannot inherit the kingdom of God" (v. 50; cf. vv. 22-24). J. C. Beker notes that Paul does not teach resurrection of "flesh" (*sarx*) but of the "body" (*soma*).[67] The resurrected *body* cannot be confined by any part of the earthly existence of *flesh* with its propensity for immorality (1 Cor 6:13-14). The earthly body, like the heavenly body, can be transformed in Christ (Rom 6:12) but it still remains ensnared by the effects of flesh, namely the power of death. In death flesh decays, and because of that, flesh can no longer hold power or influence over the body. The body that has been resurrected can then be completely free from the power of the flesh because the body is free from death and decay. Thus, there is continuity and transformation of the body. There is no loss of identity with the new body, and the body is transformed into the likeness of Christ's body and is devoid of the appetites and shortcomings of the flesh.

Conclusion, vv. 50-58

An inconsistency appears in Paul's argument that he has yet to address. Up to this point he has not successfully answered the rhetorical question asked in verse 35: "*How* are the dead raised and with what kind of body will they come?" This inconsistency concerns the spiritual and bodily natures of the resurrection. Paul may have realized this inconsistency and uses the apocalyptic term "mystery" in verse 51 to speak of the transformation of the body at the "last trumpet." The reference to the "last trumpet" is found in Jewish apocalyptic and became a circumlocution for Christ's *parousia* in early Christian circles.[68] Paul attempts to explain this "mystery" possibly to answer the rhetorical question of verse 35. His answer is inadequate because the transformation at the last trumpet still remains unknown. All he can really say about this change is that the perishable will become imperishable, and the

---

[67] Beker, *Paul the Apostle*, 153.
[68] Isa 27:13; Joel 2:1; Zeph 1:14-16; 2 Esd 6:23; Matt 24:31; Rev 9:14; 11:15.

mortal will become immortal (vv. 53-54). But the "how" of verse 35 is not answered, possibly because Paul does not know how all this will take place; to some degree it remains a mystery to him also. What he knows is based upon his experience of the risen Christ who "swallowed up death" and took away its "sting" or power to inflict harm (v. 55). This mystery is related to the wisdom of God in 2:7. The mystery of the end is the promise and fulfillment of the mystery revealed on the cross. The death and resurrection of Christ guarantees the resurrection of believers. The two "mysteries" are related because both are aspects of God's revelation in Christ.

The thought in verses 56-57 is similar to Romans 8:1-4. By step parallelism, Paul attributes the power of death to sin, and the power of sin to the law. The law gives sin opportunity which, when followed, leads to death (see Rom 7). The destruction of sin meant the destruction of the power of death. By conquering death, Christ showed his power over sin. Because of believers' solidarity with Christ, they too can have victory over the law, sin, and death. Paul describes this in the present context as that victory which comes "through our Lord Jesus Christ" (1 Cor 15:57). In Romans, no condemnation comes to those "in Christ Jesus" (8:1). The first phrase from 1 Corinthians is probably instrumental, but the second reference from Romans goes beyond that and speaks of union with Christ and existence in the sphere of Christ. The reference in 1 Corinthians also has the possible connotation of union with Christ because it is those *in Christ* who will be raised to immortality at his coming (cf. 15:23-24). Christ is both agent and location of this transformation that comes to those in fellowship with him.

Both the first and second *partitio* end in exhortation.[69] The Corinthians were to be (a present active imperative) "steadfast and immovable" "by abounding" in the work of the Lord. The motivation for this *being* was "because they knew" that their work in the Lord was not in vain. Paul ends the argument as he began it—in reference to "vain" labor in the Lord. Vain faith (v. 2) leads to vain labor (v. 58). As Hays writes, "The resurrection is the necessary foundation for faithful action in the world."[70]

Paul's agenda in chapter 15 is to convince the Corinthians that they needed to believe in the *complete* story of Christ. The completion of the divine mystery, revealed with power on the cross, entails the bodily resurrection of those in communion with Christ. Those who live in the sphere of Adam have no hope. Those who live in the sphere of Christ have the hope of im-

---

[69] Verse 58 functions as the conclusion to this chapter and, according to Mitchell, the body of the letter. Chapter 16 serves as an epistolary closing by which Paul relates an assortment of instructions for the community which are related in various ways to the body of the letter (Mitchell, *Rhetoric of Reconciliation*, 290–95).
[70] Hays, *First Corinthians*, 277.

mortality and of transformation into the image of Christ. Paul lays before the Corinthian church a choice between two very different paradigms. The Corinthians could continue in their present paradigm and accept the position of life "in Adam," or they could shift to Paul's paradigm and live "in Christ."

Paul's Scheme of Time

The rhetorical features of Paul's argument highlight his efforts to convince the Corinthians to modify their concept of resurrection of the body and accept his ideology of resurrection. Paul attempts to create order in his world by placing events in a "map of time." A map of time shows how a person perceives the order and priority of events in his or her symbolic universe. Time is a significant factor in 1 Corinthians 15. The many references to time and the sequence of events illumine Paul's ontology. In this chapter of the letter, time revolves around the mystery and revelation of Jesus Christ. According to Jerome Neyrey, Paul classifies anthropological history into two parts: old creation and new creation (1 Cor 5:17; Gal 6:15).[71] Christ inaugurated a new map of time for Paul that directly influenced Paul's symbolic universe.

❖ Fixed Moments

On a map of time there are fixed points or markers that indicate progress or movement. These fixed moments are important because they show a shift from "then" to "now." Paul's map of time is also divided into a "then" and "now."[72] The primary determining point between these two time periods is the Christ-event, the revelation of the divine mystery. This revelation has created a new "now" for Paul. The present age is governed by sin and death—the effects of Adam (15:21-22), but their power was decisively destroyed by Christ's death and resurrection. Sin became powerless because of Christ's atonement on the cross. Death, the consequence of sin, also lost its power because Christ proved his ability to overcome death. This itself is a significant matter, but for Paul in this chapter, the significance of this event is that others can be included. Christ's resurrection shows that death has been conquered, though it still holds temporary power over believers. His resurrection is a moment already fixed as an historical fact (vv. 3-11) and the first part of a process as the "first-fruits."

When Christ returns, the second point on Paul's map will be completed, and the full reality of the "then" will be revealed. When this moment in time

---

[71] Neyrey, *Paul in Other Words*, 46–47.
[72] Ibid., 48, 158.

will take place is unknown, although Paul seems to indicate that he believes it will happen in the near future (7:29; 10:11; 16:22). When this moment comes and the dead in Christ are raised, the last enemy, death, will be completely destroyed because it will have no power over those in Christ. A tension remains between the first and the second moment because believers still must face death. These two major time indicators for Paul can be diagramed in various ways. One useful representation is given by James Dunn in the following way:

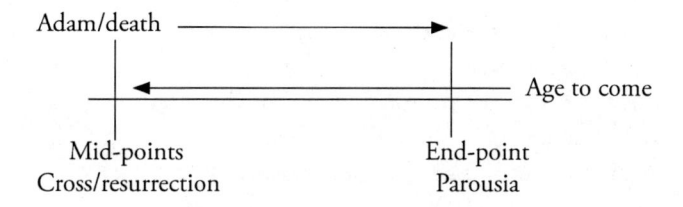

```
Adam/death  ─────────────▶
            │            │
            ├────◀───────┤── Age to come
            │            │
         Mid-points   End-point
       Cross/resurrection Parousia
```

Dunn comments, "Believers are 'in Adam' and continue to be 'in Adam'; they have not yet died. But they are also 'in Christ,' and have begun to experience life, though they have yet to share in the full experience of Christ's resurrection—in the resurrection of the body."[73] This diagram could be modified to contrast the two typologies in Paul's thought:

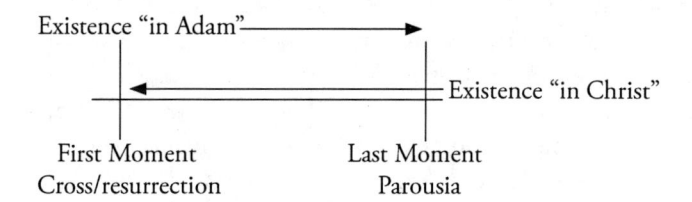

```
Existence "in Adam" ─────────▶
            │            │
            ├────◀───────┤── Existence "in Christ"
            │            │
       First Moment  Last Moment
     Cross/resurrection Parousia
```

Time indicators in the text show that this two-point map of time can be further divided into smaller moments. Paul, in quoting the early Christian tradition, divides the first moment into four steps found in verses 3-5: Christ died, was buried, was raised, and appeared. Each of these smaller moments is significant in the "Christ-event." Christ died "in behalf of our sins" (v. 3); was buried, verifying his physical death; was raised victorious over death (v. 20); and appeared to many people, verifying his resurrected state (vv. 5-8). The Corinthians then received this gospel in a process that began with the prophecies of scripture, next through the story of the life of the Lord himself, then through the agency of Paul's preaching, and finally in the reception of the community. They had not seen the risen Jesus firsthand, so knowledge

---

[73] James D. G. Dunn, *The Theology of Paul the Apostle* (Grand Rapids: Eerdmans, 1998) 464.

of him came through Paul. The first moment is described also in verse 20: Christ has been raised, guaranteeing the resurrection of those in him. Thus, the first moment insures the realization of the second moment.

In verses 21-28 Paul further breaks down the major moments into smaller moments.[74] The first part of human existence is characterized by the reign of death in Adam. After Christ was raised and the reign of death destroyed, a new alternative began. Beginning in verse 23, Paul gives an "order" to the last great moment in his scheme. The closure of the present age takes place in four smaller moments. First, Christ returns. Second, the dead are raised and death's dominion finally ends. Third, Christ delivers the conquered kingdom to God the Father. Finally, the end will come when God is all in all. Paul breaks down his major moments one other time in the chapter, in verses 37-50 when he adds the unknown minor moment in the interim period when believers die. This is described as the sowing of the *psychikon* body. This body is then raised at the close of this age as a *pneumatikon* body.

✧ The Changing of the Guard

At the first fixed moment in Paul's map there is a changing of the guard. For the first time in history, because of the Christ-event, there is another alternative to existence in Adam. For the first time since Adam's fall, sin no longer needs to be the dominant power (Rom 5:20-21) because Christ reverses the bondage resulting from Adam's fall. Christ restores the image of God lost by Adam, and those in union with him can be restored to this image (2 Cor 3:18). The effects of Adam's reign as the type and corporate head are reversed with Christ, even though these effects last until Christ takes full control over the power of death. This could be described as the "already" and "not yet" in Paul's scheme of time. The only exception to the power of Adam's sphere of existence has been Christ. For others to join with Christ in this freedom, they must be in fellowship with him and live in his sphere of influence.

The changing of the guard on the cosmic level is beyond human intervention. It is part of the divine plan and therefore cannot be stopped or modified. But the changing of this guard in the life of individual people can be stopped or frustrated. Paul may have perceived the potential for this problem in Corinth—so he wrote this chapter. There are two basic actions that the Corinthians could do to secure themselves in the sphere of Christ and experience eschatological transformation. The first is a matter of faith. The Corinthians' faith rested upon the resurrection of Christ. If this faith had no object or foundation, then it was meaningless and they remained in their sins (15:17). A similar thought is found in Romans 10:9: "If you confess

---

[74] See further Lincoln, *Paradise Now and Not Yet*, 38.

with your mouth that Jesus is Lord and if you believe in your heart that God raised him from the dead, you will be saved." The common premise in Paul's grand enthymeme suggests that there was no problem in Corinth over a basic belief in the resurrection of Jesus. The area that concerns Paul most is the second matter of lifestyle, morality, or action. His exhortations (imperatives) are based upon the kerygma (indicative). He ends each of his *partitios* with commands to stop sinning (v. 34) and to be steadfast and immovable in the work of the Lord (v. 58). The Corinthians could prove their fellowship with Christ and maturity in him by how they lived as a community of holy ones within a hostile pagan environment.

❖ The Eschatological Fulfillment of the Mystery

Paul's map of time ends with the coming of Christ, the resurrection of believers, and Christ's handing over the conquered kingdom to God the Father. Verse 24 is significant in this regard: "then comes the end." The word "end" comes from the Greek word *teleios* which describes that which has reached its intended end or design; hence, it could be said to be "perfected" or "mature." Paul uses the term earlier for those who are "mature" (*teleioi*) and "spiritual" (*pneumatikoi*; 2:6) to whom the divine mystery of God's wisdom in Christ is revealed. Those without the Spirit are not mature and so are "earthly" (*psychikos*; 2:12, 14). Those "in Christ" are said to be *teleios* (Col 1:28). Yet, perfection can be attained only to a certain degree in this life (Rom 12:2) because of the continuing effects of Adam's fall and the shortcomings and desires of the flesh (*sarx*). But Paul looks forward to a time when the imperfect will be replaced by the perfect (1 Cor 13:10). Ultimate perfection or maturity will be attained at the last major moment on Paul's map of time when death, the last enemy, is finally destroyed. Paul's goal in life is to receive the heavenly prize of resurrection (Phil 3:10-14). Perfection comes at the resurrection when all the powers of existence in Adam are finally destroyed and those in Christ are completely restored to the divine image. The Corinthians would be able to remain blameless to the end because of God's faithfulness and their fellowship with Christ (1 Cor 1:8). The mystery will be fully revealed and completed at the "last trumpet," "in a moment, in a twinkling of an eye." This will take place at Christ's return when the dead are raised and transformed, and death is destroyed forever (15:51-56). The goal in the present life, then, is to live out the hope of this mystery by fellowship with Christ. It involves pressing on, with the help of the Holy Spirit, towards spiritual maturity. This, according to Paul, is where the Corinthians had failed.

Paul's Answer for an Errant Eschatology

The Corinthians' failure to mature in their relationship with Christ prompts Paul in the last part of his letter to turn to the conclusion of the story of Christ because this part of the story offers hope and motivation for them to grow into maturity *in the present*. Paul appeals to a number of power sources to confirm his claims and to convince the Corinthians to accept his ideology. He attempts to convince the Corinthians that their spirituality rests upon a large story divided into *key periods*. One of these is the death of Jesus upon the cross, the major theme of chapters 1–4. Another is his resurrection from the dead. These two points are combined in one moment in the tradition Paul cites in 15:3-5. This Christ-event forever altered human destiny. The other major moment yet to happen is the return of Christ and the subsequent resurrection of those in communion with him. These two form the foci on Paul's map of time. Paul as maker of the map holds power and influence over the Corinthians and tries to convince them of the significance of his interpretation of the eschaton.[75] He sees two basic alternatives: living according to the ways of the world as a *psychikos* person who is "in Adam," or living as spiritually mature person called being *pneumatikos* or "in Christ."

Paul, the Kerygma, and the Corinthians

As he does throughout the letter, Paul appeals in this chapter to his authority as the basis for his rhetoric. Verses 1-11 serve to establish his authority and the authority of his message, both of which then provide authority to his letter. He gains his authority and power for persuasion from two areas. The first is the foundation of the kerygma, the death and resurrection of Jesus Christ. Paul's message agrees with the apostolic tradition which he "received" (v. 3) in a similar way that he "received" (11:23) the words of the Lord's supper, both of which had their origin with the Lord (cf. Gal 1:12). Paul's authority and message had divine origins, and because of that, should be heeded as the words of the Lord himself (14:37).

The second source of authority is Paul's own experience of seeing the risen Lord. Paul's vision proved that his message was not isolated but in line with tradition. He makes himself the link between the apostolic tradition and the Corinthian church by his position as bearer of the message. Beker writes,

> Paul's passionate temper and life-style are not the result of a personal idiosyncrasy but are part of his awareness that he is the man of the hour whose mission takes place in the last hours of world history. He

---

[75] Neyrey, *Paul in Other Words*, 48.

knows himself to be the eschatological apostle who spans the times between the resurrection of Christ and the final resurrection of the dead.[76]

Paul's ideology agrees with the other apostles and followers of Christ, the tradition and kerygma, Christ himself, and ultimately God who is the source and originator of the plan of the death and resurrection of Christ. Paul leaves no other alternative for the Corinthians than to accept his views because he places himself in this sequence of authority. It is his way or no way for the Corinthians. Fee comments,

> Paul's point is a simple one: If their present position prevails, they have neither a past nor a future. . . . The denial of their future, that they are destined for resurrection on the basis of Christ's resurrection, has the net effect of a denial of their past, that they have received forgiveness of sins on the basis of Christ's death.[77]

Paul tries to convince the Corinthians that since they were living a new existence in fellowship with Christ, they should act in a way consistent with this status (vv. 34, 58).

Christ as the Second Adam

Paul's ideology is connected with his paradigm of spiritual maturity in Christ. The divine mystery discloses the new status made possible by the sacrificial death of Christ on the cross (the indicative of redemption) and the new way of living according to God's standards revealed in Jesus Christ (the imperative of holiness). The resurrection of Christ completes the first part of God's plan. The second part involves believers living in fellowship with Christ in the present age by identifying with him in his death and resurrection through baptism and fellowship in community. The third part and completion of the plan will take place when Christ returns and all who have lived in union with him will be raised from the dead and be fully transformed into the image of God. All three parts of the mystery are important to Paul.

The choice is, then, by which of the two paradigms will one live in the interim period? Paul's calls the first choice by different terms in this chapter: a state of being in sin (v. 17), perishing (v. 18), death (v. 21), being "in Adam" (v. 22), dishonor and weakness (v. 43), *psychikos* (v. 44), confined to the earth (v. 48), and enslaved by sin and the law (v. 56). People are universally bound to this existence (v. 22) and remain there until they put their faith in the complete mystery of God in Christ. Those who deny the completion of the

---

[76] Beker, *Paul the Apostle*, 144–45.
[77] Fee, *First Corinthians*, 739, 743.

divine plan remain bound to this paradigm because they also deny the saving power of Christ's own death and resurrection (v. 17).

The other paradigm involves the voluntary association of the believer with Christ by submitting to his lordship (12:3). This involves, among other things, submitting to the way of Christ which, as Paul articulates in this letter, is love. The primary description of this paradigm in chapter 15 is resurrection. Faith in Christ's redeeming work on the cross is linked to hope in the resurrection because the two events are part of the same grand scheme of God for the complete salvation and restoration of humanity. If the Corinthians failed to believe in the future resurrection of the body, then they demonstrated that they still lived "in Adam." This is a state to be pitied because it lacks hope (15:19). The Corinthians should experience shame when they realize that by denying the resurrection of the body, they were putting themselves outside of the sphere of Christ. If they accepted the apostolic tradition as preached by Paul, then they needed to adjust their views to agree with Paul and to live in the sphere of Christ. This is a serious choice.

Paul attaches to Christ the apocalyptic hopes pinned on a reversal of the fall of Adam. He calls Christ the second or last Adam because Christ reverses the effects of Adam's fall. The first Adam introduced the curse of sin and death and trapped humanity in a *psychikos*, earthly existence. The Second Adam introduced a new order of a *pneumatikos* life in the Spirit.[78] Christ brings a new creative power to those united with him (2 Cor 5:17), leading to "newness of life" (Rom 6:4). He restores the lost divine image and glory to those who put their faith in him (2 Cor 3:18). He brings resurrection life in the present age in a spiritual sense (Rom 6:5-11) and in the eschatological age in a bodily sense (1 Corinthians 15). The first is a promise and guarantee of the second. The Corinthians may have thought that the first resurrection was enough and that their spiritual status was fully realized in the present. For Paul, however, perfection (*teleios*) is not reached until the final resurrection takes place and death is finally conquered. By denying resurrection, the Corinthians limited what God could do for them. Their denial was not simply cognitive but behavioral, proven by the numerous problems in the community that modeled too closely the *psychikos* life of the world.

Christ is both the model and source of the transformation of believers. Robin Scroggs writes, "By being 'in Christ' the believer will be changed to that same nature which now belongs to his Lord."[79] Paul writes to the Corinthians in a later letter, "And we all who with unveiled faces while reflecting the glory of the Lord are being transformed from glory to glory which

---

[78] Davies, *Paul and Rabbinic Judaism*, 49.
[79] Robin Scroggs, *The Last Adam: A Study in Pauline Anthropology* (Philadelphia: Fortress, 1966) 84.

is by the Lord who is the Spirit" (2 Cor 3:18). This transformation is both a single event and an ongoing process. The decision to identify with Christ's death and resurrection by crucifying the "old man" symbolized in baptism opens the door to new life (Rom 6:4-7). Then comes the imperative of living in Christ as transformed, new creations (Rom 6:12-13). Yet, for Paul, this is only the beginning of the story. This transformation happens by steps, "from one degree of glory to another," culminating at Christ's return when believers will completely bear the image of Christ without the hindrance of the flesh (*sarx*; 1 Cor 15:49). Fee writes, "Thus for Paul, to be truly *pneumatikos* is to bear the likeness of Christ (v. 49) in a transformed body, fitted for the new age."[80] One can only be fully *pneumatikos* by a resurrection like Christ's.

Resurrection marks the full-reversal of the effects of Adam. The one who is in Christ assumes the nature of Christ in life, while the one in Adam assumes the nature of death.[81] Only in the *pneumatikos* state of being "in Christ" can one conquer the last enemy—death (v. 26). The destiny of those in union with Christ is to experience a resurrection power like Christ. Paul writes to the Romans that not even death can separate believers from the love of God which is in Christ Jesus (Rom 8:38). For Paul, the ultimate goal for believers is to experience the "glory" of God as new, resurrected persons transformed into the image of Christ.[82]

The Fulfillment of the Mystery for the Corinthians

Paul has great hopes that the Corinthians would see his point of view and conform to his ideology about the divine mystery and plan of God. God's wisdom revealed on the cross and completed in Christ's triumphant return shows the ultimate reversal of God turning death to life. The Corinthians had experienced the power of resurrected life in Christ, but they had not seen the importance of aligning their whole lives and perspectives according to this new existence. Paul is concerned in this letter that the Corinthians had missed this fundamental conviction. His concern is that they had continued to live according to the paradigm of Adam, and because of this, he can call them *sarkinoi* (3:1-3). The real danger for the Corinthians would be to allow this immature view to continue, and they would end up regressing to be *psychikoi*, devoid of the Holy Spirit. If this happened, not only would they not know the mind of Christ (2:14-16), but they would have no hope for a resurrected spiritual body in the model of Christ's resurrected body (15:42-46).

---

[80] Fee, *First Corinthians*, 786.
[81] Scroggs, *The Last Adam*, 84–85.
[82] 1 Thess 2:2; Rom 8:18, 21; Phil 3:21; cf. Col 3:4; Dan 12:3; *2 Bar* 51:10 *1 Enoch* 62:15; 105:11, 12.

This was only a potential danger for the Corinthians. Paul is concerned that they not sin by living according to this alternative paradigm. The eschatological promise of the resurrection of the body directly impacts the way believers should live in this life. After describing the completion of God's plan in Christ, Paul exhorts the Corinthians to stop sinning (v. 38) and be steadfast in the work of the Lord (v. 58). Fee comments,

> Paul's concern is a simple one: They are to adopt the kind of behavior that should be expected of those for whom the future is both "already" and "not yet," who have been "washed from their sins" through Christ Jesus (cf. 6:11; 15:3) and who yet await the final destruction of death (vv. 24-28). They are to live as people who not only have a past in Christ, but a future as well.[83]

Beker likewise writes,

> Within this setting of pneumatic freedom and ontological participation in Christ, the Corinthians bear witness to the gospel by demonstrating their freedom by an ethic that proclaims in word and deed that they have become indifferent to the world and that history and human affairs, that is, bodily structures, cannot compromise and contaminate their mystic bond with Christ. In terms of their theology, then, a resurrection of the dead (i.e., a resurrection of dead bodies) is both disgusting (because the body is inimical to salvation) and unnecessary (because our spiritual union with Christ is the redemption of our true self).[84]

When death, as the last enemy, is finally destroyed, Christ's sovereignty will be seen and God's plan for saving humanity from the clutches of sin and death will be completed. This plan has been initiated and confirmed by Jesus' resurrection and defeat of sin and death. The cross and resurrection forever altered the way Paul thought about the completion of history. He rejoices, because he believes the victory has already been claimed "through our Lord Jesus Christ" (15:57).

The Corinthians remained spiritually immature (*sarkinos*) with the danger of forfeiting their hope in Christ (*psychikos*) if they did not believe in the whole story of God's plan in Christ. They had missed the implications of Paul's message. Without hope in the resurrection of the body, they lacked faith in the full salvation of Christ. Death was a real problem to them, but Paul had the conviction that death does not have the final say in the destiny of believers. His motivation for service and holy conduct comes from the past event of Christ's death and resurrection *and* the future hope of the resur-

---

[83] Fee, *First Corinthians*, 773.
[84] Beker, *Paul's Apocalyptic Gospel*, 166.

rection of believers. Looking *back* and peering *forward* serve to motivate a certain way of living in the *present*.

5

The Paraenesis of the Mystery for the Community *(1 Corinthians 5–14)*

Paul's Assessment of the Problems in Corinth

PAUL refers to the *past* and the *future* in order to convince the Corinthians to act a certain way in the *present*. His primary contention is over their lack of spiritual maturity evident in their divisive attitudes and fleshly behavior (3:1-3). In order to stop the community from self-destructing, he appeals to the divine mystery of Jesus Christ. This revelation brought not only redemption from the past and hope for the future but also sanctifying power in the present (1:30; 15:19). The basic problem is that as redeemed people, the Corinthians did not live by a standard consistent with the message of the cross (6:19-20). They failed to break from their cultural and religious contexts to live according to Paul's paradigm of existence in Christ.

In his second (5:1-11:1) and third (11:2-14:40) major arguments, Paul turns to practical issues facing the church. After the imperative in 4:16, "Become imitators of me," Paul gives the church some practical advice, urging them to model his imitation of the divine paradox. To do this, he uses a form of rhetoric called *paraenesis*. Paraenesis is exhortation and was often used in the Greco-Roman world to address moral issues. According to David Aune, it was sometimes used to address a behavioral problem in an indirect way. Aune writes, "Since the content of paraenesis is generally approved by society, it provides a basis of agreement in situations that are potentially divisive."[1] Paraenesis is often presented as a reminder of something that should already be known.[2] Paul and the Corinthians share the same basic starting point of faith in Jesus Christ. Paul may have chosen to begin his letter by ap-

---

[1] Aune, *The New Testament in Its Literary Environment*, 191.
[2] Seneca, *Letters* 13.15; 94.21-25; Dio Chrysostom, *Oration* 17:2, 5.

pealing to the paradox of the cross because it was the common faith between himself and the Corinthians as well as the key paradigm to be imitated.

Paul's method of paraenesis is basically three-fold. First, he deals with specific, actual, or potential problems in Corinth made known to him by letter, word of mouth, or his own memory of the situation. In this, he exhorts the church to stop living according to the practices of the world around them and to begin living according to the paradigm of being "in Christ." Second, the theoretical foundation for this appeal is his understanding of the divine mystery revealed in the crucified and risen Jesus Christ. He appeals to this past moment because it can influence the present through the power of the Holy Spirit. Third, he supports and illustrates this foundation with his own life and example. He, as steward of the divine mysteries, serves as the primary mediator of this new reality to the Corinthians (4:1).[3]

Paul shows in chapters 3–4 that the reason for the Corinthians' immaturity was their lack of living out the message of the cross. They were relying on human wisdom and power and not on what the Holy Spirit wanted to teach them about the cross. In the following chapters, he shows them how they can mature in their faith by living lives of holiness and love. For Paul, holy living is the proper response of those who have been redeemed by Christ Jesus (1:30). Some of the Corinthians, however, lived as if Christ's atonement on the cross makes no difference in one's behavior. They did not set themselves apart from the immorality around them. Their lack of concern and divisive attitudes showed their lack of love for one another.

The primary evidence of a lack of holiness in the community was the problem with *porneia*, which can be translated as "sexual immorality." The Corinthians were tolerating immoral activity in their fellowship and had not considered the significance of the union in sexual activity. Their tolerance of immorality contradicted their redemption and violated their covenantal relationship with Christ.[4] Therefore, Paul urges them with a strong command to flee sexual immorality (6:18).

Paul also deals with specific issues related to their lack of love. Some in the church showed no concern for others by participating in idol worship and eating food sacrificed to idols.[5] This problem drives Paul's response in

---

[3] Paraenesis can be exemplified in exceptional people who are models of virtue (Seneca, *Letters* 6.5-6; 11:9-10; 95.72).

[4] The term *porneia* is also used in the context of covenantal unfaithfulness in the Old Testament (Isa 1:21; Jer 3:2; 5:7; Amos 2:7; Hos 1-3; see F. Hauck and S. Schulz, "*Porneia*," *TDNT* 6:584-87). Paul may have this use of the term also in mind in 1 Cor 6:15-17 and 10:7-8, especially since the idea of covenant is present in 10:14-15 and 11:25.

[5] Paul refers to meat as part of the sacrifice but also food (*broma*) in general, therefore meat was not the only problem (8:13). Many different types of food were sacrificed to idols including grain, wine, honey, and animals. See Peter D. Gooch, *Dangerous Food: 1 Corinthians 8–10 in*

chapters 8–10 and leads him to issue another strong imperative about fleeing participation in idol worship (10:14). Some in the church overlooked others during times of worship and the Lord's supper, a problem which Paul deals with in chapter 11. Some also spoke in tongues to the detriment of community integrity and unity. Paul addresses this issue in chapters 12–14 by uttering the imperative, "seek after love" (14:1).

Problems with Holiness

Toleration of the Immoral "Brother" (5:1-13)

Paul makes an abrupt change in 5:1 from problems with "power" and "wisdom" to the problem of *porneia*. Evidently, a man in the church was having immoral relationships with his father's wife.[6] The word *porneia* typically denotes frequenting prostitutes, and in the New Testament, broadly denotes a variety of sexual sins. Paul begins this chapter with two statements of astonishment: the reported *porneia* was worse than that which occurs even among non-believers, and the Corinthians boasted about it. Paul is not specific about whether they were proud of this sin in their midst or too proud in their self-exalted spirituality to bother with such trivial matters as personal morality (5:2). His astonished reaction is more apparent. The community should have been mourning and repentant because of this sin (cf. Isa 6:5), but instead, boasted about it.

Paul's solution to this problem is rather simple: throw the immoral "brother" out of the fellowship. He gives two reasons why they should do this: for the eschatological salvation of the "brother's" spirit by the destruction of his "flesh" (*sarx*, v. 5), and for the preservation of the community (v. 6). This appeal to advantage is based upon Paul's impending presence by "spirit" in their midst (v. 3).[7] The proverb about leaven in a lump of dough in verse 6 (cf.

In Context, Studies in Christianity and Judaism 5 (Waterloo, Ont.: Wilfred Laurier University Press, 1993) 53–54.

[6] Paul is somewhat vague in v. 1 about the exact sin of this man whom he does not even call "brother," but rather the more indefinite "someone" (Greek *tina*, v. 1). The man seems to think of himself as a "brother," as v. 11 suggests. Paul simply says that this person "has" this woman. Fee comments, "The verb 'to have,' when used in sexual or marital contexts, is a euphemism for an enduring sexual relationship, not just a passing fancy or a 'one-night stand.' By his 'having' her, Paul means that the 'brother' is 'living with' (RSV) her sexually" (*First Corinthians*, 200).

[7] This is a rather difficult statement to interpret. The key to unlocking this verse can be found in the phrases, "in the name of our Lord Jesus," and "with the power of our Lord Jesus" (v. 4). There is no way Paul could be physically present with them to offer his judgment since he was in Ephesus, although his letter could serve as a partial substitute. The only way he could be present was through the agency of the corporate personality of Jesus by means of the Spirit.

Gal 5:9) serves as an analogy to illustrate the pervasive and penetrating influence of the sin of *porneia* in the community. Leaven represents the sin of the immoral "brother" and the dough represents the community; evil spreads in the community just as leaven spreads through dough. The leaven of evil had entered the community and would grow and destroy the fellowship unless it were purged. The community could dangerously grant approval to *porneia* by accepting the "brother," and this could lead to other sins, eventually undermining the integrity and holiness of the fellowship. This situation in Corinth was incompatible with Paul's paradigm of redemption in Christ.

Paul restates his solution to the problem through two commands. He gives the first in verse 7 in the form of a metaphor: "Cleanse out the old leaven in order that you might be a new lump of dough, since you are already unleavened; for Christ is our Passover lamb." This verse is a significant statement of the indicative and imperative. Hans Conzelmann writes, "The imperative is grounded in the indicative; holiness is not the goal of conduct, but its presupposition."[8] The Corinthians had failed to act as holy people redeemed by the sacrifice of Jesus upon the cross. They had divorced their ethics from God's grace.[9] Paul gives the second imperative in verse 13 in the form of a quotation found in many places in Deuteronomy (13:5; 17:7; 19:19; 21:21; 22:21; 24:7), "Expel the evil one from among you." The lists of the sins in Deuteronomy are similar to the marks of immorality Paul states in verses 9-11, but most often the punishment stated is death. Paul may have this concept in mind and may hope that exclusion from the fellowship would be a death-like punishment and drive the "brother" back to the community in shame and repentance. The shame of the immoral "brother" should replace the present shame of the Corinthians for accepting immorality in the holy community.

Paul gives his position again in verse 9 by reminding the Corinthians of what he said in a previous letter: do not associate or have anything to do with people of *porneia*. The Corinthians should have known what to do because of this previous letter. The reason they were in the present predicament was because they had not heeded his instructions. The basic problem for the community was not pollution from outside the church ("the immoral ones of the world") but from the danger of sin within a fellowship meant to be holy (6:19). Many of the vices in Paul's list in verse 11 were problems present in Corinth (immorality, chs. 5, 7; greed, ch. 6; idolatry, chs. 8–10; slanderous speech, chs. 12 and 14; and drunkenness, ch. 11). The Corinthians failed to adhere to Paul's ethical principle that those who are "in Christ" will be-

---

[8] Conzelmann, *1 Corinthians*, 98.
[9] Fee, *First Corinthians*, 217.

have consistently with transformation that happens "in Christ." Their failure to grow into maturity showed him that they were living according to the paradigm symbolized by existence "in Adam" and "in the flesh" (3:1-3; cf. 15:21-22).

Paul assumes three levels of morality in chapter 5. At the lowest level is the immoral "brother," in the middle is the world of unbelievers (vv. 1, 10), and at the highest point the redeemed, holy community (v. 12). The immoral "brother" is at the lowest point because his sin is not even accepted by the unbelieving world (v. 1). Paul puts the Corinthians at the lowest level with the immoral "brother." This serves his rhetorical strategy of shaming them and making them aware of the severity of their situation. As a result, they should repent and live by the paradoxical ethic of the cross.

Other Problems with Sexual Immorality

The Corinthians appear to have three positions concerning sexual immorality. One is their toleration and acceptance of the immoral "brother" as illustrated above. The second is ethical freedom represented in the slogans in 6:12-13. The third is asceticism and avoidance of conjugal relationships altogether, which is discussed in 7:1-40.

✧ Ethical Freedom

Paul extends his discussion of *porneia* into 6:12-20 by reminding the Corinthians that they were free from the power of sin which lies behind sexual immorality. He states in 6:19-20 that they had been purchased off the slave block of sin and had been made holy and fit to be the temple of the Holy Spirit. He begins this by stating several slogans in verses 12-13: "Everything is lawful for me, but not everything is beneficial. Everything is lawful for me, but I will not be mastered by anything. Food for the stomach and the stomach for food, but God will destroy both of them."

The punctuation of these slogans is a matter of interpretation since the original Greek text lacked any. Most commentators and translators put the first clause of each of the slogans in quotation marks to designate them as slogans current among the Corinthians; then the final clause is interpreted as Paul's reaction against these slogans. Brian J. Dodd suggests that these slogans are Paul's self-characterization in the form of his epistolary "I" statements. Paul uses the first person singular as a form of stylistic ventriloquism to involve his readers in the discussion and also to provide himself as a paradigm. These slogans provide examples of his self-limiting freedom seen more fully in chapter 9.[10] It is possible that these slogans represent teaching consistent with Paul's message and that the Corinthians misunderstood and misinterpreted them. For example, the first slogan, "All things are possible for me, but not all things are beneficial," relates to Paul's teaching on freedom from legalistic righteousness but still obedience to the law out of love for Christ (Rom 8:1-4; Gal 5:1-14).[11] The Corinthians could have taken this statement to its logical extreme and used it as support for their ethical indifference by claiming they were free from such restraints.[12] The other two slogans could also be interpreted this way. Paul may be using his own theology in the form of slogans to counter the misunderstanding of the Corinthians.[13]

❖ Asceticism

Some in the community were possibly taking an opposite perspective to the lax moral standards shown by the acceptance of the immoral "brother." Paul addresses the ascetic tendencies of some in his reaction to the letter he received (7:1).[14] In chapter 7 he refocuses his topic of a holy ethic and applies it to specific issues in the community. The question to which he responds is whether or not a man should "touch" or have sexual relations with a woman.[15] He does not deal so much with actual situations of sexual immorality in this section but rather with potential situations. If some believers refused their mate conjugal rights, then one or both of them were in danger of falling prey to sexual temptations (*porneias*, 7:2). Paul is concerned with sexual practices because they directly impact fellowship with Christ (6:15-17), and

---

[10] Brian J. Dodd, "Paul's Paradigmatic 'I' and 1 Corinthians 6:12," *JSNT* 59 (1995) 39–58.

[11] The term *exestin* (it is "permissible" or "possible") is related to the key term *exousia* ("power," "authority," or "freedom"). It was a significant term in Hellenistic philosophy of the Stoics (Dio Chrysostom, 3:10), in legal matters, and in Hellenistic Judaism of Philo (*Prob.*21, 22, 41, 59-61). See Werner Foerster, "*Exousia*," in *TDNT* 2:570.

[12] They were abusing their *exousia*. The concept of freedom is basic to the entire argument of 5:1-11:1 and can be seen in the repeated use of *exousia* and its variations. These words are *exousia* in 7:37; 8:9; 9:4, 5, 6, 12 twice, 18; *exousiazo* in 6:12 and 7:4, a word which occurs only else in Luke 22:25 in the New Testament; and *exestin* in the sense of "lawful" or "possible" in 6:12 twice and 10:23 twice.

[13] Fee comes close to this position. He argues that the error of the Corinthians was to make absolute what Paul would have qualified by his "in Christ" perspective (*First Corinthians*, 252; cf. Conzelmann, *1 Corinthians*, 110).

[14] There is actually no evidence that the topics referred to before this point are only in response to oral reports and not to the Corinthians' letter. See Archibald Robertson and A. Plummer, *A Critical and Exegetical Commentary on the First Epistle of St. Paul to the Corinthians* (Edinburgh: T. & T. Clark, 1914) 131; Hurd, *Origin of 1 Corinthians*, 6–8.

[15] The verb *haptesthai* ("to touch") is a euphemism for sexual intercourse (Fee, *First Corinthians*, 275).

he does not want the Corinthians' communion with Christ to be harmed or incomplete.[16]

Paul concedes to the basic sexual drive of humans because of the possibility of immorality. The conjugal rights of the husband and wife are equal in the marriage relationship, as the balanced parallelism in verses 2-4 suggests. The only exception is for a time of prayer (v. 5). The best situation is to remain single, like Paul, because one can then be more fully devoted to the work of the Lord (v. 7). Paul states the basis for his maxims in verse 17: let each person live in the situation to which the Lord has called him or her. He applies this principle to matters not directly related to the issue of sexual morality but logically linked to the principle itself.[17] The principle also involves in the discussion those in the church who may not have been tempted with immorality. Giving this general rule also allows Paul to develop his point beyond sexual immorality to the broader issue of "authority" (*exousia*). The problem with sexual immorality is an extension of the problem of authority. Some of the moral difficulties in Corinth could have arisen as a result of the Corinthians' sense of superiority in their own knowledge which they believed brought freedom, power, and authority (*exousia*). They may have felt secure in their own morality so that sexual relations could be altogether avoided. Paul agrees with this position in principle, but in practice realizes that such self-control is a gift of God (v. 7).

❖ Influences from the Cultural Environment

Paul's conflict with the Corinthians over *porneia* could have been influenced by the cultural context of Corinth. Sexual immorality was an issue not only for Christians and Jews in Corinth but also for Gentiles. The chastisement of the typical immorality of the period is well known and documented. For example, the philosopher Epictetus writes, "Before marriage guard yourself with all your ability from unlawful intercourse with women."[18] The teacher of Epictetus, Musonius Rufus, condemned sexual intercourse outside of marriage.[19] This morality can be seen also in Seneca who asks, "Is there any shame

---

[16] Ellis comments, "Paul regards such sexual sins as particularly abhorrent for Christians not only because they involve a sin against one's 'own body' but also because the resulting 'one body' created by the couple in such cases clashes impossibly with the 'one spirit,' that is, the corporate body existing via the Holy Spirit between the believer's body and Christ" ("*Soma* in First Corinthians," 140).

[17] He covers a number of issues for those who are married (vv. 2-7), single and widowed (vv. 8-11, 39-40), with an unbelieving spouse (vv. 12-16), circumcised and uncircumcised (vv. 18-20), slaves (vv. 20-23), and unmarried or virgins (vv. 25-38).

[18] Epictetus, *Ench.* 33.8.

[19] Musonius Rufus, *Fragment* 12 (*On Sexual Indulgence*), quoted in Malherbe, *Moral Exhortation*, 152–54.

at all for adultery now that matters have come to such a pass that no woman has any use for a husband except to inflame her paramour? Chastity is simply a proof of ugliness."[20] The incest evidenced by the immoral "brother" was viewed by many as wrong and was prohibited by Roman law. Gaius 1.63 reads, "I may not marry one who once was my stepmother. We say, who once was, since if the marriage producing that alliance were still continuing, I should be precluded from marrying her on another ground."[21] Concerning a woman who had broken up her daughter's marriage to marry her son-in-law, Cicero writes, "Oh! To think of the woman's sin, unbelievable, unheard of in all experience save for this single instance!" This was a "scandal among men" and a "disgrace."[22] The actions of the immoral "brother" in Corinth coincide with the immorality of an unbelieving world degenerating to self-destruction (cf. Rom 1:18-32).

The immorality of Corinth and other Greco-Roman cities was well known in the ancient world. The nature of the worship in some of the cults known to have existed in first-century Corinth suggests the presence of rampant immorality. For example, the presence of Aphrodite worship in Corinth implies the sensual nature of some of the city inhabitants. Worship of Aphrodite as the goddess of love and sexuality may have provided the inhabitants of Corinth an opportunity to participate in sensual enjoyment contrary to Paul's understanding of holiness. The presence of the worship of Hera Argaea, the goddess of marriage and sexuality for women and of sacred marriage, also may have influenced the immorality of the city. In addition, the worship of Dionysus, the god of wine and ecstasy, had a reputation for drunkenness and sexual immorality and eventually had to be suppressed as far away as Italy.[23] Sacred prostitution may also have existed in Corinth. The Greeks typically saw nothing wrong with prostitution. F. Hauck and S. Schulz write, "The main cause of prostitution is the Greek view of life which regards sexual intercourse as just as natural, necessary and justifiable as eating and drinking."[24] According to Athenaeus, whenever the city of Corinth would pray to Aphrodite in matters of great importance, the people would "invite as many prostitutes as possible to join in their petitions, and these women [would] add their supplications to the goddess and later [be] present

---

[20] Seneca, *Ben.* 3.16.3.
[21] Quoted by David Daube, "Pauline Contributions to Pluralistic Culture: Re-creation and Beyond," in *Jesus and Man's Hope*, ed. D. G. Miller and D. Y. Hadidian (Pittsburgh: Pittsburgh Theological Seminary, 1971) 241, n. 3.
[22] Cicero, *Clu.* 4.
[23] Wendell Willis, *Idol Meat in Corinth: The Pauline Argument in 1 Corinthians 8 and 10*, SBLDS 68 (Chico, Calif.: Scholars, 1985) 30.
[24] Hauck and Schulz, *"Porneia," TDNT* 6:582.

at the sacrifices."[25] Typical of the polemic against this morality is Josephus, who describes an all night sexual engagement between a lady named Paulina with the god Anubi (*Ant.* 18:65-80). These examples suggest that the sexual problems faced by the Corinthian believers were typical, extensive, and influential.

Problems with Love

Paul had another big problem with the church in Corinth: their immaturity appeared in their lack of love for one another. Rather than submitting to one another in love, they were neglecting and overlooking each another and possibly even causing some in the church to fall back into sin. Influences from the environment of Corinth did not help the quest for love either because those outside the church lived according to a different paradigm than the divine mystery.

Participation in Idolatry (8:1—11:1)

❖ INTERNAL PRESSURES

The Corinthians had a problem with their knowledge or lack of knowledge concerning food offered to idols. According to Joop F. M. Smit, 8:1-6 serves as the *partitio* of Paul's larger argument in 8:1-10:22. Paul gives the basic issue at stake and provides two options that he will develop through deliberative argument: the use of freedom which comes with knowledge or the use of responsibility which comes from love. The first is harmful to the community; the second builds up the community. The first option is elaborated in 8:7-12, and the second option is developed in 8:13-9:27.[26]

There were two apparent segments within the church. The "strong" included those with whom Paul agreed in principle but disagreed with their practice of that principle because of their abuse of their freedom.[27] This group is suggested in verse 1 with the words, "we know," which introduces a fact well-known to Paul and the group.[28] Paul addresses the strong because they could change their behavior towards others because of their knowledge about the true nature of idols. The statement, "we all possess knowledge," may be ironical because there was in fact another part of the church that did not have the type of knowledge to which Paul refers. This other segment is represented

---

[25] Athenaeus, *Deip.* 13.573C.
[26] Joop F. M. Smit, "1 Cor 8, 1-6: A Rhetorical Partitio," in *The Corinthian Correspondence*, ed. Reimund Bieringer (Leuven: Leuven University Press, 1996) 580, 584.
[27] Joël Delobel, "Coherence and Relevance of 1 Cor 8–10," in *The Corinthian Correspondence*, ed. Reimund Bieringer (Leuven: Leuven University Press, 1996) 178.
[28] Smit, "1 Cor 8,1-6," 596.

in the plural as "those who are weak" (v. 9), and in the singular as "the brother for whom Christ died" (v. 11). Those who were weak serve only as passive artillery in the argument of chapter 8 because they were not in a position of power. They lacked "authority" (*exousia*) because of their weak conscience. They do play an active role, however, in chapter 10 because of the temptation to associate idol food with the worship of idols (cf. 10:6-13).

The criterion for the evaluation of moral conduct, in this case eating food sacrificed to idols, is the issue of *syneidesis*, which can be roughly translated as "conscience." This word occurs fifteen times in the undisputed epistles of Paul, and of those, eight times in chapters 8 and 10 of 1 Corinthians.[29] The term is based on the word *oida*, "to know," and has the basic meaning of an awareness of both past and future actions. One's conscience can be good or bad. A bad conscience remembers one's evils deeds and sins and warns of condemnation and punishment. One's conscience can become an over-awareness of self and of various issues which leads to the development of regulations or scruples.[30] The conscience serves as the guide in moral conduct.[31] In the present context, Paul is concerned with the knowledge that idols are nothing but human-made artifacts. But he also believes that there is an evil power behind the worship of idols that can lead astray those who attach too much reality to idols. Those who are "weak" in conscience are not able to distinguish the false nature of idols and the demonic power that lies behind the worship of idols. Thus, these people become trapped by their conscience and unable to go beyond their former belief in idols.

Paul realizes that the problem and solution with eating idol food rest with knowledge. As with the term "wisdom" (*sophia*) in chapter 2, Paul will add his own definition to "knowledge" (*gnōsis*) in 8:1—11:1. He has already proven that the Corinthians' wisdom is insufficient, and now he must demonstrate that their knowledge is also incomplete and based on a faulty foundation.[32] Knowledge was the basis for the strong Corinthians' ethical freedom. The problem with this freedom was that it violated the conscience of the weaker brother or sister. In 8:1-2 Paul contrasts the "knowledge" of the strong with the love they lacked:

---

[29] 1 Cor 8:7, 10, 12; 10:25; 27, 28, 29 (twice); cf. Rom 2:15; 9:1; 13:5; 2 Cor 1:12; 4:2; 5:11.

[30] Christian Maurer comments, "It is man aware of himself in perception and acknowledgment, in willing and acting" ("*Synoida*," in *TDNT* 8:914). For further discussion, see also C. A. Pierce, *Conscience in the New Testament*, SBT 1/15 (London: SCM, 1955); Jewett, *Paul's Anthropological Terms*, 402–46.

[31] Furnish, *Theology and Ethics in Paul*, 229.

[32] Conzelmann, *1 Corinthians*, 138.

> **A** Knowledge puffs up, but
>> love builds up (v. 1).
>>> **B** If anyone thinks he knows something,
>>>> he does not yet know as he should know (v. 2).
>
> **A'** If anyone loves God,
>> this one is known by God (v. 3).

In "A" Paul states that the basic problem of the Corinthian strong was that they boasted in their knowledge and overlooked the better alternative of love. "B" shows the futility of this position because the Corinthians' knowledge was inferior to the better knowledge given in "A'." For Paul, knowledge consists in being known by God in a relationship of love. Paul grounds the morality of believers in love and not knowledge, and he redefines what knowledge is. The love of the strong stands in antithesis to their knowledge. The strong may have allowed their knowledge to supersede their love for the weaker members of the community. Paul attempts to replace this with a synthesis between love and knowledge.

Paul accepts the basic premise of the strong but *not* the logical conclusion. A different type of logic must be used, and this logic is the paradox of the mystery of the cross. That improper knowledge is the real issue behind eating idol food is shown by Paul's returning to the issue of idol food in verse 4, where he gives the basic theological principle and content of the knowledge described in verse 3. The content of the shared knowledge between Paul and the strong is that there is only one God and one Lord; all others exist only as objects of worship and as inferior, created beings (cf. 10:19-21). This knowledge may have created a sense of freedom for the strong who may have come out of a polytheistic environment.[33]

According to verse 7, however, not all the Corinthians shared this liberating knowledge. The logic of the stronger members is that since there is no God but one, then idols are nothing; therefore, it is permissible to eat the food sacrificed to these idols. The issue at stake for Paul is that the weak brothers or sisters might be in danger of falling back into idolatry if they ate idol food. Their conscience or awareness was too weak to break the tie between the objective eating of food and the subjective worship of the idol to which the food was offered in dedication. The strong could be guilty of leading the weak into sin if they violated the conscience of the weak. Food itself was not the problem because it is morally neutral (v. 8).

Paul is concerned about this potential, that the strong in the community might violate the conscience of the weak and cause them to sin (v. 9). The re-

---

[33] Conzelmann comments that Paul's attitude was that "the gods *become* gods by being believed in, and faith in the *one* God and the *one* Lord creates freedom no longer to recognize these powers" (*1 Corinthians*, 145).

sult, then, would be sin on the part of the strong (v. 12), and everyone would come out losers. The assumption is that the "strong" had violated or were in danger of violating the law of love and were unconcerned about the welfare of their brothers and sisters in Christ. Paul encourages the strong to avoid this practice by using double negatives (*ou mē*) in verse 13 to show emphasis: "I will never ever eat meat if it causes my brother to fall." The shift to the first person singular makes a smooth transition to his personal example in the next chapter. The principle developed in this section will govern Paul's rhetoric for the remainder of this part of the letter and will be restated in 10:24 to cover any circumstance that violates the ethic of love.

After providing himself as an example of love in chapter 9, Paul returns to matters of eating "food sacrificed to idols" (*eidōlolatrias*) and violating the conscience of the weak in chapter 10. He shows both segments of the church the dangerous implications of the actions discussed in chapter 8. He presents the view opposite to his own in the worst possible way with a negative typology from the history of Israel. The climax of this illustration occurs in verse 4 with the statement that all of the Israelites drank from the spiritual drink that flowed out of the Rock which was Christ. In spite of these special gifts of grace, the Israelites experienced God's displeasure because of their idolatry (v. 7).

Paul next shows that the things that happened to Israel serve as patterns, examples, or warnings for the Corinthians.[34] He distinguishes four points of comparison between Israel and the Corinthians: the Corinthians should not be like the Israelites who participated in idolatry (v. 7), sexual immorality (v. 8), testing the Lord (v. 9), and grumbling (v. 10).[35] The basic problem with the Israelites and the danger for the Corinthians was in desire for evil (v. 6) which is antithetical to love (cf. Gal 5:16-24).

Paul shifts his attention again to the Corinthians in his application of this typology in verse 11. The Israelites had special privileges that they forfeited because of their disobedience, and the Corinthians were at a similar point of decision. What paradigm they followed would determine how they would be treated by God. One of the underlying goals of Paul's argument on idol food appears in verse 12: the Corinthians should watch lest they fall like the Israelites. The answer and way to escape from troubles (v. 13) comes in fellowship with Christ, the theme of verses 14-22. At this point Paul un-

---

[34] According to Witherington, "The idea behind typology is that since God's character never changes God acts in similar ways in different ages of history and, perhaps more importantly, provides persons and events that foreshadow other later persons and events in salvation history" (*Conflict and Community*, 217).

[35] Paul uses here a number of texts from Jewish tradition including Exod 14:19-22; 16:4-30; 17:1-7; Num 14; 16; 21; Wis 11.

dermines the false security of the strong who relied on their knowledge for their morality and spirituality, while at the same time also challenging the weak in their temptations to idolatry. In verse 14 he shifts to surface issues that concern the weak, but the deeper problem could only be addressed by a paradigm shift of the strong. Thus, he moves beyond the issue of idol food to the principle behind it.

Paul is concerned about two issues in 10:14-22. The first is the obvious spiritual danger of fellowship with demons when one eats food sacrificed to an idol. The second concern is the social danger of schism within the community. The cup and the bread unite believers with Christ (v. 17) and with each other (v. 18). Paul's rhetorical questions in verse 19 challenge and clarify the supposed "knowledge" of the Corinthian strong (8:1): "What then should I say? That food sacrificed to idols is anything or that an idol is anything?" Although idols are nothing to both Paul and the strong, idols are controlled by demons and offer demons an open door to draw a person away from God (10:20). Verse 21 is a call to exclusive loyalty and functions as the culmination of Paul's argument in this section. The Corinthians could not have fellowship with demons and the Lord at the same time but had to make a choice between the two.[36] Paul does not want them to slip back into idolatry and thereby apostatize.[37]

Paul begins the conclusion in verse 23 by speaking directly to both the weak and the strong.[38] First, he speaks to the indifference of the strong by repeating the neutral slogans of 6:12 because now the strong can attach the proper meaning to these statements. The individualism of the strong—or of those confident in their own interpretation of community integrity—has been debunked and replaced by the greater concern for social holiness and the well-being of the weak brother or sister.[39] Paul's central goal for the strong is for them humbly to love their weak sister or brother (vv. 23-24).

With verse 25, Paul turns his attention to the concerns of the weak. He provides two hypothetical but possible situations common in the social interaction of the time. He introduces the first by way of ethical maxim by saying that anything in the meat market is suitable for eating without consideration

---

[36] Joop Smit comments, "All participants in the Lord's Supper, without exception, enter into an alliance with the one Lord and may not enter into additional relationships with other so-called 'lords'" ("'Do not be Idolaters': Paul's Rhetoric in First Corinthians 10:1-22," *NovT* 39 [1997]: 45). Paul's call to loyalty here is similar to Exod 20:32 and Deut 6:4.

[37] Willis, *Idol Meat*, 160.

[38] Duane Watson writes that "in 10:23-11:1 Paul is gathering together the points he has tried to make beginning in 8:1" ("1 Corinthians 10:23-11:1 in the Light of Greco-Roman Rhetoric: The Role of Rhetorical Questions," *JBL* 108 [1989] 312).

[39] According to Conzelmann, the term *oikodomei* in verse 23 "denotes first and foremost the building up of the community, not the edification of the individual" (*1 Corinthians*, 176).

of conscience. He follows this up with confirmation from scripture (Ps 23:1, LXX). The second hypothetical situation takes place in the private home of an unbeliever (vv. 27-30). Paul is subtly challenging the weaker believers to grow in their awareness (*syneidēsis*) that indeed food sacrificed to idols is not a concern since all food is created by the Lord. Paul's basic concern for the Corinthians is their lack of fellowship and concern for *everyone* in the community. He continues this concern in his next major argument in chapters 11–14 by discussing other issues related to love.

❖ External Forces

Archeological evidence suggests that there may have been significant external pressures upon the church from the cultural environment of Corinth that contributed to the problems with idol food. First, food sacrificed to idols was widely available. Dining facilities have been found at the temple of Demeter and Core located on the road to the Acrocorinth. According to Peter D. Gooch, cultic meals were probably eaten in these dining rooms. The cult of Demeter and Core, which had a strong presence in Corinth, was related to the cultivation of food with attention given to the yearly agricultural cycle, the burial and rebirth of dead seeds, and the growth and harvest of abundant food.[40] This cult was also related to the Eluesinian Mysteries which had the eating of religious food as one of the central rites of initiation. The use of food at Demeter worship at Eleusis suggests the same at Corinth. Gooch concludes, based on archeological evidence, that since food was a sacred part of the Demeter worship, any food eaten within the precincts of the temple most likely would be sacred to her.[41] The Temple of Askelpeion located on the northern wall of Corinth and the fountain of Lerna found nearby also suggest the availability of idol food in Corinth. The dining facilities found there may not have been part of the worship of Asklepios, but played a part possibly through the incubation and pursuit of health. Gooch writes concerning these facilities,

> Three aspects of this use of food are attested. First, sacred food was used in the rites of the cultus. Second, sacred food was eaten by priests and worshipers inside the sanctuary, and taken outside the sanctuary for consumption elsewhere. Finally, there is attested the use of ordi-

---

[40] For archeological evidence of the presence of Demeter and Core worship in Corinth, see N. Bookides and J. E. Fischer, "The Sanctuary of Demeter and Core," *Hesperia* 41 (1972) 283–331; N. Bookides and R. S. Stroud, *Demeter and Persephone in Ancient Corinth* (Princeton: ASCSA, 1987).
[41] Gooch, *Dangerous Food*, 1–13.

nary food (that is, food not sacrificed) either prescribed or prohibited by the god to effect a cure.[42]

The *macellum* ("meat market," 10:25) was a common feature in Hellenistic cities during the Roman Imperial period.[43] Archeologists have for some time tried to locate the *macellum* of Corinth but have not found it yet, although a location based on a pair of Latin inscriptions has been suggested.[44] Three things typically happened to sacrificial meat: the god's portion was burned on the altar, a certain part was allotted to worshipers for consumption, and a third part was put on a table and dedicated to the god but consumed by worshipers or priests.[45]

Second, the evidence suggests that idol food was available to people of all social levels. The typical diet of a poor person during the period did not usually consist of meat because of its expense. Only on special occasions, such as at feasts, or with money could one afford this luxury. The typical diet of the time consisted of grain products, porridge, olives, and occasionally fish.[46] Gerd Theissen identifies five occasions when the poorer citizen could have eaten meat: (1) special celebrations of victory, funerals, or to win the public's goodwill, (2) sacrificial meals for particular days, (3) the great religious feasts, (4) participation in one of the many associations, and (5) invitation to dine at a temple.[47] Theissen goes on to argue that for lower status people, the eating of meat was typically associated with some type of ceremonial occasion. This led him to conclude that social-stratification existed in the church in Corinth between the economically poor and the more well-to-do resulting in problems of division.[48] As Gooch has shown, the food sacrificed to idols need not have been only meat, thus the issues may not have been socio-economic as Theissen has argued. Archeological evidence also disputes Theissen's claim that food was a significant difference in social classes, and suggests that even the lower classes used the various dining facilities at sacred sites.[49]

---

[42] Gooch, *Dangerous Food*, 21.
[43] See for further description Ned P. Nabers, "Macella: A Study in Roman Archeology" (Ph. D. diss., Princeton University, 1967).
[44] Henry J. Cadbury, "The Macellum of Corinth," *JBL* 53 (1934) 134-41; David W. J. Gill, "The Meat-Market at Corinth (1 Corinthians 10:25)" *TynBul* 43 (1992) 389–93.
[45] Willis, *Idol Meat*, 16–17; Gooch, *Dangerous Food*, 22.
[46] See P. Garnsey, "Mass Diet and Nutrition in the City of Rome," in *Hourir la plebe*, ed. A. Giovanni (Basel: Herder, 1991) 67–101. Peter Tomson writes, "In antiquity meat was expensive and very difficult to keep . . . it was eaten only at special events such as festivals and ceremonies, certainly by the lower classes . . . fish, bread, vagetables [sic], cakes and fruit were the regular diet"(Peter J. Tomson, *Paul and the Jewish Law: Halakha in the Letters of the Apostle to the Gentiles*, CRINT 3/1 [Minneapolis: Fortress, 1990] 189).
[47] Theissen, *Social Setting*, 127–28.
[48] Ibid., 121–43.
[49] Gooch, *Dangerous Food*, 53–54, 149–50.

Third, the evidence indicates that eating food sacrificed to idols was a significant part of the social interaction of many people in ancient cities such as Corinth. Many social events besides cultic worship were held at the dining facilities associated with various temples. Richard E. Oster comments, "The dining facilities at Corinth provide architectural evidence for a situation in which 'monotheistic' believers . . . could attend and participate in activities indigenous to their religio-cultural matrix but which did not require overt participation in the central *cultus* and sacrifices of the religion itself."[50] Sacrifice was often part of many social meals, especially those during some type of social transition (e.g., births, weddings, funerals, or reunions). Willis writes, "The assessment of the cult meals as occasions of good company, good food, and good fun makes it obvious why the Corinthian Christians would not have wanted to miss out."[51] Eating at sacrificial meals was a civic responsibility and failure to do so brought social isolation.[52] Gooch estimates,

> If Corinthian Christians following Paul's advice were to attempt to avoid any situation where they would be asked to eat food explicitly identified as idol-food, then it is very likely that they could not accept invitations to frequent and important occasions. . . . It would not be possible to maintain social relationships with those outside the Christian circle without major adjustment and the serious possibility of misunderstanding and hostility.[53]

As Bruce N. Fisk offers, there may have been a continuum of involvement in various pagan temple activities. "At the one end was harmless fun and social convention; at the other end was raw idolatry."[54]

The availability of eating food sacrificed to idols and the social implications of eating meat may have adversely influenced the formation of community in the Corinthian church. According to Willis, there were two classes of eating idol food in 1 Corinthians 8 and 10: (1) Paul strictly forbids eating at the table of sacrifice, which could lead to fellowship with demons; and (2) he permits eating in other situations when qualified by consideration for others (10:31-32).[55]

The above evidence suggests that the Corinthians had food sacrificed to idols readily available to them, whether that be meat or some other type of food. Paul appears to be more concerned about communal and personal fel-

---

[50] Oster, "Use, Misuse," 66–67.
[51] Willis, *Idol Meat*, 63.
[52] Smit, "1 Cor 8,1-6," 582.
[53] Gooch, *Dangerous Food*, 37, 46.
[54] Bruce N. Fisk, "Eating Meat Offered to Idols: Corinthian Behavior and Pauline Response in 1 Corinthians 8–10," *TJ* 10 (1989) 63.
[55] Willis, *Idol Meat*, 244.

lowship in holiness and love. He agrees with the strong that idols are nothing before the one God and one Lord (cf. Deut 6:4; 4:35, 39; Isa 44:8; 45:5), but qualifies this by stating that there is a source of power behind idols that should not be overlooked. He also does not want the worship in the church to become indistinguishable from its environment. It is impossible to be certain, but some of the weak may have been Gentiles who formerly worshiped idols and who still had some form of emotional or psychological attachment to them.[56] Paul's concern is with Christ's exclusive ownership of the believer (6:20a). Smit comments, "Within Hellenistic religion people freely participate in sacrificial meals of several deities. An exclusive relationship with one of them is unknown. Alternation is the general and undisputed practice."[57] Food itself was not evil, only the religious and social context made food the instrument of demonic forces.

Problems with Community Solidarity

Paul appears disappointed in the Corinthians because their gatherings were doing more harm than good (11:17). In response to this, he tries to offer guidelines for orderly worship (14:40). The deeper problem was that the Corinthians lacked love for one another. They were not measuring up to Paul's ideology of the *pneumatikos* person (12:1). He adduces several problems in the church in support of his basic conflict with them over ideology: certain men and women had abused their new freedom in Christ in regard to propriety in worship (11:2-16); the church had overlooked some in the community during the Lord's supper (11:17-34); and, the individualism of certain people who spoke in tongues caused the church and the gospel to be questioned by outsiders and led to division within the church (chs. 12–14).

❖ Order in the Community

One issue related to community formation concerns conformity to traditional hairstyle. The opening, middle, and closing of Paul's argument in chapter 11 reveals his progression of thought. After calling for imitation of himself and ultimately of Christ in 11:1, Paul then praises the Corinthians in verse

---

[56] Barrett, *First Corinthians*, 194–95; Willis, *Idol Meat*, 91–95. James Dunn suggests that the weak were Jewish. He writes, "For the fear of idolatry as a Jewish concern was primarily the fear of contamination, and eating was strictly governed by taboos against unclean food; idol meat entering the body through the mouth could render spiritually unclean. Hence in 8:7 the fear of defilement, in 10:6-8 the association between idolatry, eating and drinking, and sexual immorality, and in 10:14-22 the abhorrence of any thought of partnership with idols and demons through eating and drinking" (*1 Corinthians* [Sheffield: Sheffield Academic, 1995] 66).

[57] Smit, "Do not be Idolaters," 48.

2 for remembering his ways and keeping his traditions. This statement is full of irony because some of the Corinthians had failed to imitate, remember, and keep his commands and traditions. The middle of his argument verifies this when he says in verse 17, "But in this, I do not praise you." The reason why he blames the Corinthians here becomes evident by his rhetoric. Finally, in his closing, he gives the way to avoid shame or condemnation: by looking out for the interests of others, thus modeling the paradigm of the cross (vv. 33-34; cf. Phil 2:3-4).

Paul has a problem with how some of the Corinthians wore their hair in public gatherings. He uses epideictic rhetoric in 11:2-16 by censuring the actions of certain people in the church and urging them to reaffirm traditional values.[58] He begins by commending the Corinthians for keeping his traditions, but apparently there is one tradition they had not kept. He begins to address this lack of convention by covertly stating a basic principle in verse 3: "The head of every man is Christ, the head of every woman is the man, and the head of Christ is God." The specific problem in Corinth is suggested in verses 4-5, that some men prayed with head coverings and some women without head coverings. The key word in these verses is the verb "dishonor." Both men and women dishonor their heads (taking Paul literally, these being men, Christ, and ultimately God) by improper attention to their heads (hair or veils) while praying.[59] Paul then provides support for his contention through the use of an analogy from creation in verses 6-9.

His attention to matters of personal propriety has deeper concerns than simply hairstyle. Some in the community may have taken their new-found freedom in Christ too far and blurred sexual distinctions and/or cultural propriety (cf. 10:23). Paul is concerned with order of creation and not subordination, with distinction and not discrimination (vv. 8-9).[60] He demonstrates that his real point is propriety in worship, and not gender issues, by an important clarification in verses 11-12. He makes a significant shift with verse 11 and writes, "Nevertheless, the woman [does not exist] without the man nor the man without the woman *in the Lord*. For just as the woman [came] from the man, so also the man [came] through the woman" (emphasis added, verbs supplied). Existence "in the Lord" is the optimal condition for relationships in the community (Gal 3:28). There is mutual dependence and no hierarchy "in the Lord." Hierarchy and superiority should not exist in a

---

[58] See Kennedy, *New Testament Interpretation*, 19.
[59] Jerome Murphy-O'Connor, "Sex and Logic in I Corinthians 11:2-16," *CBQ* 42 (1980) 483. Fee represents the differing view that Paul is speaking to women and not men in the church (*First Corinthians*, 495).
[60] Jerome Murphy-O'Connor, *1 Corinthians* (Wilmington, Del.: Glazier, 1979) 107–8.

community where modeling the love of Christ is present. The sphere of the Lord should be a sphere where love is the norm.

There is no mention of "weak" brothers or sisters here, but some in the community may have been violating others'—including Paul's—sense of decorum and raised questions of spirituality in the community. Below the surface of the text lies the primary problem in the church of individualism without regard for others (a good definition of *sarx*), which was leading to a break down of community (*koinōnia*).[61] Imitation of Paul—and hence of Christ (11:1)—directly impacts worship in the church. If the Corinthians would recognize their mutual dependence "in the Lord" (11:11), then they would also realize the significance of their impropriety.

❖ The Neglect of Some

The tone of the passage changes with verse 17 where Paul shifts to another issue related to a lack of love. There is a chiastic structure to 11:17-34:

> **A** 11:17-22 The situation at Corinth (Problem)
>   **B** 11:23-26 Eucharist and appeal to tradition
> **A'** 11:27-34 The situation at Corinth (Solution).[62]

At the center of this arrangement stands the tradition of the Lord's supper. This emphatic position draws attention to the self-giving, sacrificial death of Christ that Paul has mentioned previously in the letter (1:18; 5:7; 6:20). The paradigm of the cross provides for Paul the answer to problems in the church. He uses epideictic rhetoric cloaked in judicial terms to shame the Corinthians into heeding his call for unity.

Beginning with verse 17, Paul presents his case against the Corinthians with the charge that their times of gathering were doing more harm than good. His controversy with them is revealed in the words "come together" in verses 17, 18, 20, 33, and 34, and repeated again in 14:23 and 26. Verse 18 gives the evidence of this with the rumor of division within the fellowship. The primary surface symptom with the church was that the members had failed to take one another into consideration, and some in the fellowship were being overlooked. The deeper disease was a lack of love and concern for all in the community. They had failed to imitate Paul's modeling of Christ through consideration of others in the community, the same problem addressed in chapters 8–10 with the "weak brother." The problems they were experiencing as a community were affecting their times of corporate worship.

---

[61] Cf. Conzelmann, *1 Corinthians*, 191.
[62] Murphy-O'Connor, *1 Corinthians*, 114.

Love was the key to their unity. Thus, Paul condemns the Corinthians' selfishness in eating before others could partake.

Paul uses the tradition of the Lord's supper to develop some basic principles in verses 27-29 that he applies to the problems in the community. These principles center around active participation in the communal Lord's supper. The problem is more than simply manners in eating and drinking, but involves "discerning the body" (v. 29). To which "body" is Paul referring here, the Lord's, the corporate body of the church, or even the individual body of believers? This question has challenged interpreters from early on, as the textual variations imply. The simplest reading leaves "body" undesignated and is attested by the best manuscripts. The words "of the Lord" could have been added in certain manuscripts to clarify "body." Fee suggests that Paul is speaking of the community here as he did in 10:17.[63] Paul wants the Corinthians to participate in the Lord's supper in a "worthy" manner. Considering 10:16-17, it may be that Paul is concerned about community integrity and wholeness. The word "body" could be intentionally vague here. Paul does not want the Corinthians to be guilty of violating the central theme of the Lord's supper, which is sacrificial love. They could sin against one another by overlooking some in the community and thereby becoming guilty of sinning against Christ (cf. 8:12). Paul places their shame on two levels. First, their shame is evidenced by their having experienced judgment in that some had become ill and others had died (v. 30). The second and more real danger of shame is that they could suffer the same fate as "the world" (v. 32). Both of these could be avoided by heeding Paul's instructions.

❖ The Divisiveness of Tongues

Still on the subject of corporate worship, Paul turns his attention to another issue about which he has heard or read: "now about *pneumatikon*" (12:1). Unfortunately, it is impossible to know whether the genitive *pneumatikon* is either masculine ("spiritual people") or neuter ("spiritual things").[64] The context supports both alternatives.[65] One of Paul's concerns in this letter is the definition of spiritual maturity. His stated goal in this section is to free the Corinthians from their ignorance about the meaning of spirituality. He has already foreshadowed the present discussion in 8:1-3 where he gives the key words "knowledge" (*gnōsis*) and "love" (*agapē*). The ignorance of the Corinthians was already proven in chapter 8 by their lack of love for

---

[63] Fee, *First Corinthians*, 563.
[64] Barrett, *First Corinthians*, 278.
[65] The masculine is used five times in 2:13, 15; 3:1; 14:37; cf. Gal 6:1. The neuter appears in 2:13; 9:11; and 14:31.

the weaker members of the community. In chapters 12–14, Paul goes on to condemn a wrong interpretation of spirituality.

In 12:2 Paul attributes the ignorance of the Corinthians to their former lives as Gentiles. As Gentiles, some of them were led aimlessly about, as in a pagan *pompe* or procession.[66] According to C. K. Barrett, the verb "led about" "suggests moments of ecstasy experienced in heathen religion, when a human being is (or is believed to be) possessed by a supernatural."[67] The prophetic ecstasy of the Dionysiac festivals or of the Oracle of Delphi could have influenced some of the Corinthians. The possible influence of the pagan environment becomes even more of an issue in chapter 14, as will be suggested later. In a subtle way, Paul reminds the Corinthians throughout chapters 12 and 14 that their behavior modeled that of unbelieving Gentiles around them and was not consistent with the revelation of Jesus Christ (cf. 14:23).

✣ Internal Pressures

Paul crafts his argument carefully in these chapters lest he create too much friction and cause the Corinthians to burn his letter. In order to avoid this, he uses a rhetorical feature called *insinuatio*. *Insinuatio* is used in difficult situations when the audience may be hostile and the speaker must criticize something highly favoured by the audience. The author hides the subject matter behind something else at the beginning and later articulates it.[68] Paul here hides the problem of speaking in tongues behind the issues of spiritual gifts and unity in the Spirit. The more pressing issue for him is the Corinthians' faulty understanding and practice of community.

The unifying force in the community is the Holy Spirit who empowers those who confess Jesus as Lord. Paul claims that a significant sign of being "spiritual" is to recognize Jesus as Lord. Being "unspiritual" is shown by cursing Jesus. The Holy Spirit always points to Jesus as Lord (cf. John 16:13-15). The Spirit gives "spiritual gifts" (*charismata*) and brings unity in the church. Response to the gospel of Jesus Christ can be proclaimed only by the Spirit. Likewise, the Spirit leads believers to proclaim the content of the gospel.[69]

The real issue with this church from Paul's perspective is spiritual maturity, or better stated, maturity in the Spirit, and so he attempts in these

---

[66] Terence Paige suggests that verse 2 recalls the many pagan *pompe* or processions where the crowds were led about in cultic worship ("1 Corinthians 12.2: A Pagan *Pompe*?" *JSNT* 44 [1991] 57–65).

[67] Barrett, *First Corinthians*, 278; see also Fee, *First Corinthians*, 576.

[68] Joop F. M. Smit, 'Argument and Genre of 1 Corinthians 12–14,' in *Rhetoric and the New Testament*, ed. Stanley E. Porter and Thomas H. Olbricht (Sheffield: JSOT Press, 1993) 213, referring to Cicero, *De inventione* 1.15, 20–21; 1.17.23–24.

[69] F. F. Bruce, *1 and 2 Corinthians*, NCB (Grand Rapids: Eerdmans, 1971) 118.

chapters to define further what it means to be "spiritual" (*pneumatikos*) by discussing "spiritual gifts" (*charismata*). The word *charismata* basically denotes the manifestation of *charis* or "grace." This is a uniquely Pauline word, with half of all uses of the term occurring in 1 Corinthians.[70] Paul gives three different lists of "spiritual gifts" in this chapter (vv. 8-10, 28, and 29-30). Three of the listed gifts appear at the center of discussion and contention between Paul and the Corinthians: knowledge, tongues, and prophecy. The position of tongues as last in all the lists in this chapter (12:8-10, 28, 29, 30) is significant since it is the major evidence of a lack of love in this part of the letter.[71] By putting tongues last and giving prophecy a more prominent place, Paul may be preparing his audience for his argument in chapter 14.[72]

In chapter 14, Paul compares tongues and prophecy. He uses the verb "to speak" (*laleo*) 24 times in various forms in this chapter, which suggests that his problem with the Corinthians lies with communication.[73] Evidently, the Corinthians gloried in their ability to speak in tongues just as they boasted in their wisdom (*sophia*, chs. 1–4) and freedom or authority (*exousia*, chs. 5–10). They may have sought to speak in tongues because of the impressive nature of tongues and their eschatological orientation to understand "mysteries" (14:2).[74] Paul attempts to put the outwardly seen gifts of prophecy and tongues into the greater context of community edification and, by this, offer the Corinthians an example of how love within the community overcomes personal preferences (14:18-19; see further 8:13).

Chapter 14 begins and ends with an appeal to "keep on seeking love" (14:1, 39). Paul gives love as the goal of "spiritual gifts" in 12:31, and in 14:1 he applies this to the communication problems at Corinth. He shifts his attention in 14:1 from "spiritual gifts" to "spiritual matters." The spiritual matter or gift of the Spirit that the Corinthians should pursue relative to love is the ability to prophesy. Paul emphasizes the gift of prophecy in this context as a better gift for the community because it edifies the church. He states this as a thesis in verses 2 and 3, and summarizes it in verse 4: "The one who speaks a tongue edifies one's self, but the one who prophesies edifies the church."

This is a significant assessment of tongues in the context of the letter because of Paul's insistence on placing the concerns of others over those of oneself. He recognizes tongues as a divine gift and does not attempt to hinder

---

[70] Rom 1:11; 5:15, 16; 6:23; 11:29; 1 Cor 1:7; 7:7; 12:4, 9, 28, 30, 31; 2 Cor 1:11; 1 Tim 4:14; 2 Tim 1:6; 1 Pet 4:10.
[71] Robertson and Plummer, *First Corinthians*, 280.
[72] Prophecy is the only consistent gift listed by Paul in all his lists of spiritual gifts (1 Cor 12:8-11; 28-30; 13:1-2; Rom 12:6-8).
[73] Verse 2 thrice, 3, 4, 5 twice, 6 twice, 9 twice, 11 twice, 13, 18, 19, 21, 23, 27, 28, 29, 34, 35, 39.
[74] D. L. Baker, 'The Interpretation of 1 Cor 12-14,' *EvQ* 46 (1974) 230.

the Spirit by totally disregarding speaking in tongues, but by his numerous qualifications of it, especially the significant one given in verse 4, he basically assigns it an inferior position in the life of the gathered community.[75] Tongues speaking can become useful to the community *only if it is interpreted*, which then makes it equivalent to prophecy. In the remainder of this chapter, Paul develops this thought through veiled logic: speaking in tongues fails the test of being intelligent and understandable, and thus the building up of the community (vv. 6-19), but prophecy meets this test (vv. 20-25). Therefore, prophecy should be the means of communication within the community (vv. 26-33a).

In the first step of his logic, Paul claims that speaking in tongues by itself serves no purpose in the community because it does not build up the community. Communication that benefits the church comes by "revelation, knowledge, prophecy, or teaching" (v. 6). He could be implying here that tongues cannot be described with any of these words unless it is made intelligible. He uses several illustrations to demonstrate the unintelligibility of tongues (flute, harp, horn, voices or languages) and then applies these images to the community in verses 9 and 12. His basic point is that speaking in tongues fails the test of intelligibility and therefore has no value for the gathered community. He does give one exception to this principle: there must be someone to interpret the meaning of the tongues (v. 13). He presses the unintelligibility theme in verses 14-17. The speaker in tongues loses control of the mind even though his or her spirit is praying. Likewise, others (literally, "the one who fills the place of the *idiotes*"[76]) cannot understand the message. Paul then describes his personal use and evaluation of speaking in tongues in verses 18-19. His statement in verse 18 that he speaks in tongues more than any of the Corinthians is qualified by a strong adversity in verse 19: "BUT in the church I would rather speak five intelligible words to instruct others than ten thousand words in a tongue." Although he speaks in "myriads" or ten thousand words in a tongue, he would rather speak five words that make sense and edify the community.

Paul then moves on to show how prophecy meets the test of intelligibility and edification. In verse 20, he makes a possible association between

---

[75] Jerome Murphy-O'Connor, *1 Corinthians* (Wilmington, Del.: Glazier, 1979) 106. Perhaps the critical interpretive issue of the debate is the divine-human mix in the modern phenomenon of "speaking in tongues." We also need to allow that Paul may not blatantly condemn speaking in tongues here as part of his rhetorical strategy. See Smit, "Argument and Genre," 211–30.

[76] The term can mean an amateur or non-specialist. It can refer to non-members who participate in sacrifices (BAGD, 370). It is difficult to determine whether Paul is referring to "outsiders" who visit the community or those who are amateurs at speaking in tongues. More to the point is that whoever they were, they could not understand what the speakers in tongues meant.

speaking in tongues and being immature (cf. 3:1-4). Because the Corinthians emphasized speaking in tongues, they were immature in their thinking. Christian maturity is governed by love, not the display of certain spiritual gifts. He then begins to distance tongues from prophecy with a quotation from Isaiah 28:11-12 that stresses the nonsense of speaking in tongues for those who do not know its meaning. He gives the real danger with tongues in the community in verses 23-25: speaking in tongues fails to convict and lead to worship of God. Unbelievers will call tongues speakers mad or insane and be repelled from the message of the gospel (v. 23). Prophecy, on the other hand, confronts unbelievers with the power of God and leads to salvation (cf. 12:3).

In verses 26-33, Paul goes on to qualify the only positive use of tongues in the church. His logic is rather straightforward. For tongues to have any value in the church it must be interpreted. In other words, *tongues must become like prophecy and be intelligible to the community* in order that the community might be edified, convicted, or encouraged. If there is no interpreter, then tongues should not be spoken. Speaking in tongues must involve more than one person, while prophecy has no such restriction (v. 31). Possibly one of Paul's most stinging rebukes of the tongue speakers comes in verse 33: "For God is not one of disorder or confusion but of peace." Prophecy contributes to God's purpose of love in the community, while uninterpreted *glossolalia* leads only to the breakdown of community and witness.

Paul then shows in verses 34-36 that his discussion about tongues is meant to make some in the church uncomfortable. Apparently there was a group of women in the church who did not submit in love to the needs of the community and may have been exalting themselves by speaking out in the times of gathering. They were creating the same type of confusion evidenced by the tongues speakers.

Verse 37 begins the conclusion to Paul's argument. A conclusion in letters of this time served as an author's last opportunity to convince the readers to accept his or hers views. The conclusion often also gives the good and the bad alternatives.[77] Paul likewise states the two alternatives in his discussion in verse 39 by way of two infinitive clauses: seek the gift of prophesying, and use the gift of speaking in tongues in the right way. The bottom line is that all things should be done decently and in order (v. 40). The potential for division existed if the Corinthians accepted tongues speaking without qualification. Thus, Paul has subtly side-lined tongues speaking and left the better choice to be love in community.

---

[77] Quintilian, *Inst.* 4.1.28-30; 6.1.9-13.

❖ External Pressures

A question often asked of these chapters is, why does Paul deal with tongues speaking only in this letter and only with this church? This question is probably impossible to answer with certainty, but understanding a bit of the religious and cultural environment of these early believers gives us more of an appreciation for their struggles towards Christian maturity.

The tongues speaking by the Corinthians has parallels in the Hellenistic world of the first century, which may have influenced this practice by some in the church. One possible source for this practice may have been the Platonic view of prophecy. Plato distinguished two types of prophecy, the first being *mantic* prophecy, seen in divine possession and inspiration where the prophet serves as the mouthpiece for the divine. The mantic goes into a trance and becomes the passive instrument of the divine. The second type of prophecy is *interpretation,* where skill is acquired through practice, and the prophet remains in control of him or herself.[78] Losing one's mind is part of the process of divination. Cicero (c. 43 BCE) described this as a soul in frenzy without any reason.[79] Plutarch (c. 60–127 CE) wrote that the soul of the mantis expels sense or mind.[80]

Noteworthy similarities can also be seen between the Corinthians and the Hellenistic Jew, Philo. Philo was a Platonist who viewed prophecy in a way similar to Plato. He distinguished four types of ecstasy: frantic delirium, excessive consternation, tranquillity of the mind, and divinely inspired enthusiasm. The last type is the best for a person to have and involves the inspiration of God.[81] It is also the characteristic of the prophets in the scriptures of whom Moses is the chief example.[82] One of Philo's goals was prophetic ecstasy, according to the model of Moses, which came by inspiration of the Holy Spirit.[83] When the mind is "agitated and drawn into a frenzy by heavenly love," it can enter into prophetic ecstasy, leave the body, and discern the things of God.[84] Speech in this state stumbles about vainly, "being unable by common expressions to give a clear representation and understanding of the peculiar properties of the subjects with which it was dealing."[85] The mindless state of the Corinthians' speaking in tongues, as Paul describes it in 14:14-15, is similar to Philo's understanding of ecstatic prophecy.[86]

---

[78] Plato, *Tim.* 71E–72B; *Phdr.* 244A–B.
[79] Philo, *Her.* 1.2.4.
[80] Plutarch, *De def. or.* 432C.
[81] Philo, *Her.* 249.
[82] Philo, *Her.* 260–63.
[83] Philo, *Leg.* 3.100–104; *Migr.* 34–35; *Deus* 1–3; *Gig.* 47.
[84] Philo, *Her.* 69–70.
[85] Philo, *Her.* 72.
[86] For links between Philo and the Corinthians at this point, see Pearson, *Pneumatikos-*

Two nearby practices that may also have influenced the Corinthian believers were the Oracle at Delphi and the worship of Dionysus. One of the most famous places of prophetic activity in the Greco-Roman world was the Oracle at Delphi located less than 50 kilometres from Corinth. A priestess, known as the Pythia, was the medium of revelation at Delphi.[87] There is some debate as to what happened with the priestess, but apparently she descended into a pit and sat upon a tripod whereupon she entered into a trance or some form of ecstasy. Tatian wrote, "Some woman by drinking water gets into a frenzy, and loses her senses by the fumes of frankincense, and you say that she has the gift of prophecy."[88] The prophetess would speak "strange words" that she did not understand and that needed the interpretation of a priest who would then reveal the message to the inquirer.[89]

Connected with the activity at Delphi was the worship of Apollo. Apollo was an important deity in Corinth since a temple to him was located next to the Lechaeum Road, the main road through Corinth. Apollo was the god of prophecy and one of the most important gods in Greek epic. As the son of Zeus, Apollo interpreted the signs of his father.[90] He was the god of healing and the father of Asclepius (another god of healing), as well as the god of purification and cryptic oracles. Often disease was viewed as pollution that needed to be purified. Purification came through prescribed action made known through super-human knowledge gained from oracles. Indirect and veiled revelation belonged especially to Apollo who was called *Loxias* or Oblique.

A second source of prophetic activity in Corinth possibly known to the Christians there was the cult of Dionysus. A wooden image of Dionysus covered with gold was seen in the Agora (marketplace) of Corinth by Pausanias who lived in the second century CE.[91] Dionysus was the god of fertility, animal maleness, wine, drama, and ecstasy. He was believed to be present in raw animal flesh, the wine goblet, theatre performance, and ecstasy. Images show Dionysus always surrounded by frenzied male and female worshipers. The Dionysus cult was known for its ritual ecstasy. The worshipers often danced to music until in a frenzied state when they believed they became filled with the god and the god could speak and act through them.

These examples show some curious similarities. For example, the Corinthians' speaking in tongues is similar to Plato's first category of ecstatic

---

psychikos Terminology, 45–46.
[87] Euripides, *Ion* 42, 91, 321.
[88] Tatian, *Or. ad Graec.* 19.
[89] Plutarch, *Mor.* 406. For a different interpretation of the evidence, see F. J. Fontenrose, *The Delphic Oracle* (Berkeley: University of California Press, 1978) 10, 217–18.
[90] Walter Burkert, *Greek Religion* (Cambridge: Harvard University Press, 1985) 111.
[91] Pausanias, *Desc. of Gr.* 2.2.6.

prophecy. To counter this, Paul urges them to seek the gift of prophecy which uses the mind (14:14). Like the oracles at Delphi, tongues must be interpreted to have any meaning for others (v. 13). It is not beyond possibility that some of the women in the fellowship had visited the oracle and had been inspired by the prophetesses there. These women may have been a major cause of dissension in the church (vv. 34-36).[92] Could Paul have had in mind the mindless worship of Dionysus when he refers to tongues speaking? It is impossible to tell, but the similarities between the Corinthians and these cults are striking.[93]

Thus, Paul's letter implies that the Corinthians' speaking activities had been influenced to some degree by their Hellenistic environment. Philo or Platonism, the Oracle of Delphi, the Dionysiac cult, or any combination of these could have provided examples of prophetic inspiration to the Corinthians, not to exclude the possibility that some of the Corinthians may have even practiced such prophetic activity before they joined the church.[94] The assumption behind Paul's claim in 14:23 is that if outsiders visited the church and saw such activity, they would associate the Corinthians with the frenzy of the *manic* prophets of the time. Paul's aim is to point the Corinthians to the superior goal of "having the mind of Christ" and not modelling the world around them.

Conclusion

Paul's assessment of the Corinthians after receiving news of the church focuses upon a lack of holiness and love. Paul is concerned with the present behavior of the Corinthians since this behavior did not follow his standard of life in Christ. The Corinthians were being adversely effected by their environment and had not grown into spiritual maturity. Their acceptance of immorality in their midst demonstrated that they were no different from the unbelievers around them and were still fleshly and not spiritually mature (3:1-3). They were more concerned about individual exhibition than community edification. The problems resulting from speaking in tongues, overlooking some during the Lord's supper, violating the weaker brother or sister's conscience, and even disregard for traditional hair style all proved to Paul that the Corinthians had failed to see the implications of his teaching

---

[92] This is the thesis of Antoinette Clark Wire in *The Corinthian Women Prophets: A Reconstruction through Paul's Rhetoric* (Minneapolis: Fortress, 1990).

[93] See also Terrance Callan, "Prophecy and Ecstasy in Greco-Roman Religion and in 1 Corinthians," *NovT* 27 (1985) 125–40; Christopher Forbes, "Early Christian Inspired Speech and Hellenistic Popular Religion," *NovT* 28 (1986) 257–70.

[94] See further H. W. House, "Tongues and the Mystery Religions of Corinth," *BSac* 140 (1983) 134–50.

and preaching and to grow into mature believers in fellowship with Christ. Paul's judgment of the situation led to a conflict of ideology between them and him. He attempts to resolve this conflict by urging them to accept his interpretation of spirituality. By doing this, they could heal the divisive attitudes in the church and live as redeemed people in an unholy culture. They could either continue in the foolish ways of the world or adhere to the way of the cross (1:18).

6

Paul's Boundaries of Holiness and Love

PAUL attempts to persuade the Corinthians to erect boundaries between themselves and their environment that could lead to healing the fractured nature of their fellowship and resolve their differences with him. The conflict in Corinth lay in the wrong place. The Corinthians should have been uncomfortable about the activities of the immoral "brother" in their midst, but instead, were accepting him and his behavior. They were in conflict with Paul's view of morality but not with the "brother's" actions. Furthermore, the friction between the weak and strong over eating idol food should not have existed. Paul addresses those who could change the situation and who had the power of conscience to forego their freedom of eating such food. The strong could resolve this difference by following Paul's example of love and concern. The basic problem with the Corinthians was that they failed to grow into maturity according to Paul's standards of holiness and love. This lack of maturity could eventually lead to the breakdown of the community and to certain individuals falling back into sin.

Paul's relationship with this church was characterized by a basic conflict between his own christologically informed ethic and the Corinthians' lack of conformity to this ideal. If they would conform to Paul's ways, conflict with him could be resolved and conflict with the world would result. To shift the difference to where it should lie, Paul attempts to set up boundaries of holiness and love for the community that coincide with his view of the paradox of the divine mystery. Without these boundaries in place, the Corinthian church would not survive long as an organization.[1]

---

[1] Meeks writes, "In order to persist, a social organization must have boundaries, must maintain structural stability as well as flexibility, and must create a unique culture" (*First Urban Christians*, 84).

The Boundary of Holiness

Paul's Purity and the Corinthians' Dirt

Jerome Neyrey's cultural reading of Paul's letters again offers a useful method for delineating the friction between Paul and the Corinthians. Neyrey utilizes the anthropological methods of Mary Douglas to explore the boundaries that Paul develops in his letters. Paul attempts to persuade the Corinthians to come over to his "map" by aligning with the divine paradox of the cross-event. He attempts to create a new social order for the Corinthians based on his symbolic universe by putting everything in its proper place.

The term "purity" describes this effort to put things in their proper place. According to Neyrey, it is the "term used to describe the patterns of order and the system of labeling and classification."[2] Various terms can be used including pure/polluted, clean/unclean, and holy/profane. Neyrey writes, "In general, an object or action is pure (or clean, holy) when it conforms to the specific cultural norms that make up the symbolic system of a particular social group."[3] That which is pure is in its place; that which is polluted is out of place in the particular symbolic universe. This corresponds to the label "dirt" in the anthropology of Mary Douglas.[4] What constitutes dirt is group specific and varies from context to context. Authority and discipline help a less structured group adhere to social norms of purity.

Paul and the Corinthians share the same starting point of faith in Christ but express this faith through different ethics. A point of conflict between the maps of Paul and the Corinthians appears with the concern over personal and community purity. Paul urges the Corinthians to adhere to his concept of purity because it is the ideal of existing in the sphere of Christ. He is primarily concerned in 5:1—11:1 with purity of the body through avoidance of sexual immorality (*porneia*) and idol food (*eidōlolatria*). Such purity would lead to holy individuals and a community fit to be filled with the presence of the Holy Spirit.

According to Mary Douglas, the human body represents the social body on a small scale through boundaries (defense of the body), structure (the relationship of body parts), and margins (entrance, exits, bodily exuviae). In order to control a group, one must control the bodies of the individuals in that group. Douglas writes, "Consequently I now advance the hypothesis that bodily control is an expression of social control—abandonment of bodily control in ritual responds to the requirements of a social experience which is

---

[2] Neyrey, *Paul in Other Words*, 23.
[3] Ibid.
[4] Mary Douglas, *Purity and Danger* (London: Routledge and Kegan Paul, 1966) 35, 40.

being expressed."[5] Paul attempts to define group boundaries concerning the standard of holiness by distinguishing behavior of those on the outside from those on the inside. Dirt for Paul is everything that is not consistent with the standard of the gospel. By keeping dirt out of the body on the individual level and subsequently on the corporate level, the Corinthians would be able to keep themselves pure and establish distinct group boundaries. Michael Newton comments, "Paul's concern is with the unity of the Church and it is to that end, within the Church, that he makes use of the concept of purity."[6]

Paul uses insider/outsider language to make the Corinthians aware of group boundaries. Those on the outside of the boundary are stigmatized in order to develop group identity and to resocialize individuals.[7] Wayne Meeks writes, "The insider/outsider language invariably implies a negative perception of the outside society, even when the immediate function of the dualistic expressions is to reinforce the internal ordering of the group."[8] The following chart sets in contrast some of Paul's dualistic language and will aid in understanding his emphasis on community holiness. Not every term has its opposite in the text, therefore, the parallelism is incomplete.

Outside	Inside
Chapter 5	
Gentiles (1)	Paul
Satan (5)	
Old leaven (7)	New leaven (7)
Immoral, greedy, robbers, idolaters, revilers, drunkards, robbers (9-11)	
Outsiders (12)	
Immoral "brother" potentially (13)	
Chapter 6	
Unrighteous (1, 9)	Saints (2)
World (2)	
Those despised by the church (4)	

---

[5] Mary Douglas, *Natural Symbols: Explorations in Cosmology* (New York: Pantheon, 1982) quoted by Neyrey, *Paul in Other Words*, 105.
[6] Michael Newton, *The Concept of Purity at Qumran and in the Letters of Paul* (SNTSMS 53; Cambridge: Cambridge University Press, 1985) 101.
[7] Meeks, *First Urban Christians*, 86.
[8] Ibid., 95.

Wrong and defraud (7-8)
Adulterers, greedy (9-10; cf. 5:9-11)   Washed, sanctified, justified (11)
Prostitute (15-16)   Members of Christ (15)
Sin in the body (18)   Temple of the Holy Spirit (19)

Chapter 7
Sexual Immorality (2)   Prayer and self-control (5)
Inflamed passion (9)   Marriage (9)
Unbelieving spouse (12)
Unclean (14)   Sanctified (14)
Unbeliever (15)   Brother or sister (15)
                                        Shortened time and
                                        distance from the world (29)
Anxiety with Life (30-31)   Free from anxiety about
                                        life (32-34)
Divided loyalties (33-34)   Undivided loyalties (35)

Chapter 8
Knowledge (1)   Love (1)
Many gods and lords (5)   One God and one Lord (6)

Chapter 9
Use of freedom (1-14)   Setting aside personal
                                        freedom through
                                        discipline and flexibility (15-27)

Chapter 10
Disobedient, seekers of evil,   "We" the obedient (8, 9)
idolaters, immoral, grumblers (5-10)
Participation in idols (14, 21)   Participation in Christ (16-17, 21)
Unbelievers (27)

Paul compares the Corinthians' actions with the outside world since the ways of the "outside" were a problem for the Corinthians. The language he uses is reminiscent of the two categories in 1:18: "those who are perishing and us who are being saved." He does not want them to leave their world—for that would be impossible—but to be different from their world (5:10). By personal and group discipline they could erect boundaries that would lead to the purity of the community. The letter implies that they were confused about where the boundary lines should be drawn. He uses group pressure to move those on the fringe either outside the boundary (the immoral "brother") or inside (the so-called "strong" of the community). The individual must move away from everything considered dirt. This would lead to stronger social control and group unity.

Developing Group Boundaries

Paul differs with the Corinthians over matters of the physical body of the individual and the corporate body of the community. His view about the physical body can be seen in his letter to the Romans. He writes that the physical body can be controlled either by sin or by the Holy Spirit. How one lives in the body shows to what or to whom one gives allegiance. The person who lives in the sphere of Christ will live a life in submission to the ways of the Spirit (Rom 6:12-13; 8:11). Paul's argument is similar in 1 Corinthians. The Corinthians' physical body showed where their allegiance laid. Living within the boundaries of the divine mystery through submission to the paradigm of the cross would lead them to relationship with God and one another, and also keep impurity from entering the corporate body of the church. This was to be an exclusive commitment. Meeks writes, "For Paul and his co-workers, the corollary of unity in the body of Christ is strict exclusion from all other religious connections. That is, group solidarity entails strong boundaries."[9]

According to Douglas, many ancient religions developed rules for ritual purity in order to keep negative forces from keeping them from communing with God. It was believed that pollution kept people from God. To keep the community pure, rules were developed to govern the actions of the individual's body. Douglas writes,

> When rituals express anxiety about the body's orifices the sociological counterpart of this anxiety is a care to protect the political and cultural unity of a minority group. The Israelites were always in their history a hard-pressed minority. In their beliefs all the bodily issues were polluting, blood, pus, excreta, semen, etc. The threatened boundaries of their body politic would be well mirrored in their care for the integrity, unity and purity of the physical body.[10]

According to Douglas' theory, control of the social body can be accomplished by controlling the bodies of individuals. Paul may have consciously or intuitively realized this since he sought to maintain strict boundaries for the bodies of individuals. Stephen C. Barton comments that Paul's instructions "have to do with how individual physical bodies are to represent and grow

---
[9] Ibid., 159.
[10] Douglas, *Purity and Danger*, 124.

together in an identifiable social body and how that social body (the church) is to conduct itself as the body of the crucified and risen Christ in the city of Corinth."[11] Douglas has also developed a model that explores the control or lack of control of the individual within a "group" (Douglas' term for the pressure of the corporate body) using the classifications of "weak" and "strong." In Neyrey's summary of Douglas, a strong "group" indicates "a high degree of pressure to conform to group norms as well as a strong degree of pressure for order and control." With a strong "group," the body is disciplined and strongly controlled, and group values dominate. A weak "group" shows "a low degree of pressure to conform to societal norms." There is little discipline, and bodily orifices are porous.[12]

Neyrey distinguishes two views on the physical body present in Corinth. First is Paul's view which strives for strong group control. Neyrey writes,

> It is a bounded system, to be strongly controlled; it is a pure or holy body and so must guard its orifices. Its concern for order and clarity make it fear unconsciousness or loss of control; it takes a negative view of spirit possession. It is a regulated and harmonious body whose parts are clearly differentiated and co-ordinated for the good of the whole body. No individual member is allowed to disrupt the body's disciplined functioning.

The second view is that of the so-called Corinthian strong:

> Fearing no pollutants around the body, they see no need for control of the bodily orifices. Accordingly, the bodily boundaries are porous. Porosity is accompanied by celebration of freedom of movement and spontaneity. Trances and spirit possession are looked upon favorably.[13]

Although the strong were in the position of strength to regulate their own actions, they had a weak group boundary.

A third segment not presented by Neyrey is that of the weak of the community who had a strong group boundary that they could not cross without

---

[11] Stephen C. Barton, "Historical Criticism and Social-Scientific Perspectives in New Testament Study," in *Hearing the New Testament*, ed. Joel B. Green (Grand Rapids: Eerdmans, 1995) 79.

[12] Jerome H. Neyrey, "Body Language in 1 Corinthians: The Use of Anthropological Models for Understanding Paul and His Opponents," in *Social-Scientific Criticism of the New Testament and Its Social World*, ed. John H. Elliott, *Semeia* 35 (1986) 132. Douglas also includes the variable called "grid" which shows how the individual assents to the social patterns of the group. For further discussion, see Robert A. Atkins Jr., *Egalitarian Community: Ethnography and Exegesis* (Tuscaloosa: University of Alabama Press, 1991).

[13] Neyrey, *Paul in Other Words*, 116.

violating the boundary of their conscience.[14] Unlike Paul, they did not have the power (*exousia*) to overcome the influences of their pagan environment—outside of fellowship with Christ—and so had to adhere to strict eating habits in order to avoid sin. Paul invites all groups to move to the higher plane of love and concern for the entire community by adhering to his system or map. The strong would then recognize the need for group boundaries and the weak would rise above the symbolism involved in eating food offered to idols.

Paul's Better Alternative

Paul attempts to provide a better alternative to the Corinthians by exhorting them to have more control of their bodies. Their lack of bodily control of genital orifices appears in the disregard of *porneia* in chapters 5–7. That the community boasted and tolerated the presence of immorality demonstrates to Paul its lack of a strong group boundary. Paul, however, wants a strong boundary of purity to be upheld by the purging of the pollution of sin. By expelling the immoral "brother" and accepting Paul's ethic, the community could be preserved. Paul sees the potential for the bodies of individual believers to be holy since they are intended for fellowship with Christ (6:13) and can serve as the temple of the Holy Spirit (6:19). Paul develops rules that govern the orifices of the body so that nothing impure crosses these boundaries. Sexual sins threaten the holiness of the inside of the body because they cross that bodily border. The Corinthians showed little control of the body by allowing their freedom in Christ to lead to abandonment or disregard for certain morals. Paul wants them to guard the orifices of their mouths and genitals, and by this, protect the interior of their bodies from pollution.[15]

Paul's concern with sexual orifices appears in chapter 7 as he discusses issues related to marriage. The optimum position for him is not to allow anything to cross the genital orifices except in marriage, and especially not by immoral behavior, because such activity limits total devotion to Christ. But Paul concedes to marriage as the option for avoiding the temptation of immorality. The key is not to cross the boundary of bodily holiness but to be self-controlled (7:5). Divorce is unacceptable because it tears apart a holy unity.[16] Celibates or virgins are concerned with how to be holy in body and spirit, in other words, their concern is with strong, bodily boundaries. But the married are concerned with worldly affairs, that is, they have weak bodily boundary because of their limited loyalty (vv. 32-34). According to Dunn, this chapter shows relationships in transition towards a new loyalty to

---

[14] Cf. Meeks, *First Urban Christians*, 98.
[15] Neyrey, "Body Language," 139–40.
[16] Ibid., 140–42.

Christ where "the new relationships of church were cutting across the more established relationships of the wider society (in a way analogous to 6:1-8) and causing friction and uncertainty as to role and responsibility for which conventional counsel was inadequate."[17] Paul guides this community formation by helping the Corinthians establish boundaries of purity.

The Boundary of Love

Paul also builds a boundary of love around the Corinthians. Love defines the community as distinct from its environment, but it is much more the characteristic of those within the boundary of holiness. In chapters 5–7 Paul is concerned with issues *outside* the community and the differences between those "inside" and "outside" the church. In chapters 8–14 he moves on to define what should happen *inside* the community, yet without disregarding the community's relationship with those outside the church (14:23-25).[18] He confronts the same underlying problems in chapters 8–14 as he does elsewhere in the letter. The surface problems of spiritual enthusiasm and individualism without regard for others were evident in their disregard for the weaker brothers and sisters, ignoring customs, overlooking some during the Lord's supper, and speaking in tongues. The deeper problem was simply a lack of love for others. The Corinthians' individualistic spirituality could be seen in their defective fellowship (*koinōnia*). The best way they could prove their spirituality was by their fellowship of love.[19]

Paul turns his attention to the orifice of the mouth in chapters 8–10 with issues over food sacrificed to idols in an effort to establish love as the norm for those within the boundary of holiness. The mouth of the individual determines to a significant degree the holy integrity of the fellowship. Neyrey comments, "If what goes in is good, it renders the body holy and does not contaminate; so it is prescribed. But if what is ingested is corrupting, like leaven, it pollutes the holy inside of the body, and so it is proscribed."[20] Paul presents both the Corinthian "weak" and "strong" a choice by way of general principle: one can eat the holy food of the Lord or the contaminated food of idols/demons (10:15-20). The choice is really between the holy and the profane (v. 21). The solution to impurity is exclusive communion with Christ, which is also the test of whether or not someone is polluted. Neyrey further states, "Sharing the body and blood of Christ means *koinōnia* with the holy Lord; and this one body is holy. But sharing the cup and table with demons means *koinōnia* with an unholy demon; this union is polluting. Paul's meta-

---

[17] Dunn, *1 Corinthians*, 55.
[18] This is also Mitchell's approach to dividing the text (*Rhetoric of Reconciliation*, 152).
[19] Bo Frid, "Structure and Argumentation in 1 Cor 12," *SEÅ* 60 (1995) 95.
[20] Neyrey, *Paul in Other Words*, 121.

phor manifests the same analogy."[21] For the strong, this meant seeking the good of the weak brother or sister who might be violated through eating idol food (v. 24). For the weak, this meant developing their conscience by recognizing the superiority of the one God and one Lord (v. 25). The meeting place for both is participation in the divine mystery through eating the Lord's supper together in unity and love.

The Corinthians as a community of individuals did not control the orifices of their mouths very carefully. The "strong" had a freedom, based on their claimed knowledge, that caused them not to control what went in their mouths. Their low, personal boundaries threatened the boundary of the community. Neyrey assesses, "No holiness, no group concerns, no regulations of freedom colors their thinking."[22] Paul develops rules to set up clear boundaries to protect the holiness of the community. He builds his ethic of freedom not upon knowledge leading to a lack of rules but upon love that self-imposes rules upon the self for the sake of the community (8:1; 10:23). The "weak" were spiritually immature because they had not recognized that there is only one God and one Lord. They had not made a radical break from their past involvement in idolatry. Paul invites them to rise above their environment by living according to a new paradigm of exclusive loyalty to Christ.

A boundary of love is also Paul's answer to the divisive nature of the Corinthians' times of gathering. The disregard of some in the church during the Lord's Supper harmed unity by setting up barriers between themselves and others, and between themselves and Christ (11:20-22; cf. 10:16-17). There should be no barriers between members of Christ's body; rather, love should be the bond of unity between these various parts (12:27, 31b). The Corinthians claimed to be spiritual (*pneumatikos*) based on their display of spiritual gifts (*charismata*). Paul changes the focus of their spirituality and puts it through the filter of love.

Love is the ultimate paradigm for relationship within community and will also be the mark of the age to come (13:10-12). Paul wants the Corinthians to apply this future ethic in their present community since they had been redeemed and freed from the powers of this world. They were to live not according to an ethic found in this world or this age but one characteristic of the age to come when Christ will conquer everything once and for all (15:24-28). Paul wants them to realize that they had been washed from the corruptions of sin. He attempts to resocialize them in light of the new reality in Christ. He tries to create a new community based on an ethic of holiness and love by placing boundaries around the community and by enhancing fellowship within the community. The Corinthians needed to appropriate

---

[21] Ibid., 122.
[22] Ibid., 126.

on an individual and corporate level the new reality brought by the event of the divine mystery in Christ. They could conform their ideology to Paul's by aligning themselves with his definition of purity. They could not leave the world (5:10), but their community boundary could be clarified. Vincent L. Wimbush comments, "The world was affirmed by Paul as the *sphere* of Christian existence . . . but the world was rejected by him as a *source* of value and identity."[23]

---

[23] Vincent L. Wimbush, "The Ascetic Impulse in Ancient Christianity," *ThTo* 50 (1993) 427.

7

The Essential Paradigm Shift

PAUL creates conflict with the Corinthians in order to convince them to accept his own view of spirituality. He builds his case by demonstrating that their behavior revealed that they were following the ways of the world by living as "fleshly" people (*sarkikoi*, 3:1-3). They had not grown in their fellowship with Christ by allowing the Spirit of holiness to teach them the ways of Christ. Their individual and group boundaries were fluid and not fixed, leading to problems of immorality and lack of love. Paul prompts them on to spiritual maturity through deeper fellowship with Christ. Paul's own example of love, his attempts at shaming the Corinthians for their own lack of love, and the indicative of the divine mystery serve as the basis for his paraenesis.

Paul's Example of Ethical Freedom Bound by Love

Paul builds his ethic upon the kerygma of the divine mystery described in 1:18-2:16. Throughout the letter, he gives the Corinthians practical ways to avoid being *sarkikoi* and how to be *pneumatikoi* in Christ. But this ethic of freedom is conditioned with the responsibility of love. Paul illustrates this love by his willingness to forego his rights (*exousia*) as an apostle. He lays aside these rights in order to demonstrate the strength resident in the divine paradox of Christ as the wisdom of God (9:1). By refusing to patronize the Corinthians for his support, Paul shows his identification with the humiliation of the crucified Christ.[1] Thus, he contends, as Troels Engberg-Pedersen writes, that "the gospel is one of love, of giving up oneself for others and of willing that and willing it alone. Therefore, 'believing' the gospel ('subscribing' to it) is a matter of *living* in a certain way."[2] Paul offers himself as me-

---

[1] Richard A. Horsley, "1 Corinthians: A Case Study of Paul's Assembly as an Alternative Society," in *Paul and Empire: Religion and Power in Roman Imperial Society*, ed. Richard A. Horsley (Harrisburg, Pa.: Trinity, 1997) 250.
[2] Troels Engberg-Pedersen, "The Gospel and Social Practice According to 1 Corinthians,"

diator and example of the ethic of Christ. He uses scripture throughout his argument to support his views of morality, but more significantly, he appeals to his own life and teaching as authoritative for conduct.

His authority to serve as an example comes in his modeling of Christ by identifying with the weakness and foolishness of the cross (4:16) and having the mind of Christ (2:16). In 5:3-5 he uses his full authority as ambassador of Christ to pass judgment on the immorality infiltrating the church. His presence in Corinth by "spirit" or the "Spirit" (5:3) allows him to command the church to cast the immoral "brother" out of the fellowship. Furthermore, his statement in 6:7 about being wronged rather than taking other believers to court recalls his suffering described in 4:12-13 and serves in the context as an invitation to suffer willingly in order to save the integrity of the church. In 7:7 he provides another example of personal abstinence when he says, "I wish all were like I am," that is, that all could be celibate and free to serve the Lord unhindered. He restates the basis of his charismatic authority in 7:40: "And I too think that I have the Spirit of God."

Paul's self-example in chapter 9 is a significant rhetorical tool for motivating the Corinthians to accept his ideology. The primary purpose of the digression in chapter 9 is to provide an example of his theological and ethical foundation of imitating Christ (cf. 11:1).[3] He establishes his *ethos* in this section by demonstrating that his example models the divine mystery of the cross.[4] He uses sixteen rhetorical questions to advance his argument in this chapter. He begins with a series of four questions, all of which expect positive answers. The obvious answers to his questions bring out his points: of course he is free, an apostle who has seen the Lord, and the fact of the existence of the Corinthian church verifies this (vv. 1-2). The shift to the first person singular in verses 1 and 15 guides the argument until the inclusion of and ap-

---

NTS 33 (1987) 583.

[3] Wendell Willis, "An Apostolic Apologia? The Form and Function of 1 Corinthians 9," *JSNT* 24 (1985) 33–48; David M. Stanley, "'Become Imitators of Me': the Pauline Conception of Apostolic Tradition," *Bib* 40 (1959) 874. A digression in an argument can serve to the advantage of the speaker. According to Quintillian, "this form of digression can be advantageously appended . . . . Indeed such a practice confers great distinction and adornment on a speech, but only if the digression fits in well with the rest of the speech and follows naturally on what has preceded, not if it is thrust in like a wedge parting what should naturally come together" (Quintillian, *Inst.* 4.3.4).

[4] George Lyons argues that Paul's primary purpose in his autobiographical statements is to establish his *ethos*. Lyons writes, "Paul's rhetorical approach, not his opponents' reproaches, is responsible for the form in which he presents his 'autobiography'" (George Lyons, *Pauline Autobiography: Toward a New Understanding*, SBLDS 73 [Atlanta: Scholars, 1985] 3). This assessment holds true at least for 1 Corinthians 9. Paul's rhetoric here is deliberative but cloaked in forensic terms. He demonstrates his position of innocence as apostle only to refute it for the sake of the gospel.

plication to the Corinthians in verse 24. He has two topics in mind: freedom (*eleutheros*, v. 1) and "authority" or "power" (*exousia*, v. 4). His defense of his authority, which is based on his vision of the risen Jesus, directly influences what he does with his freedom, and he expects the Corinthians to respond in the same way. He chooses to curtail a number of rights in order to clarify what he means by true freedom. In verses 4-14 he defends his rights as an apostle only to refute them in verses 12b and 15. He accomplishes his defense by the use of arguments from analogy that focus on the right of support for labor in ministry. The rhetorical power of his argument comes in his association with other apostles who have the right to receive compensation for their labors in ministry (vv. 4-6). The God-given right for compensation is supported through analogies from secular employment (soldier, vinedresser, shepherd, v. 7), scripture (oxen in Deut 25:4, vv. 8-9), and religious life (priests, v. 13).

Paul restates his ethical principle in verse 12b in terms of his apostolic ministry: "But we have not made use of this authority (*exousia*), but endure all things in order that we might not give any hindrance to the gospel of Christ." The only restraint or control upon Paul's *exousia* is the proclamation of the gospel. Like his call for imitation in 4:16, here he again aligns himself with the divine paradox by forfeiting his God-appointed rights of support in ministry. This is a rather broad ethical statement, which Paul may have realized, so he further explains in verses 15-18 what he means. He personalizes the principle in verse 15 by shifting again to the first person singular and then gives the motivation for his principle in verses 16-18 by stating that the only compensation he wants for being an apostle is to preach without hindering the gospel. It is a significant advance in the argument when he attaches his *exousia* with the gospel in verse 18 because by doing this, he redefines *exousia* in terms of the paradox of the divine mystery. In other words, he puts his personal rights and freedoms beyond the plane of the wisdom and strength of the world and onto the peak of divine wisdom and strength.

Paul next gives the method by which he fulfills his motivation. This method can be divided into three parts. First, he accommodates himself to his context by becoming all things to all people in order to win them to Christ (vv. 19-22). His real freedom comes with the ability *not* to choose to use his right. Second, he makes sure that he does not hinder the gospel by what he does (v. 23). He rises above issues of patronage and demonstrates that the true power of the divine paradox comes in the freedom to be used without attachments of obligation. Finally, he does all of this in order to share in the fellowship of the gospel. He associates himself with the weakness and foolishness of the cross in order to experience the power and wisdom of God. The outcome of this will be that he receives an eternal reward described in verse 25 as an "imperishable wreath."

Paul's final rhetorical move in this chapter is to provide an illustration of his ethical motivation taken from the games with direct application to the Corinthians. The illustration of the athlete in training adds weight to his example, draws the Corinthians into the discussion, and serves as a *conclusio* to his example. To win the reward, Paul must use self-discipline and self-sacrifice by voluntarily curtailing his rights and liberties. He invites the Corinthians to share his motivation by using an imperative in verse 24: "Therefore, *run* in order that you might receive [the prize]." This imperative stands out as the only command in the entire chapter. The Corinthians may have had a certain amount of moral authority, but they should also have refuted it for the sake of the weaker brother or sister and for the sake of community unity. Verse 26 is another radical shift to the first person singular as Paul identifies himself as a runner in this race. He is moving towards his significant imperative in 11:1, "Imitate me as I imitate Christ." The ultimate motivation of an ethic consistent with the divine mystery is to receive an eternal reward which is fellowship with Christ (Phil 3:12-14).

The imperative in 11:1 is based on the paradigm of the cross-event and is the summary of Paul's efforts at giving a self-example of an ethic of love.[5] According to Ernest Best, when Paul calls for imitation of Christ, he is providing a control over imitating himself.[6] He is concerned about a specific area of imitation. He does not command the Corinthians to imitate him in every way, for example, in his celibacy.[7] Rather, the primary way he imitates Christ is by putting his own wishes beneath those of others. Victor Paul Furnish comments that Paul does not single out any specific attributes of the earthly Jesus. "Rather, it seems always to be the humble, giving, obedient *love* of the crucified and resurrected Lord to which the final appeal is made."[8] This appeal to love forms the foundation of Paul's ethic.

In addition, Paul may be subtly calling for imitation of himself in 13:1 when he changes again to the first person singular. Carl R. Holladay points out the similarities between chapters 13 and 9 and contends that Paul uses the first person singular in chapter 13 to offer himself as an example of love. In chapter 9, "Paul adduces himself as the concrete paradigm of voluntary, responsible self-restraint for the self-indulgent Corinthians."[9] He then uses this same apostolic paradigm in chapter 13 in the context of worship to show

---

[5] Paul appeals a number of times in his second major argument to the paradigm of the cross-event, cf. 5:7; 6:11, 20; 7:23; 8:11; 9:12-23; 10:16.
[6] Best, *Paul and His Converts*, 59.
[7] Ibid., 65.
[8] Furnish, *Theology and Ethics in Paul*, 223.
[9] Carl R. Holladay, "1 Corinthians 13: Paul as Apostolic Paradigm," in *Greeks, Romans, and Christians: Essays in Honor of Abraham J. Malherbe*, ed. David L. Balch et al. (Minneapolis: Fortress, 1990) 84.

the blameworthiness of the behavior of the Corinthians. Holladay argues that behind 13:1-3 can be discerned Paul's own self-presentation. Of the seven attributes of the rhetorical "I" given in the passage, all of them can be attributed to Paul: Paul spoke in "tongues" (14:18), functioned as a prophet (2:2-16; 7:40; 14:6; Gal 1:15-16), knew mysteries (1 Cor 2:1, 7),[10] had knowledge especially of the ways of God (2:12, 16), could perform miracles (2 Cor 12:12; Rom 15:19; cf. Acts 14:3; 16: 16-24; 19:11; 28:3-6), and gave up himself for Christ (2 Cor 4:7-15).[11]

Love could heal the fractious nature of the Corinthians' behavior and could create unity within the God-ordained diversity in the church. The Corinthians may have wanted to be "something"—they may have been trying to be "spiritual" but had been going about it in the wrong way. Since they acted in the fellowship without love, they could be called "nothing" like Paul (the "I") calls himself in 13:1-3. Not all the Corinthians may have had problems with tongues and prophecy (ch. 14), but Paul's solution for the church is inclusive of all in the community. All had been given gifts by the Spirit (12:7), therefore, all must love or these gifts remained useless for the community. Paul models for them how not to seek one's own good but to seek the good of the neighbor, and he expects them to follow his example (10:23; 11:1). By providing this example he tries to foster and regulate community life.[12]

Paul's Appeal to Shame and Honor

A second means by which Paul attempts to motivate the Corinthians to accept his position is by creating moments for them to feel ashamed because of their conduct in order to challenge them to erect boundaries of holiness and love around the church. He gives a new definition to honor in the midst of a society where honor and shame were some of the most significant social forces. There was substantial social pressure for people to conform to social norms, standards, or concepts within a particular group or location. A person of position or power could cause shame in order to motivate and persuade others to accept his or her views.[13] Shame resulted when a person or group failed to meet the test of honor, and it was to be avoided at great cost. Paul assesses the Corinthians as immature and as living according to the paradigm of the world (i.e., being *sarkikos*, 3:1) in order to shame them into accepting his

---

[10] According to Barrett, "mystery" should not have any specific meaning attached to it (*First Corinthians*, 301).
[11] Holladay, "1 Corinthians 13," 89-91. See also Witherington, *Conflict and Community*, 268.
[12] Helmut Koester, *Introduction to the New Testament* (Philadelphia: Fortress, 1982) 2.110.
[13] Malina, "'Religion' in the World of Paul," 98.

own position of honor. As Ben Witherington states, Paul offers them "a *counter*culture with a set of values often at odds with that of the larger society."[14]

The position of shame for Paul exists outside the boundary of holiness. The fact that he identifies some of the actions of the Corinthians with those of the "outsiders" should have caused the Corinthians to feel ashamed. For example, by tolerating immorality in their midst, they were no different than "this world" (5:9-11). That they brought lawsuits against other believers as if the "church" had no impact on relationships should have made them feel ashamed (6:5). Moreover, they acted as if their washing, sanctification, and justification made little difference in their morality (6:11). Paul gives himself as an example in chapter 9 in order to show the "strong" that their own position of superiority over the weaker sister or brother was inconsistent not only with his view but also with that of Christ (11:1). Paul's paradigm leads to honor before God because it is based on love which edifies community and not knowledge which erodes (8:1). In interaction with others, Paul takes a position of weakness, much as he did in chapter 4, not to identify with people of lower status, the "weak brother," but because this position is consistent with the paradox of the divine mystery (cf. 11:29).[15] It is the starting point of an ethic of love. He possesses a knowledge even superior to the Corinthian strong because his knowledge is based upon love for God and love for the brother and sister. The place to begin to receive this knowledge is at the Lord's table where all are unified.

Paul uses his position of power which comes in association with the example of Christ to coerce the Corinthians to conform to his standard of honor, but he does this ironically by reversing common perceptions of power, gender, and social status. Believers can find a common ground in Christ and become a unified community where the typical positions of shame—poor, female, and slave—are put on a par with positions of honor—rich, male, and free. The same is true about the valued, more visible spiritual gifts—tongues and prophecy. Paul offers the paradigm of love as the highest position of honor. He uses the Corinthians' acceptance of shame as a motivational force to pressure them to assume his position of honor.[16] Although being in Christ abolishes some distinctions (cf. Gal 3:28), Paul cannot completely get around the social norms of honor and shame concerning propriety at worship. Even though men and women are mutually dependent "in the Lord" (11:8-9, 11-12), they are distinct, and this distinction should be obvious while praying or

---

[14] Witherington, *Conflict and Community*, 155.
[15] Cf. Dale B. Martin, *Slavery as Salvation: The Metaphor of Slavery in Pauline Christianity* (New Haven: Yale University Press, 1990) 123.
[16] Peter Marshall, *Enmity in Corinth: Social Conventions in Paul's Relations with the Corinthians*, WUNT 2/23 (Tübingen: Mohr/Siebeck, 1987) 389–95.

prophesying. A woman "dishonors" or shames her head (the man), by looking like a man while at worship, and the same can be said about a man who looks like a woman (vv. 4-7).

Paul also attempts to shame the Corinthians in 11:17-34 because some in the community were overlooked during the Lord's supper. He can find nothing for which to "praise" them in their eating of the meal (vv. 17, 22). The problem was a lack of concern by some who overindulged while others went hungry.[17] This individualism and factionalism resulted in a breakdown in community (vv. 18, 20). The tradition of the Lord's supper given in 11:23-26 challenges the behavior of the Corinthians and offers them the opportunity to live according to this paradigm of honor. If those who had gorged themselves would assume a weaker position and share with those who had not eaten yet, then they could avoid judgment and the outcome would be no more factions in the church. The honorable thing to do would be to love and not to be self-seeking or rude (13:5).

Paul also alters typical understandings of power and prestige in chapter 12. Speaking in tongues represented a position of power for the Corinthians and a possible source for boasting. Those who spoke in tongues might think of themselves as the outwardly "presentable" parts of the body of Christ since tongues is a gift all can see (12:23). Paul takes this "treasured" gift of the Corinthians and puts it last in his map of spiritual gifts, thereby taking it from a position of honor to one that could, by analogy, be considered shameful.[18] He reverses this position of power and wants the Corinthians to give more honor to the "unpresentable" parts of the church. The outwardly "honorable" gifts of tongues, prophecy, knowledge, faith, and even martyrdom (13:1-3) count as nothing without love. The position of honor for Paul is to defer these outward gifts to other gifts so that the effect upon the church is edification and not stratification.

This same thought is carried over into 13:1-3 where Paul puts himself in the position of honor by his willingness to allow love to take precedence over all the great or honorable gifts that the Corinthians cherished. Love supersedes all other gifts and will be the mark of the age to come. The immaturity of the Corinthians was evidenced by their lack of love. Paul realizes that we can love only in part in this life, but that is not to set aside the goal (v. 12, cf. Phil 3:12-14).

In chapter 14, Paul continues to seek to shame the Corinthians for their spiritual immaturity by associating speaking in tongues with unintelligible communication that does not edify the church but only the individual.

---

[17] Whether or not this was due to social or economic stratification as Theissen argues is not directly relevant to the purpose of this study (*Social Setting*, 145–74).
[18] Neyrey, *Paul in Other Words*, 38–39.

Prophecy builds up community, but tongues builds up the individual; prophecy creates unity, but tongues creates alienation.[19] By assigning tongues a lesser role than prophecy and by qualifying the necessity for interpretation, Paul puts tongues on the sideline of the life of the church.[20] He takes this highly acclaimed, individualistic gift of the Corinthians and places it beneath prophecy which meets the test of community edification. Prophecy, like love, is useful to everyone in the church. Paul associates prophecy with love and puts tongues outside of love. Love is the sign of being in Christ, and prophecy is the means by which the existence in Christ is disclosed to both believers and unbelievers.

Paul gives the highest place of honor to Christ and the attributes Christ showed on the cross. Those who wish also to be honored in Paul's scheme should emulate Christ. The Corinthians should have been ashamed for their behavior contrary to the cross. Honor comes from love and unity in the community; shame results from division and lack of concern for others. The Corinthians acted as if the cross made no difference in the way they lived. Paul, however, expects love to be the fruit that comes from lives submitted to the lordship of Christ (Gal 5:22). His letter is all about change and conformity to this pattern of life which he himself exemplifies. He as patron of the divine mystery (2:1, 7; 4:1) has in his mind a model for the Corinthians that could influence social and religious standards within the community. The indicative of being in Christ should influence the imperative for communion with Christ and with others in the church.

The Indicative of the Divine Mystery as the Basis for Paul's Imperatives

Thus, Paul defines spiritual maturity according to his understanding of the transformation that fellowship with Christ through the Holy Spirit brings in the life of the believer. The Corinthians could be spiritually mature (*pneumatikos*) if they would allow the Spirit to grow within them the mind of Christ. Paul's basic paradigm is the indicative and imperative of existence *in Christ*. He shares with the Corinthians the common premise that Christ's sacrifice on the cross offers a new existence to those who put their faith in him (2 Cor 5:17). This newness leads to living according to Christ's standards of holiness and love. When one lives in the sphere of Christ, one is no longer under the control of sin or the desires of the flesh (Gal 5:16). The new existence made possible in Christ transforms the present situation into conformity to the

---

[19] Karl O. Sandnes, "Prophecy–A Sign for Believers," *Bib* (1996) 4.
[20] Dale B. Martin, "Tongues of Angels and Other Status Indicators," *JAAR* 59 (1991) 569.

ways of Christ. Believers belong to a new reality (Phil 3:20) and a new creation (2 Cor 5:17). Fee writes,

> Ethics for Paul is ultimately a *theological* issue pure and simple. Everything has to do with God and with what God is about in Christ and the Spirit. Thus (1) the *purpose* (or basis) of Christian ethics is the glory of God (10:31); (2) the *pattern* for such ethics is Christ (11:1); (3) the *principle* is love, precisely because it alone reflects God's character (8:2-3; 13:1-8); and (4) the *power* is the Spirit (6:11, 19).[21]

The Corinthians divorced the imperative (the *doing*) from the indicative (the *being*) by not allowing the Spirit to teach them that being a believer in Jesus Christ should impact the way a person lives. They were stuck at the first stage, with the basic elements of the gospel (3:2), but Paul wants them to realize that they had all the power they needed in the Holy Spirit to live a holy life.

The Holy Spirit is the means of fellowship with Christ and makes living as community possible. Dunn states, "The one Spirit which unites believers is precisely the reality of their union with Christ, and the reality of that union is demonstrated by whether or not they begin to take on the character of their heavenly partner."[22] This unity by the Spirit involves and affects the physical body (6:17). Paul makes this explicit in 6:19: "Do you not know that your body is the temple of the Holy Spirit who is in you and whom you have from God?" This is an important qualifier to the freedom which comes through Christ (see 6:12-13). The logic for Paul's ethic is simple: behavior that is incompatible with being a vessel fit for the divine Spirit, such as immoral sexual activities, cannot be acceptable to one who is in Christ. Being united with Christ involves a break from the control of the flesh. As John A. T. Robinson states, "To go back to that is to break the possibility of being *in* Christ."[23] Paul's goal is the holiness of both the community (3:16) and the individual (6:19). This goal is stated in the form of an imperative in 6:18b, "Flee sexual immorality," and the more inclusive imperative in 6:20b, "Glorify God in your body." The basis for this ethic rests upon the indicative of 19b-20a: "You are not your own, for you were purchased for a price." Paul assumes that the Corinthians would realize that the purchase price was Christ's death upon the cross (1:30). With this, he again rests his ethic firmly upon the divine mystery.

Paul's ethic is also influenced by his future hopes of the *parousia* of Christ and the resurrection of believers. Albert Schweitzer writes, "Again and

---

[21] Gordon D. Fee, "Toward a Theology of 1 Corinthians," in *Pauline Theology: 1 and 2 Corinthians*, ed. David M. Hay (Minneapolis: Fortress, 1993) 53.

[22] Dunn, *Jesus and the Spirit*, 323.

[23] John A. T. Robinson, *The Body: A Study in Pauline Theology*, SBT 1/5 (Chicago: Regnery, 1952) 52.

again he exhorts the believers to continue steadfastly in the good, because eternal life at the coming of Christ is promised to them as a consequence."[24] For Paul, the power of the present evil age and all it represents has ended and has been overcome by the power of Christ (15:56-57). Ethically, this gives believers power over the desires of the flesh. Paul uses this eschatological viewpoint to influence the present conduct of the Corinthians. The strong in the community showed a detachment from social concerns through indifference to the weak. The community as a whole showed indifference to the immorality of the sinful "brother" involved in an illicit relationship with his step-mother. The Corinthians had misappropriated the eschatological ethic. Fee comments, "Since salvation is essentially eschatological, always pointing toward its final consummation at the *parousia*, the future is understood to condition everything in the present. This is why ethical life is not optional; life in Christ in the present age is but the life of the future already begun."[25] Some of the Corinthians had mistakenly used their freedom (*exousia*) to the detriment of the community. They thought their power gave them a certain degree of liberty (*eleutheria*). Paul knew that the eschatological power of the indwelling Spirit brought liberty (2 Cor 3:17), but he surrendered his freedom to love; his ethic was one of strength through weakness. He qualified his ethical freedom by the gospel and by concern for others. He urges the Corinthians to join him in this ethic for their own salvation and for the preservation of community. Being in the realm of Christ by aligning with the divine paradox and living as vessels fit for the Holy Spirit makes this ethic possible. Schweitzer writes, "Since with the dying and rising again of Christ the super-earthly world has already begun to be, the believers who through the being-in-Christ already belong to it, can already exercise the temper of mind appropriate to their liberation from the natural world."[26]

Paul knew that the only way the Corinthians could effectively overcome the "desires of the flesh" was by becoming fit vessels for the Holy Spirit and by being empowered by the Spirit to live a holy ethic. They could grow into spiritual maturity by being *pneumatikos* ("spiritual") as he defines it in chapters 1–4. The Spirit is the key to understanding the mystery of God. This is a Pauline way of saying that the Spirit makes it possible to appropriate the lifestyle that is demanded by living in communion with Christ. The presence of the Holy Spirit in the believer makes sinning against one's body a violation of the temple concept. Only the Spirit makes love and community possible.

The primary way personal holiness becomes community holiness is through love. For Paul, the character of the believer is not based on authority

---

[24] Schweitzer, *Mysticism*, 310.
[25] Fee, "Toward a Theology," 56.
[26] Schweitzer, *Mysticism*, 296.

to do something (*exousia*) or knowledge (*gnōsis*), but on love (13:2; Gal 5:13). His own example demonstrates that true freedom comes in love. Richard Horsley writes, "In his response to the problem posed by the 'freedom of consciousness,' Paul insists on the 'real ethical question' at the interpersonal level. Both the structure and the substance of Paul's response makes the effect of one's behavior on others the criterion of ethics."[27] Unbounded freedom does one of two things: it destroys one's self or destroys community.[28] R. Pickett writes, "Ethics is never just a matter of what people do, but a question of the interplay between their identity, attitudes and beliefs, and behaviour."[29]

Paul's ethic of holiness and love addresses the need for community solidarity in Corinth. His conflict with the Corinthians can be narrowed down to community versus individual concerns. Horsley writes, "For the Corinthians, therefore, the eating of idol meat and other matters were issues only in an internal personal sense, for one's individual consciousness, and not in a truly ethical, i.e., relational sense." For Paul, "such issues are ethical, that is, matters of relationships between people, not of one's own inner consciousness."[30] The individualism of the strong threatened community (chs. 8–10). The lack of concern for the immoral "brother" (ch. 5), the indifference about matters of internal strife (ch. 6), and sexual and marital issues (ch. 7) all threatened the solidarity of the community since these all violated the holiness expected of a transformed people. Christ's sacrifice makes fellowship in community possible and demands exclusive loyalty in return. Love is the mark of spiritual maturity, and not spiritual gifts that edify the individual (cf. 2:6-3:3). For some of the Corinthians, their liberating "knowledge" had puffed them up in arrogance to the detriment of their love for one another and their love for God (8:1-3). Paul's answer to this problem is to allow love the more excellent position and put knowledge and all other gifts of the Spirit below love in priority (13:1-3). The great gifts of the Corinthians—even the gift of knowledge—could be quite useful for the church if the Corinthians would only first love one another. When Paul shows the more excellent way of love to them, he grounds all the gifts of the Spirit in love, and by this solves the competition and divisiveness within the community.

Love in the community is possible by experiencing the mystery of Christ. The believer identifies with Christ's death and resurrection symbolized in baptism, and the result is "newness of life" (Rom 6:4). Paul begins the

---

[27] Richard A. Horsley, "Consciousness and Freedom among the Corinthians: 1 Corinthians 8–10," *CBQ* 40 (1978) 586.
[28] See Foerster, "*Exousia*," in *TDNT* 2:570.
[29] R. Pickett, *The Cross in Corinth: The Social Significance of the Death of Jesus*, JSNTSup 143 (Sheffield: Sheffield Academic, 1997) 87.
[30] Horsley, "Consciousness and Freedom," 589.

letter with the best example of love that he can—the revelation of God's love upon the cross. The "paradox" of the divine wisdom and strength disclosed in Christ serves as Paul's paradigm for the problems in the community. Love in Christ is the one attribute that bridges present reality to eschatological reality.[31] Paul contends that love outlasts prophecy, tongues, and knowledge (13:8) since it is the characteristic of the "perfect" or "mature" (*teleioi*). The Corinthians gave permanence to things impermanent and had neglected love which is the true mark of the eschaton.

---

[31] Witherington, *Conflict and Community*, 272.

8

Conclusion

Paul consistently applies his interpretation of the divine mystery of Jesus Christ as the model and means for the Corinthians to grow into spiritual maturity. First, his purpose for describing the "divine wisdom in mystery" in the first section of the letter (1:18-2:16) becomes clear as he calls for imitation of himself at a number of key points (4:16; ch. 9; 11:1, 13:1-3). The reason he can serve as an example to the Corinthians is because he himself follows the example of Jesus Christ. He describes this model in terms of a paradox from a human perspective. The divine mystery revealed with the death and resurrection of Christ appears as foolishness and weakness from a human standpoint because it opens a way of life that contradicts the typical behavior of those "in Adam," offering holiness to replace immorality, and love to replace selfishness.

Paul uses the indicative mood in the Greek to describe the effect of the death and resurrection of Jesus Christ upon those who believe, demonstrating that it is a past event that influences present and future reality. Moreover, it forms the first of two foci of time for him. His apocalyptic hopes had been significantly modified with his encounter with the resurrected Christ. He saw the longed-for revelation of God's plan as having been fulfilled with the death and resurrection of Jesus. He contextualizes and references this past moment to remind the Corinthians of the new relationship they had with God. They had been redeemed, sanctified, and justified by means of the cross of Christ (1:30). As a result of this past event, they were enabled to live as holy, justified, and redeemed people (6:11). They were no longer under the power of sin and confined to the sphere of Adam. Rather, they now could live in the sphere of Christ where love and holiness are the ethical ideals.

Because of this indicative of new existence, believers also have hope for the future. Paul refers to the completion of the divine plan in Christ in order to motivate the Corinthians to stop sinning (15:34, 58). If they continued in sin, they were in danger of forfeiting their hope of resurrection. If they denied the bodily resurrection of believers, they proved their disbelief in the power of Christ over sin and death, hence, they remained in their sins (15:12-20). Paul's hope, based on the apostolic kerygma, is that those who live in fellowship with Christ will someday rise from the dead because Christ will finally and completely defeat death. After this, he will hand the conquered kingdom over to God and the divine plan revealed as a mystery will be completed (15:24-28). Since the Corinthians were already in communion with Christ through the Holy Spirit, they should live according to the paradigm of the divine mystery.

Furthermore, Paul's letter shows significant concern with the present behavior of the Corinthians. Paul creates an intentional conflict of ideology with the Corinthians in order to motivate them to live according to a certain paradigm. He uses a paraenetic style of writing in order to exhort them to live as persons fit to be indwelt with the Holy Spirit. The church faced a number of diverse moral and community issues which, if not addressed, could eventually lead to schism and a loss of salvation by some (e.g., the "weak brother"). Paul provides one answer to these problems with various applications. His answer is simply to imitate him as he imitates Christ by living as transformed people. To live by this ethical ideal is more than simply a human endeavor. Importantly for Paul, this emulation involves fellowship with Christ through the Holy Spirit on an on-going basis (Phil 1:21; Gal 2:20). The Spirit is the means for this communion with Christ and directs believers into conformity to this ideal by teaching them "the mind of Christ" (1 Cor 2:16).

Second, Paul attempts to deal with the many apparent problems in the Corinthian community by addressing deeper issues of spiritual immaturity. Immediately after providing his kerygmatic foundation in 1:18-2:16, he assesses the Corinthians as spiritually immature (3:1-3). This assessment is significant and revealing for understanding the intention of Paul's rhetoric. He attributes to the Corinthians the descriptions of those on the "outside" of the church. He must call them fleshly (*sarkinoi*) because of their jealousy and dissension, and more inclusively, for their lack of living according to the ways of Christ. This categorization is rhetorically useful because it attempts to shame them into seeing the foolishness and weakness of their behavior. If they truly wanted to boast, they would boast like Paul in their weakness and reliance upon Christ and one another in community. Their conduct revealed their motives and their immature spiritual condition.

Paul works with two basic paradigms in this letter. The first paradigm can be simply characterized as existence "in Adam." A person enters this paradigm involuntarily and remains in it unless one puts one's faith in Jesus as Lord. The second paradigm for Paul is existence "in Christ." This for Paul is the best sphere in which to be. The immature behavior of the Corinthians corresponded with Paul's description of life "in Adam." They were living according to the paradigm of Adam where sin dominates and love is neglected. They had failed to allow the Holy Spirit to mature them into conformity to the mind and image of Christ (2:16). To solve the various problems in the community they needed to act upon the indicative of relationship with Christ. Their failure to mature (to be *teleios*) put them in danger of being *psychikos* and devoid of the Spirit because they were not acting as temples fit for God's presence (3:16; 6:19). The problem with the Corinthians, then, was that they did not allow the Spirit to continue to transform them based upon the indicative of redemption, sanctification, and justification in Christ. There is no evidence in the letter that they lacked a basic belief in Christ; they only failed to appropriate the divine mystery of communion with Christ in their lives and community.

Third, Paul uses the power of his written words with intended results. He expects the Corinthians to heed his letter and conform to his intentions for them. His position as founder, apostle, steward of the divine mysteries, and imitator of Christ provide him with significant power and authority over the Corinthians. Since the relationship between him and the Corinthians is voluntary, he must appeal to his position of power by using his rhetorical skills to convince them to accept his words. Therefore, he uses a number of different rhetorical devices in the letter such as irony, sarcasm, shame, example, and others to accomplish his purposes. His paradoxical language in chapters 1–4 is more than simply stylistic. Beginning with 4:14 and on into the following chapters, his intention becomes clear as he expects a change of behavior and a repositioning of faith on the part of the Corinthians. He attempts to blame and shame them for not living and acting as people who had been redeemed by Christ. Their association with immorality threatened their status as temples of the Holy Spirit (6:12-20). Their lack of love threatened their communion with Christ (10:14-22).

Fourth, the issues considered central to the letter by some interpreters such as schism within the church are only *results* of a more basic problem of spiritual immaturity. The failure of the Corinthians to grow into the likeness of Christ by loving one another would lead to schism if they did not change their behavior. They were living as mere humans who do not rely on the Spirit for understanding the deeper truths of God. Their lack of wisdom, as defined by Paul, led to their inability to understand the ways of Christ. They could not grow into maturity because they relied on the wrong source for their wisdom. Their behavior modeled the world around them and even went beyond the accepted standards of the time. They failed to see the implications of Paul's kerygma, and the result was a breakdown of the community and acceptance of sin, jealousy, and boasting.

Finally, the method of this study allows the modern interpreter to peer into the thoughts and intentions of Paul for the formation of early Christian communities. Although it is impossible to know exactly what Paul was thinking when he wrote this letter, it is possible to catch a glimpse of the fruit of this thinking. His paradigm for the Corinthian community centers upon a call to follow a different way of life than the paradigm of the world. The divine mystery, as interpreted by Paul, offers transformation. The believer who identifies with the death and resurrection of Christ by putting to death the old way of life (Rom 6:5-11; Gal 2:20) enters into a new sphere of influence characterized by intimate fellowship with Christ. One who is in this sphere is free from the snare of Adam and the world and is no longer bound by the power of sin and death. The divine mystery also offers a new source of power by the indwelling Holy Spirit. The Spirit brings gifts to those in Christ that enable them to function as community. The highest and most significant of these is love which brings diversity together into unity. The indicative is that the Spirit graces believers with love. The imperative is that they should follow after the example of Paul and hence, Christ, in loving others. The divine Spirit is described as holy and makes holiness possible for those in Christ. The indicative is that fellowship with Christ is possible because of redemption. The imperative is that Christ demands loyalty which cannot be shared with any other, particularly with prostitutes who represent the ways of the world or idols that open doors for demons.

Paul has a two-part goal for the Corinthians. First, they should grow in their fellowship with Christ. They could do this by honoring God with their bodies by becoming fit temples for the Holy Spirit. Second, they should grow in their fellowship with one another. By loving each other and looking out for the welfare of the "weaker" members, they could grow into a unified community. If they failed to love one another, they faced the judgment of God and the mockery of people. Paul's interpretation of the divine mystery of Christ for the Corinthian community allows the text of 1 Corinthians to speak as a conversation of concern for maturation.

Bibliography

Primary Sources

Aristides, P. Aelius. *The Complete Works*. Translated by Charles A. Behr. Leiden: Brill, 1981–86.

Aristotle. *The "Art" of Rhetoric*. Translated by John Henry Freese. LCL. Cambridge: Harvard University Press, 1926.

Athenagoras. *On Resurrection of the Dead*. Translated by William R. Schoedel. Oxford: Clarendon, 1972.

Athenaeus. *Deipnosophists*. Translated by Charles Burton Gulick. LCL. Cambridge: Harvard University Press, 1937.

Biblia Hebraica Stuttgartensia. Edited by K. Elliger, W. Rudolf, et al. Stuttgart: Deutsche Bibelgesellschaft, 1983.

Charlesworth, James H., editor. *The Old Testament Pseudepigrapha*. Garden City, N.Y.: Doubleday, 1983–85.

Cicero. 28 vols. Translated by G. L. Hendrickson, H. M. Hubbell, et al. LCL. Cambridge: Harvard University Press, 1912–72.

[Cicero]. *Ad C. Herennium De Ratione Dicendi (Rhetorica ad Herennium)*. Translated by H. Caplan. LCL. Cambridge: Harvard University Press, 1954.

Demetrius. *On Style*. Translated by W. Hamilton Fyfe. LCL. Cambridge: Harvard University Press, 1927

Dio Chrysostom. 5 vols. Translated by J. W. Cohoon and H. L. Crosby. LCL. Cambridge: Harvard University Press, 1932–51.

Epictetus. 2 vols. Translated by W. A. Oldfather. LCL. Cambridge: Harvard University Press, 1925–28.

Epictetus. *Enchiridion*. Translated by Thomas W. Higginson. New York: Bobbs Merrill, 1948.

Euripides. 4 vols. Translated by A. S. Way. LCL. New York: Macmillan/Putnam's Sons, 1912.

The Greek New Testament. 3rd ed. (corrected). Edited by Kurt Aland, et al. Stuttgart: United Bible Societies, 1983.

Herodotus. 4 vols. Translated by A. D. Godley. LCL. Cambridge: Harvard University Press, 1921–25.

Hippolytus. *The Refutation of All Heresies*. Translated by J. H. MacMahon. Edinburgh: T. & T. Clark, 1986.

Homer. *The Odyssey*. 2 vols. Translated by A. T. Murray. LCL. Cambridge: Harvard University Press; London: Heinemann, 1942–45.

Irenaeus. *Against Heresies*. Translated by Alexander Roberts and W. H. Rambaut. Edinburgh: T. & T. Clark, 1868–69.

Isocrates. 3 vols. Translated by G. Norlin and L. Van Hook. LCL. Cambridge: Harvard University Press, 1928–45.

Josephus. *The Works of Josephus*. Translated by William Whiston. Peabody, Mass.: Hendrickson, 1987.
Justin. *First and Second Apologies*. Translated by Leslie William Barnard. New York: Paulist, 1966.
Lucan. *The Civil War*. Translated by J. D. Duff. LCL. Cambridge: Harvard University Press, 1928.
Minucius Felix. *Octavius*. Translated by G. W. Clarke. New York: Newman Press, 1974.
Pausanius. *Description of Greece*. Translated by W. H. S. Jones. LCL. New York: Putnams, 1918–35.
Philo. *The Works of Philo*. Translated by C. D. Yonge. Peabody, Mass.: Hendrickson, 1993.
Plato. *Plato: Works* 12 vols. Translated by H. N. Fowler, W. R. M. Lamb, et al. LCL. Cambridge: Harvard University Press, 1914–37.
Pliny the Younger. *Letters, Panegyrius*. 2 vols. Translated by B. Radice. LCL. Cambridge: Harvard University Press, 1969.
Plutarch. 15 vols. Translated by F. C. Babbitt, W. Helmbold, et al. LCL. Cambridge: Harvard University Press, 1927–69.
Pseudo-Philo. *Biblical Antiquities*. Translated by M. R. James. London: SPCK, 1917.
Quintillian. 4 vols. Translated by H. E. Butler. LCL. Cambridge: Harvard University Press, 1920–22.
Schneemelcher, Wilhelm, editor. *New Testament Apocrypha*. Translated by R. McL. Wilson. Louisville: Westminster John Knox, 1991.
Scott, Walter, editor. *Hermetica*. 2 vols. Oxford: Claredon, 1924–25.
Seneca. *Ad Lucilium Eistulae Morales*. Translated by R. M. Gummere. LCL. Cambridge: Harvard University Press, 1918–25; rev. ed. 1943, 1953.
Suetonius. 2 vols. Translated by J. C. Rolfe. LCL. Cambridge: Harvard University Press, 1914.
Sophocles. 2 vols. Translated by F. Storr. LCL. Cambridge: Harvard University Press, 1912–13.
Tatian. *Oratio ad Graecos and Fragments*. Translated by Molly Whittaker. Oxford: Clarendon, 1982
Vermes, Geza. *The Dead Sea Scrolls in English*. 4th ed. Baltimore: Penguin, 1995.

Secondary Literature

Atkins, Robert A. Jr. *Egalitarian Community: Ethnography and Exegesis*. Tuscaloosa: University of Alabama Press, 1991.
Aune, David E. *The New Testament in Its Literary Environment*. LEC 8. Philadel-phia: Westminster, 1987.
———. *Prophecy in Early Christianity and the Ancient Mediterranean World*. Grand Rapids: Eerdmans, 1983.
Baker, D. L. "The Interpretation of 1 Cor 12–14." *EvQ* 46 (1974) 224–34.
Barrett, C. K. *A Commentary on the First Epistle to the Corinthians*. London: A. & C. Black, 1971.
———. *Essays on Paul*. Philadelphia: Fortress, 1982.
———. *The Second Epistle to the Corinthians*. London: A. & C. Black, 1973.
Barth, Karl. *The Resurrection of the Dead*. Translated by H. J. Stenning. London: Hodder and Stoughton, 1933. Reprinted, Eugene, Ore.: Wipf & Stock, 2003.
Barton, Stephen C. "Historical Criticism and Social-Scientific Perspectives in New Testament Study." In *Hearing the New Testament*, edited by Joel B. Green, 61–108. Grand Rapids: Eerdmans, 1995.

———. "Paul and the Cross: A Sociological Approach." *Theology* 85 (1982) 13–19.

Bauer, Walter. *A Greek-English Lexicon of the New Testament and Other Early Christian Literature*. Second revision by William F. Arndt, F. W. Gingrich, and Frederick W. Danker. Chicago: University of Chicago Press, 1979.

———. *Rechtgläubigkeit und Ketzerei im ältesten Christentum*. Tübingen: Mohr/Siebeck,1934.

Beker, Johan Christiann. *Paul the Apostle: The Triumph of God in Life and Thought*. Minneapolis: Fortress, 1980.

———. *Paul's Apocalyptic Gospel: The Coming Triumph of God*. Philadelphia: Fortress, 1982.

Best, Ernest. *One Body in Christ*. London: SPCK, 1955.

———. *Paul and His Converts*. Edinburgh: T. & T. Clark, 1988.

———. "The Power and the Wisdom of God, 1 Corinthians 1:18—2:5." In *Paolo a Una Chiesa Divisa (1 Cor. 1–4)*, edited by L. De Lorenzi, 9–41. Rome: St. Paul Abbey,1980.

Betz, Hans Dieter. *Galatians: A Commentary On Paul's Letters to the Churches in Galatia*. Hermeneia. Philadelphia: Fortress, 1979.

———. "The Problem of Rhetoric and Theology According to the Apostle Paul." In *L' Apôtre Paul: Personalitié, style et conception du ministère*, edited by A. Vanhoye,16–48. BETL 73. Leuven: Leuven University Press, 1986.

Bieringer, Reimund. "Paul's Divine Jealousy: The Apostle and His Community in Relationship." In *Studies on 2 Corinthians*, edited by Reimund Bieringer and Jan Lambrecht, 223–53. BETL 112. Leuven: Leuven University Press, 1994.

Bieringer, Reimund, editor. *The Corinthian Correspondence*. BETL 125. Leuven: Leuven University Press, 1996.

Bitzer, Lloyd F. "The Rhetorical Situation." *Philosophy and Rhetoric* 1 (1968) 1–14.

Bookides, N., and J. E. Fischer. "The Sanctuary of Demeter and Core." *Hesperia* 41 (1972) 283–331.

Bookidides, N., and R. S. Stroud. *Demeter and Persephone in Ancient Corinth*. Princeton: ASCSA, 1987.

Bousset, Wilhelm. *Kyrios Christos: A History of the Belief in Christ from the Beginnings of Christianity to Irenaeus*. Translated by John E. Steely. Nashville: Abingdon, 1970.

Bouttier, Michel. *En Christ: Etude D' Exegese et de Theologie Pauliniennes*. EHPR 54. Paris: University of France, 1962.

Brown, Alexandra R. *The Cross and Human Transformation: Paul's Apocalyptic Word in 1 Corinthians*. Minneapolis: Fortress, 1995.

Brown, Raymond E. *The Semitic Background of the Term "Mystery" in the New Testament*. Philadelphia: Fortress, 1968.

Bruce, Frederick F. *1 and 2 Corinthians*. NCB. Grand Rapids: Eerdmans, 1971.

———. *The Epistle to the Galatians*. NIGTC. Grand Rapids: Eerdmans, 1982.

Büchsel, Friederich. "'In Christus' bei Paulus." *ZNW* 42 (1949) 141–58.

Bultmann, Rudolf. *Existence and Faith: Shorter Writings of Rudolf Bultmann*. Translated by Schubert M. Ogden. New York: Meridian, 1960.

———. *Primitive Christianity in Its Contemporary Setting*. Translated by Reginald H. Fuller. New York: Meridian, 1957.

Burkert, Walter. *Ancient Mystery Cults*. Cambridge: Harvard University Press, 1987.

———. *Greek Religion*. Cambridge: Harvard University, 1985.

Cadbury, Henry J. "The Macellum of Corinth." *JBL* 53 (1934) 134–41.

Callan, Terrance. "Prophecy and Ecstasy in Greco-Roman Religion and in 1 Corinthians." *NovT* 27 (1985) 125–40.

Castelli, Elizabeth A. *Imitating Paul: A Discourse of Power*. Louisville: Westminster John Knox, 1991.

Chow, John K. *Patronage and Power: A Study of Social Networks in Corinth.* Sheffield: JSOT Press, 1992.

Collins, John J. *The Apocalyptic Imagination: An Introduction to the Jewish Matrix of Christianity.* New York: Crossroads, 1992.

———, editor. *Apocalypse: The Morphology of a Genre. Semeia* 14. Missoula, Mont.: Scholars, 1979.

Collins, Raymond F. "Reflections on 1 Corinthians as a Hellenistic Letter." In *The Corinthian Correspondence*, edited by Reimund Bieringer, 39–61. Leuven: Leuven University Press, 1996.

Conzelmann, Hans. *1 Corinthians: A Commentary on the First Epistle to the Corinthians.* Translated by James W. Leitch. Hermeneia. Philadelphia: Fortress, 1975.

Coser, Lewis. *The Function of Social Conflict.* Glencoe, Ill.: Free Press, 1956.

Court, John M. "Paul and the Apocalyptic Pattern." In *Paul and Paulinism: Essays in Honour of C. K. Barrett*, edited by M. D. Hooker and S. G. Wilson, 57–66. London: SPCK, 1982.

Daube, David. "Pauline Contributions to Pluralistic Culture: Re-creation and Beyond." In *Jesus and Man's Hope*, edited by D. G. Miller and D. Y. Hadidian, 223–45. Pittsburgh: Pittsburgh Theological Seminary, 1971.

Davies, William David. *Paul and Rabbinic Judaism: Some Rabbinic Elements in Pauline Theology.* London: SPCK, 1980.

Davis, Christopher A. "'The Trust which is the Gospel': The Coherent Center of Paul's Theology." Ph.D. diss., Union Theological Seminary, 1992.

Davis, James A. *Wisdom and Spirit: An Investigation of 1 Corinthians 1.18—3.20 against the Background of Jewish Sapiential Traditions in the Greco-Roman Period.* Lanham, Md.: University Press of America, 1984.

de Boer, Marcus C. *The Defeat of Death: Apocalyptic Eschatology in 1 Corinthians 15 and Romans 5.* JSNTSup 22. Sheffield: JSOT Press, 1988.

Deissmann, G. Adolf. *Die Neutestamentliche formel "In Christo Jesu."* Marburg: Elwert, 1892.

———. *Paul: A Study in Social and Religious History.* Translated by William E. Wilson. New York: Harper, 1957.

Delobel, Joël. "Coherence and Relevance of 1 Cor 8–10." In *The Corinthian Correspondence*, edited by Reimund Bieringer, 177–90. BETL 125. Leuven: Leuven University Press, 1996.

DeMaris, Richard E. "Corinthian Religion and Baptism for the Dead (1 Corinthians 15:29) Insights from Archeology and Anthropology." *JBL* 114 (1995) 661–82.

Dennison, William D. "Indicative and Imperative: The Basic Structure of Pauline Ethics." *CTJ* 14 (1979) 55–78.

———. *Paul's Two-Age Construction and Apologetics.* Landham, Md.: University Press of America, 1985.

Dodd, Brian J. "Paul's Paradigmatic 'I' and 1 Corinthians 6.12." *JSNT* 59 (1995) 39–58.

Doty, William G. *Letters in Primitive Christianity.* GBS. Philadelphia: Fortress, 1977.

Douglas, Mary. *Natural Symbols: Explorations in Cosmology.* New York: Pantheon, 1982.

———. *Purity and Danger.* London: Routledge and Kegan Paul, 1966.

Dunn, James D. G. *1 Corinthians.* Sheffield: Sheffield Academic, 1995.

———. *Jesus and the Spirit.* Philadelphia: Westminster, 1975. Reprint, Grand Rapids: Eerdmans, 1997.

———. *The Theology of Paul the Apostle.* Grand Rapids: Eerdmans, 1998.

Elliott, John H. "Social-Scientific Criticism of the New Testament and Its Social World: More on Methods and Models." *Semeia* 35 (1986) 1–34.

———. *What is Social-Scientific Criticism?* GBS. Minneapolis: Fortress, 1993.

Ellis, E. Earle. *Paul's Use of the Old Testament*. Grand Rapids: Baker, 1957.

———. "*Soma* in First Corinthians." *Int* 44 (1990) 132–44.

Engberg-Pedersen, Troels. "The Gospel and Social Practice According to 1 Corinthians." *NTS* 33 (1987) 557–84.

Engels, Donald. *Roman Corinth: An Alternative Model for the Classical City*. Chicago: University of Chicago Press, 1990.

Evans, Christopher Francis. *Resurrection and the New Testament*. Naperville, Ill.: Allenson, 1970.

Fee, Gordon D. *The First Epistle to the Corinthians*. NICNT. Grand Rapids: Eerdmans, 1987.

———. "Toward a Theology of 1 Corinthians." In *Pauline Theology: 1 and 2 Corinthians*, edited by David M. Hay, 37–58. Minneapolis: Fortress, 1993.

Fiore, Benjamin. "'Covert Allusion' in 1 Corinthians 1–4." *CBQ* 47 (1985) 85–104.

Fisk, Bruce N. "Eating Meat Offered to Idols: Corinthian Behavior and Pauline Response in 1 Corinthians 8–10." *TJ* 10 (1989) 49–70.

Flemming, Dean. "Essence and Adaptation: Contextualization and the Heart of Paul's Gospel." Ph.D. diss., University of Aberdeen, 1987.

Fontenrose, J. *The Delphic Oracle*. Berkeley: University of California, 1978.

Forbes, Christopher. "Early Christian Inspired Speech and Hellenistic Popular Religion." *NovT* 28 (1986) 257–70.

Francis, James A. "'As Babes in Christ'—Some Proposals Regarding 1 Corinthians 3.1-3." *JSNT* 7 (1980) 41–60.

Frid, Bo. "Structure and Argumentation in 1 Cor 12." *SEÅ* 60 (1995) 95–113.

Funk, Robert W. "The Apostolic *Parousia*: Form and Significance." In *Christian History and Interpretation: Studies Presented to John Knox*, edited by William R. Farmer et al., 249–68. Cambridge: Cambridge University Press, 1967.

———. "Word and Word in 1 Corinthians 2:6-16." In *Language, Hermeneutic, and the Word of God: The Problem of Language in the New Testament and Contemporary Theology*, 275–305. New York: Harper and Row, 1966.

Furnish, Victor Paul. *Theology and Ethics in Paul*. Nashville: Abingdon, 1968.

Gaffin, Richard B. "Some Epistemological Reflections on 1 Cor 2:6-16." *WTJ* 57(1995) 103–24.

Gager, John G. *Kingdom and Community: The Social World of Early Christianity*. Englewood Cliffs, N.J.: Prentice-Hall, 1975.

Garnsey, P. "Mass Diet and Nutrition in the City of Rome." In *Hourir la plebe*, edited by A. Giovanni, 67–101. Basel: Herder, 1991.

Gill, David W. J. "The Meat-Market at Corinth." *TynBul* 43 (1992) 389–93.

Gooch, Peter D. *Dangerous Food: 1 Corinthians 8–10 in Its Context*. Studies in Christianity and Judaism 5. Waterloo, Ontario, Canada: Wilfred Laurier University Press, 1993.

Goodenough, Erwin Ramsdell. *By Light, Light: The Mystic Gospel of Hellenistic Judaism*. New Haven: Yale University Press, 1935.

Goulder, Chael. "Already?" In *To Tell the Mystery: Essays on New Testament Eschatology in Honor of Robert H. Gundry*, edited by Thomas E. Schmidt and Moisés Silva, 21–33. JSNTSup 100. Sheffield: JSOT Press, 1994.

Hammerton-Kelly, Robert G. *Sacred Violence: Paul's Hermeneutic of the Cross*. Minneapolis: Fortress, 1992.

Harvey, Anthony E. "The Opposition to St. Paul." In *Studia Evangelica* IV, edited by F. L. Cross, 319–32. Berlin: Akademie, 1968.

Hays, Richard B. *First Corinthians*. IBC. Louisville: Westminster John Knox, 1997.

Hengel, Martin. *Crucifixion in the Ancient World and the Folly of the Message of the Cross*. Translated by John Bowden. Philadelphia: Fortress, 1977.

Hill, C. E. "Paul's Understanding of Christ's Kingdom in 1 Corinthians 15:20-28." *NovT* 30 (1988) 297–320.

Holladay, Carl R. "1 Corinthians 13: Paul as Apostolic Paradigm." In *Greeks, Romans, and Christians: Essays in Honor of Abraham J. Malherbe,* edited by David L. Balch et al., 80–98. Minneapolis: Fortress, 1990.

Holmberg, Bengt. *Paul and Power: The Structure of Authority in the Primitive Church as Reflected in the Pauline Epistles.* Philadelphia: Fortress, 1980. Reprint, Eugene, Ore.: Wipf & Stock, 2004.

Hooker, Morna D. *From Adam to Christ: Essays on Paul.* Cambridge: Cambridge University Press, 1990.

———. "Hard Sayings: I Corinthians 3:2." *Theology* 69 (1966) 19–22.

Horrell, David A. *The Social Ethos of the Corinthian Correspondence: Interests and Ideology from 1 Corinthians to 1 Clement.* Edinburgh: T. & T. Clark, 1996.

Horsley, Richard A. "1 Corinthians: A Case Study of Paul's Assembly as an Alternative Society." In *Paul and Empire: Religion and Power in Roman Imperial Society,* edited by Richard A. Horsley, 242–52. Harrisburg, Pa.: Trinity, 1997.

———. "Consciousness and Freedom among the Corinthians: 1 Corinthians 8–10." *CBQ* 40 (1978) 574–89.

———. "Gnosis in Corinth: 1 Corinthians 8:1-6." *NTS* 27 (1980) 32–51.

———. "'How Can Some of You Say That There is No Resurrection of the Dead?' Spiritual Elitism in Corinth." *NovT* 20 (1978) 203–31.

———. "Wisdom of Word and Words of Wisdom in Corinth." *CBQ* 39 (1977) 224–39.

House, H. W. "Tongues and the Mystery Religions of Corinth." *BSac* 140 (1983) 134–50.

Hurd, John C. *The Origins of I Corinthians.* New York: Seabury, 1965.

Hyldahl, N. "The Corinthian 'Parties' and the Corinthian Crisis." *ST* 45 (1991) 19–32.

Jewett, Robert. *Paul's Anthropological Terms.* AGJU 10. Leiden: Brill, 1971.

Johnson, E. Elizabeth. "The Function of Apocalyptic and Wisdom and Traditions in Romans 9–11." Ph.D. diss., Princeton Theological Seminary, 1987.

———. "The Wisdom of God as Apocalyptic Power." In *Faith and History: Essays in Honor of Paul W. Meyer,* edited by John T. Carroll et al., 137–48. Atlanta: Scholars, 1990.

Kabisch, Richard. *Die Eschatologie des Paulus in ihren Zusammenhängen mit dem Gesamtbegriff des Paulinismus.* Göttingen: Vandenhoeck & Ruprecht, 1893.

Käsemann, Ernst. *Perspectives on Paul.* Translated by Margaret Kohl. Philadelphia: Fortress, 1971.

Keck, Leander E. "Paul and Apocalyptic Theology." *Int* 38 (1984) 229–41.

Kennedy, George A. *New Testament Interpretation through Rhetorical Criticism.* Chapel Hill: University of North Carolina Press, 1984.

Knox, Wilfred L. *Saint Paul and the Church of the Gentiles.* Cambridge: Cambridge University Press, 1939.

Koester, Helmut. *Ancient Christian Gospels: Their History and Development.* Philadelphia: Trinity, 1990.

———. *Introduction to the New Testament.* 2 vols. Philadelphia: Fortress, 1982.

———. "The Structure and Criteria of Early Christian Beliefs." In *Trajectories through Early Christianity,* James M. Robinson and Helmut Koester, 205–31. Philadelphia: Fortress, 1971.

Koperski, Veronica. "Knowledge of Christ and Knowledge of God in the Corinthian Correspondence." In *The Corinthian Correspondence,* edited by Reimund Bieringer, 377–96. BETL 125. Leuven: Leuven University Press, 1996.

Ladd, George Eldon. *A Theology of the New Testament.* Grand Rapids: Eerdmans, 1974.

Lim, Timothy H. "Not in Persuasive Words of Wisdom, but in the Demonstration of the Spirit and Power." *NovT* 29 (1987) 137–49.

Lincoln, Andrew T. *Paradise Now and Not Yet: Studies in the Role of the Heavenly Dominion in Paul's Thought with Special Reference to His Eschatology*. SNTSMS 43. Cambridge: Cambridge University Press, 1981.

Litfin, A. Duane. *St. Paul's Theology of Acclamation: 1 Corinthians 1–4 and Greco-Roman Rhetoric*. SNTSMS 79. Cambridge: Cambridge University Press, 1994.

Lyons, George. *Pauline Autobiography: Toward a New Understanding*. SBLDS 73. Atlanta: Scholars, 1985.

Mack, Burton L. *Rhetoric and the New Testament*. GBS. Minneapolis: Fortress, 1990.

Malherbe, Abraham J. *Moral Exhortation: A Greco-Roman Sourcebook*. LEC 4. Philadelphia: Westminster, 1986.

Malina, Bruce J. "'Religion' in the World of Paul." *BTB* 16 (1986) 92–101.

———. "The Social Sciences and Biblical Interpretation." *Int* 36 (1982) 229–42.

———. "Why Interpret the Bible with the Social Sciences?" *ABQ* 2 (1983) 119–33.

Marshall, Peter. *Enmity in Corinth: Social Conventions in Paul's Relations with the Corinthians*. WUNT 2/23. Tübingen: Mohr/Siebeck, 1987.

Martin, Dale B. *The Corinthian Body*. New Haven: Yale University Press, 1995.

———. *Slavery as Salvation: The Metaphor of Slavery in Pauline Christianity*. New Haven: Yale University, 1990.

———. "Tongues of Angels and Other Status Indicators." *JAAR* 59 (1991) 547–89.

McRay, John. *Archeology and the New Testament*. Grand Rapids: Baker, 1991.

Meeks, Wayne A. *The First Urban Christians: The Social World of the Apostle Paul*. New Haven: Yale University Press, 1983.

Merritt, Benjamin, editor. *Greek Inscriptions, 1896–1927, vol. 8, part1 of Corinth: Results of Excavations Conducted by the American School of Classical Studies at Athens*. Cambridge: Harvard University Press, 1931.

Mitchell, Margaret M. "Concerning *Peri De* in 1 Corinthians." *NovT* 31 (1989) 229–56.

———. *Paul and the Rhetoric of Reconciliation: An Exegetical Investigation of the Language and Composition of 1 Corinthians*. Louisville: Westminster John Knox; Tübingen: Mohr/Siebeck, 1991.

———. "Rhetorical Shorthand in Pauline Argumentation: The Functions of the 'The Gospel' in the Corinthian Correspondence." In *Gospel in Paul: Studies in Corinthians, Galatians and Romans for Richard N. Longenecker*, edited by L. Ann Jervis and Peter Richardson, 63–88. JSNTSup 108. Sheffield: Sheffield Academic, 1994.

Murphy, James J. "Early Christianity as a 'Persuasive Campaign': Evidence from the Acts of the Apostles and the Letters of Paul." In *Rhetoric and the New Testament: Essays from the 1992 Heidelberg Conference*, edited by Stanley E. Porter and Thomas H. Olbricht, 90–99. JSNTSup 90. Sheffield: JSOT Press, 1993.

Murphy-O'Connor, Jerome. *1 Corinthians*. NTM 10. Wilmington, Del.: Glazier, 1979.

———. *Paul: A Critical Life*. New York: Clarendon, 1996.

———. "Sex and Logic in I Corinthians 11:2-16." *CBQ* 42 (1980) 482–500.

———. *St. Paul's Corinth: Texts and Archaeology*. GNS 6. Wilmington, Del.: Glazier, 1983.

———. "Tradition and Redaction in 1 Cor 15:3-7." *CBQ* (1981) 582–89.

Mylonas, George E. *Eleusis and the Eleusinian Mysteries*. Princeton: Princeton University Press, 1961.

Nabers, Ned P. "Macella: A Study in Roman Archeology." Ph.D. diss., Princeton University, 1967.

Neugebauer, Fritz. *In Christus = En Christoi: Eine Untersuchung zum paulinischen Glaubensverstandnis*. Göttingen: Vandenhoek & Ruprecht, 1961.

Newton, Michael. *The Concept of Purity at Qumran and in the Letters of Paul.* SNTSMS 53. Cambridge: Cambridge University Press, 1985.

Neyrey, Jerome. "Body Language in 1 Corinthians: The Use of Anthropological Models for Understanding Paul and His Opponents." *Semeia* 35 (1986) 129–70.

———. *Paul in Other Words: A Cultural Reading of His Letters.* Louisville: Westminster John Knox Press, 1990.

———. "Social Science Modeling and the New Testament." *BTB* 16 (1986) 107–15.

O'Day, Gail. "Jeremiah 9:22 and 1 Corinthians 1:26-31: A Study in Inter-textuality." *JBL* 109 (1990) 259–67.

Oster, Richard E. "Use, Misuse and Neglect of Archaeological Evidence in Some Modern Works on 1 Corinthians (1 Cor 7,1-5; 8,10; 11,2-16; 12,14-26)." *ZNW* 83 (1992) 52–73.

Pagels, Elaine H. *The Gnostic Paul: Gnostic Exegesis of the Pauline Letters.* Philadelphia: Fortress, 1975.

Paige, Terence. "1 Corinthians 12:2: A Pagan *Pompe?*" *JSNT* 44 (1991) 57–65.

Painter, John. "Paul and the *Pneumatikoi* at Corinth." In *Paul and Paulinism: Essays in Honour of C. K. Barrett,* edited by Morna D. Hooker and Stephen G. Wilson, 237–50. London: SPCK, 1982.

Pearson, Birger A. "Hellenistic-Jewish Wisdom Speculation and Paul." In *Aspects of Wisdom in Judaism and Early Christianity,* edited by Robert L. Wiken, 43–66. University of Notre Dame Center for the Study of Judaism and Christianity in Antiquity 1. Notre Dame: University of Notre Dame Press, 1975.

———. *The Pneumatikos-psychikos Terminology in 1 Corinthians; A Study in the Theology of the Corinthian Opponents of Paul and Its Relation to Gnosticism.* SBLDS 12. Missoula, Mont.: Society of Biblical Literature, 1973.

Pickett, Raymond. *The Cross in Corinth: The Social Significance of the Death of Jesus.* JSNTSup 143. Sheffield: Sheffield Academic, 1997.

Pierce, C. A. *Conscience in the New Testament.* SBT 1/15. London: SCM, 1955.

Pogolof, Stephen M. *Logos and Sophia: The Rhetorical Situation of 1 Corinthians.* SBLDS 134. Atlanta: Scholars, 1992.

Porter, Stanley E. and Thomas H. Olbricht, eds. *Rhetoric and the New Testament: Essays from the 1992 Heidelberg Conference.* JSNTSup 90. Sheffield: JSOT Press, 1993.

Powell, Benjamin. "Greek Inscriptions from Corinth." *AJA* 7 (1903) 60–61.

Ramsaran, Rollin A. *Liberating Words: Paul's Use of Rhetorical Maxims in 1 Corinthians 1–10.* Harrisburg, Pa.: Trinity, 1996.

Randall, J. H. *Hellenistic Ways of Deliverance and the Making of the Christian Synthesis.* New York: Columbia University Press, 1970.

Reiling, J. "Wisdom and the Spirit: An Exegesis of 1 Corinthians 2, 6-16." In *Text and Testimony: Essays on NT and Apocryphal Literature in Honour of A. F. J. Klijn,* edited by T. Baarda et al., 200–11. Kampen: Kok, 1988.

Reitzenstein, Richard. *Hellenistic Mystery-Religions: Their Basic Ideas and Significance.* Translated by John E. Steely. PittsTMS 15. Pittsburgh: Pickwick, 1978.

Robbins, Vernon K. *Exploring the Texture of Texts: A Guide to Socio-Rhetorical Interpretation.* Valley Forge, Pa.: Trinity, 1996.

Robertson, Archibald, and A. Plummer. *A Critical and Exegetical Commentary on the First Epistle of St. Paul to the Corinthians.* ICC. Edinburgh: T. & T. Clark, 1914.

Robinson, John A. T. *The Body: A Study in Pauline Theology.* SBT 1/5. Chicago: Regnery, 1952.

Sanders, Boykin. "Imitating Paul: 1 Cor 4:16." *HTR* 74 (1981) 353–63.

Sandnes, Karl O. "Prophecy–A Sign for Believers." *Bib* (1996) 1–15.

Saw, Insawn. *Paul's Rhetoric in 1 Corinthians 15: An Analysis Utilizing the Theories of Classical Rhetoric*. Macon, Ga.: Mellen Biblical, 1995.

Schmithals, Walter. *Gnosticism in Corinth: An Investigation of the Letters to the Corinthians*. Translated by John E. Steely. Nashville: Abingdon, 1971.

Schütz, John. *Paul and the Anatomy of Apostolic Authority*. SNTSMS 23. Cambridge: Cambridge University Press, 1975.

Schweitzer, Albert. *The Mysticism of Paul the Apostle*. Translated by William Montgomery. New York: Holt, 1931.

———. *Paul and His Interpreters*. Translated by William Montgomery. London: A. & C. Black, 1912.

Scroggs, Robin. *The Last Adam: A Study in Pauline Anthropology*. Philadelphia: Fortress, 1966.

———. "Paul: *Sophos* and *Pneumatikos*." *NTS* 14 (1967) 33–55.

Segal, Alan F. *Paul the Convert: The Apostolate and Apostasy of Saul the Pharisee*. New Haven: Yale University Press, 1990.

Sider, R. J. "The Pauline Conception of the Resurrection Body in 1 Corinthians XV.35-54." *NTS* 21 (1974–75) 428–39.

Simmel, George. *Conflict*. Glencoe, Ill.: Free Press, 1955.

Smit, Joop F. M. "1 Cor 8,1-6: A Rhetorical Partitio." In *The Corinthian Correspondence*, edited by Reimund Bieringer, 577–91. BETL 125. Leuven: Leuven University Press, 1996.

———. "Argument and Genre of 1 Corinthians 12–14." In *Rhetoric and the New Testament: Essays from the 1992 Heidelberg Conference*, edited by Stanley E. Porter and Thomas H. Olbricht, 211–30. JSNTSup 90. Sheffield: JSOT Press, 1993.

———. "'Do not be Idolaters': Paul's Rhetoric in First Corinthians 10:1-22." *NovT* 39 (1997) 40–53.

Spittler, Russell. "The Limits of Ecstasy: An Exegesis of 2 Corinthians 12:1-10." In *Current Issues in Biblical and Patristic Interpretation*, edited by Gerald F. Hawthorne, 259–66. Grand Rapids: Eerdmans, 1975.

Stanley, David M. "Become Imitators of Me: The Pauline Conception of Apostolic Tradition." *Bib* 40 (1959) 859–77.

Stowers, Stanley K. "Social Status, Public Speaking and Private Teaching: The Circumstances of Paul's Preaching Activity." *NovT* 26 (1984) 59–82.

Sturm, Richard E. "Defining the Word 'Apocalyptic': A Problem in Biblical Criticism." In *Apocalyptic and the New Testament: Essays in Honor of J. Louis Martyn*, edited by Joel Marcus and Marion Soards, 17–48. JSNTSup 24. Sheffield: JSOT Press, 1989.

Theissen, Gerd. *The Social Setting of Pauline Christianity: Essays on Corinth*. Translated and edited with an introduction by John H. Schütz. Philadelphia: Fortress, 1982.

Thiselton, Anthony C. "Realized Eschatology at Corinth." *NTS* 24 (1978) 510–26.

Tomson, Peter J. *Paul and the Jewish Law: Halakha in the Letters of the Apostle to the Gentiles*. CRINT 3/1. Minneapolis: Fortress, 1990.

Tuckett, Christopher M. "'No Resurrection of the Dead' (1 Cor 15:12)." In *The Corinthian Correspondence*, edited by Reimund Bieringer, 247–75. BETL 125. Leuven: Leuven University Press, 1996.

Vorster, Johannes N. "Resurrection Faith 1 Corinthians 15." *Neot* 23 (1989) 287–307.

Vos, Johan S. "Die Argumentation des Paulus in 1 Kor 1,10—3,4." In *The Corinthian Correspondence*, edited by Reimund Bieringer, 87–119. BETL 125. Leuven: Leuven University Press, 1996.

Watson, Duane F. "1 Corinthians 10:23—11:1 in the Light of Greco-Roman Rhetoric: The Role of Rhetorical Questions." *JBL* 108 (1989) 301–18.

———. "Paul's Rhetorical Strategy in 1 Corinthians 15." In *Rhetoric and the New Testament: Essays from the 1992 Heidelberg Conference*, edited by Stanley E. Porter and Thomas H. Olbricht, 231–49. JSNTSup 90. Sheffield: JSOT Press, 1993.

Weber, Max. *Economy and Society: An Outline of the Interpretive Sociology*. Edited by Guenther Roth and Claus Wittich. Translated by Ephraim Fischoff. New York: Bedminster, 1968.

Wedderburn, Alexander J. M. *Baptism and Resurrection: Studies in Pauline Theology against Its Graeco-Roman Background*. WUNT 1/44. Tübingen: Mohr/Siebeck, 1987.

Welborn, Laurence L. "On the Discord in Corinth: 1 Corinthians 1–4 and Ancient Politics." *JBL* 106 (1987) 85–111.

White, John L. "Saint Paul and the Apostolic Letter Tradition." *CBQ* 45 (1983) 433–44.

Whiteley, Denys E. H. *The Theology of St. Paul*. Philadelphia: Fortress, 1964.

Wilckens, Ulrich. *Weisheit und Torheit: Eine exegetisch-religions-geschichtliche Untersuchung zu 1. Kor. 1 und 2*. BHT 26. Tübingen: Mohr/Siebeck, 1959.

Williams, Michael. *Rethinking "Gnosticism": An Argument for Dismantling a Dubious Category*. Princeton: Princeton University Press, 1996.

Willis, Wendell. "An Apostolic Apologia? The Form and Function of 1 Corinthians 9." *JSNT* 24 (1985) 33–48.

———. *Idol Meat in Corinth: The Pauline Argument in 1 Corinthians 8 and 10*. SBLDS 68. Chico, Calif.: Scholars, 1985.

———. "The 'Mind of Christ' in 1 Corinthians 2:16." *Bib* 70 (1989) 110–22.

Wilson, R. McL. "Gnosis at Corinth." In *Paul and Paulinism: Essays in Honour of C. K. Barrett*, edited by Morna D. Hooker and Stephen G. Wilson, 102–14. London: SPCK, 1982.

Wimbush, Vincent L. "The Ascetic Impulse in Ancient Christianity." *ThTo* 50 (1993) 417–28.

Wire, Antoinette Clark. *The Corinthian Women Prophets: A Reconstruction Through Paul's Rhetoric*. Minneapolis: Fortress, 1990.

Witherington, Ben III. *Conflict and Community in Corinth: A Socio-Rhetorical Commentary on 1 and 2 Corinthians*. Grand Rapids: Eerdmans, 1995.